Coerced Labour, Forced Displacement,
and the Soviet Gulag, 1880s-1930s

Social History of Punishment and Labour Coercion

This book series is a platform for expansive understandings of practices of punishment and labour coercion. The books published in this series concern all forms of punishment which were meted out by any type of State apparatus, by individuals such as slave holders, fathers and husbands, and by social institutions such as kin and elderly councils. At the same time, labour is understood here as comprising not only wage labourers, but also enslaved, indentured, tributary and convicted workers, together with unemployed and unpaid individuals.

The series addresses the ways in which workers were punished; it deals with the role of punishment in mobilizing and immobilizing workers; and it highlights the punitive aspects of key dynamics of labour coercion, such as debt, tribute, war and anti-vagrancy laws. Punishment and labour coercion are seen here as open-ended processes: the focus lies on their practices, and how they are entangled in distinctive ways in relation to different social groups, vis-à-vis gender, age and ethnicity/race/citizenship, and across time and space.

Series Editors
Christian G. De Vito, University of Vienna, Austria
Margo De Koster, University of Ghent, Belgium
Johan Heinsen, Aalborg University, Denmark
Katherine Roscoe, University of Liverpool, UK
Paulo Terra, Universidade Federal Fluminense, Niterói, Brazil

Editorial Board
Clare Anderson (University of Leicester)
Sidney Chalhoub (Harvard University)
Chris Eyre (University of Liverpool)
Tyge Krogh (Rigsarkiver, Copenhagen)
Alex Lichtenstein (Indiana University Bloomington, US)
Marcel van der Linden (IISG, Amsterdam)
Chiara Lucrezio Monticelli (University of Rome-Tor Vergata)
Hamish Maxwell-Stewart (University of New England)
Paola Revilla (University of La Paz)
Juliane Schiel (University of Vienna)
Arjan Zuiderhoek (University of Ghent)

Coerced Labour, Forced Displacement, and the Soviet Gulag, 1880s-1930s

Zhanna Popova

Amsterdam University Press

Cover illustration: "Types from a party of convicts on the road, near Tomsk". 1885–1886.
George Kennan Papers, Library of Congress

Cover design: Coördesign, Leiden
Lay-out: Crius Group, Hulshout

ISBN	978 90 4856 035 6
e-ISBN	978 90 4856 036 3 (pdf)
DOI	10.5117/9789048560356
NUR	697

In a correctly organized society, not a single healthy and able-bodied
member should count on the privilege of being exonerated from the
labour that is obligatory for everyone.
—Nikolai Luchinskii, "Arestantskie raboty vo Frantsii i v Rossii",
Tiuremnyi vestnik, 1 (1906), pp. 39–56, 40.

It makes me laugh when [people] talk about bourgeois sabotage, when
they point the finger at a terrified bourgeois and call him a saboteur.
We have national, popular, proletarian sabotage.
—Aleksei Gastev, quoted in *Trudy I Vserossiiskogo s'ezda Sovetov
narodnogo khoziaistva, 25 maia–4 iunia 1918 g.*
(Moscow, 1918), p. 382.

Table of Contents

Introduction*

The glory days of the Western Siberian town of Tobolsk are long gone.[1] Once the centre of the Russian imperial presence in Western Siberia, a booming administrative and commercial town, by the beginning of the twentieth century Tobolsk had lost much of its significance to the city of Tyumen some 250 kilometres to its southwest. Standing on the mighty Irtysh River, Tobolsk fell victim to the modernization of infrastructure. As railroads replaced rivers as the main arteries of commerce, the Trans-Siberian Railroad became the chief route that connected Siberia and the Far East with the European part of the empire. Tobolsk could not profit from this breakthrough in connectivity: the Trans-Siberian went through Tyumen and other towns much to the south, while Tobolsk was connected to it only in the 1970s. Reaching the town by car is still tricky, with snowfall in winter and floods in spring regularly obstructing the roads.

In 2016, when I visited Tobolsk for my archival research, the town had a stagnating population of around 100,000 inhabitants and sought to attract tourists by showcasing its imperial past. Tobolsk boasts the easternmost white kremlin, a tell-tale sign of the early modern Russian military presence. The newly renovated kremlin, located on the high shore of Irtysh, dominates the town and forms the core of its museum complex. Just a stone's throw away was another museum, and one of the goals of my journey to Tobolsk: the Museum of Siberian Katorga and Exile. The Tobolsk prison castle, built in 1855 as a hard labour facility and a node of convict transportation, was used as a prison continuously until 1989. Part of this prison complex now hosts

*   Research for this book was funded by the Dutch Research Council (NWO) as part of the research programme "Four Centuries of Labour Camps. War, Rehabilitation, Ethnicity". Travel funds for archival research were generously provided by the University of Amsterdam. The Hoover Institution Library and Archives (Stanford University) funded my participation in the 2015 Workshop on Authoritarian Regimes, thanks to which I was able to consult microfilmed copies of the collections of the Gulag Administration held at the State Archive of the Russian Federation (*Gosudarstvennyi Arkhiv Rossiiskoi Federatsii*, herein abbreviated as GARF).
1   Throughout the book, I have used the simplified Library of Congress transliteration system for Russian, except for geographical and personal names that have a conventional spelling in English (hence Tobolsk and not Tobol'sk, Trotsky and not Trotskii).

Popova, Zhanna: *Coerced Labour, Forced Displacement, and the Soviet Gulag, 1880s–1930s*. Amsterdam: Amsterdam University Press, 2024
DOI: 10.5117/9789048560356_INTRO

Figure 1   Inner courtyard of the Tobolsk Museum of Siberian Katorga and Exile. Photo of the author

the museum, while the former solitary confinement block was refurbished as a hostel. Despite my better judgement, I stayed in this hostel for several weeks, partly out of research interest and partly because of convenience, as the state archive where I spent most of my days was right around the corner. Most of the time I was the only guest there.

On several occasions, I left the hostel and was surprised to find out that it was raining outside, because the tiny window at the top of the cell barely let any light or sound in. This nineteenth-century prison building inhibited any contact with the outside world in the ways its architects could not have predicted: the walls were so thick that they blocked cell phone signals, making it impossible to have calls inside. Although the place had been renovated, was kept clean, and was well-lit, it was invariably terrifying. I kept on imagining how destructive solitary confinement there must have been during the long Siberian winters.

The prison complex as a whole evoked further malaise. One could see direct material continuities between the tsarist and Soviet carceral practices, and witness how the Soviet authorities built, in very practical terms, upon the imperial heritage of repression. Soviet-era additions included window covers for regular cells, replicating the effect of total isolation that the thick walls created in the imperial prison. Watchtowers were perched over tiny, caged courtyards, measuring no more than 3 metres by 3 metres, where inmates were supposed to do their daily walks.

Continuities between the imperial penal system and the gigantic network of repressive institutions known as the Gulag, that are hard to pinpoint on the level of the entire systems, become visible, even palpable, when we are faced with concrete penal sites. Penal system and extrajudicial practices of repression have become the symbol of arbitrariness and tyranny of the state. Penal sites were, and continue to be, places where villains could turn into victims, punishment and its consequences were disproportionate to the offence, and political activism was often persecuted harsher than violent crimes.

Discussing continuities and ruptures between the imperial and the Soviet systems has been a highly politicized matter since the emergence of the Soviet state and continues to be so. Both the Soviet authorities and their critics continuously underlined the rupture between the imperial and the Soviet practices of repression, albeit for different reasons. In the immediate aftermath of the 1917 revolution, Soviet authorities highlighted the differences of the new Marxist penal system that, as they claimed, was built on profoundly different foundations than the bourgeois prison and exile complex of the Russian empire, offering criminals a true promise of return to the proletarian society as its useful productive members. Critics, meanwhile, also focused on the Soviet system's distinctions, underlining its extreme brutality as well as the widespread torture, starvation, and rape in the camps.[2]

In the public consciousness, "Gulag" designates the whole Soviet repressive system, above all camps and prisons. The word has become the denomination for any exceptionally brutal carceral institution and is commonly used beyond the Soviet context in the scholarly context and in public discussions. In the narrow sense, however, the abbreviation "GULAG", which stands for *Glavnoe upravlenie lagerei*, or Main Camp Administration, denotes a Soviet agency that officially existed between 1930 and 1960 and was responsible for running the vast system of various carceral institutions. The exact name of the agency changed several times: between 1934 and 1938, it was officially called Main Administration of Camps, Labour Settlements and Places of Confinement, while between 1939 and 1956 its name changed to Main

---

2   Among the early examples are the memoirs of two former White officers: Iu. Bezsonov, *Mes vingt-six prisons et mon évasion de Solovki* (Paris: Payot, 1928) and S.A. Malsagoff, *An Island Hell: A Soviet Prison in the Far North* (London: A.M. Philpot, 1926). For an extended list of memoirs of inmates of the early Soviet camps, see: Jonathan D. Smele, *The Russian Revolution and Civil War, 1917–1921: An Annotated Bibliography* (London, New York: Continuum, 2003).

Administration of Corrective-Labour Camps and Colonies. Regardless, the abbreviation continued to be used in the official documents and in everyday life alike. For convenience and simplicity, throughout the book I will refer to this agency as Main Camp Administration, while the term Gulag will be used for the Soviet system of carceral institutions as a whole, a system that also included a vast network of settlements for peasants deported during the collectivization and other places of confinement.

The Soviet heritage of repression casts a long shadow over contemporary Russian society and continues to be a controversial, troubling, and largely taboo subject. Crucial efforts to bring the discussion of this heritage into the public space first started during the late Soviet times. During the perestroika and the immediate post-Soviet period, the Gulag briefly came into the focus of public discourse: the significant opening of classified party and state archives, the publication of Gulag fiction and memoirs, intensive academic investigations, and discussions in the press made it seem that Russian society was starting to work through this traumatic past. However, these discussions did not lead to the establishment of an institutional framework that could bring justice to the victims of the Stalinist repression, and eventually the conversation was marginalized and testimonies of survivors silenced, and the Gulag legacy remained contested. In the 2000s and early 2010s, non-governmental organizations and regional associations of Gulag survivors continued to function, and academic research produced robust narratives on various facets of the Stalinist repression, but the discussion became increasingly dominated by state actors. The new state-sponsored GULAG History Museum opened in Moscow in 2015 and pursued a rich programme of public outreach, seeking to ignite and guide a public conversation about the Soviet camps. Its permanent exhibition accurately, if selectively, presented historical facts about the camp system, but remained full of omissions that downplayed the role of Stalin in its creation and barely mentioned political repression beyond the GULAG.[3] In the last decade, pressure against the NGOs and activists working on the history of the Gulag has been mounting. Individual activists in the regions faced direct persecution.[4] In April 2022, Memorial, the major public association that

---

3   Andrei Zavadski and Vera Dubina, "Eclipsing Stalin: The GULAG History Museum in Moscow as a Manifestation of Russia's Official Memory of Soviet Repression", *Problems of Post-Communism* 70, no. 5 (2023): 531–543.

4   In December 2021, Karelian activist and historian Iurii Dmitriev was sentenced to fifteen years in a penal colony. For a detailed account of the trials, see: https://dmitrievaffair.com, last accessed 4 July 2022.

collected, preserved, and researched testimonies and documents on the Soviet camp system, was forcibly dissolved, as state actors effectively monopolized the ways in which the Gulag can be discussed, researched, and remembered in Russia.

Historicizing and contextualizing the Gulag is rendered challenging by the long-running politization of this past, but it is necessary to inscribe the Soviet repressive system within the global history of repression beyond perpetuating the narrative of its exceptionalism. Although it was indeed exceptional in many ways, it was also firmly embedded within the global context of mass confinement, forced displacement, and coerced labour.[5] Mass confinement is discussed throughout the book, but the main focus is the latter two elements of the penal-repressive system. As I argue, confinement could be an often unachievable goal for state officials faced with financial shortages, but both displacement and forced labour were the mainstay of their punitive repertoire due to these measures' flexibility and a host of other reasons into which I delve in detail throughout the book. The emphasis of this research is primarily on tracing how forced displacement and coerced labour, used both as punishment and extra-judicially, were tightly interconnected. Both instruments long predated not only the emergence of the camp network, but also the creation of a modern prison system in imperial Russia. Tracing their developments gives an opportunity to look into the establishment of the camps beyond the Bolsheviks' arrival in power. As much as possible, this book looks at the repressive system beyond the legal acts, as it seeks to highlight the regional tensions, bureaucratic and legal inconsistencies, and contingent arrangements dictated by war, revolution, financial penury, or regional particularities: sometimes, ad hoc or temporary solutions would markedly change the places of confinement.

I approach the nexus between coerced labour and forced displacement in punitive policies in Russia and the USSR from two complementary angles: conceptual and legal production in the capitals and regional developments and practices. For state officials, both coerced labour and forced displacement bore a variety of meanings beyond the straightforward punitive goals. The meanings of forced labour were generally made explicit and theorized, while the purposes of forced displacement remained unarticulated beyond the agenda of colonization. Exploration of the evolution of these meanings helps to paint a wider backdrop against which the development of repressive

5   The term "forced displacement" is used here to designate together tsarist exile, Soviet mass deportations, and the transportation of individual inmates.

practices took place, and helps to explain why certain options were adopted, while other practices were discarded.

In the domain of punishment, the gap between proclaimed official policies and the realities of the punished was harrowingly wide in imperial and Soviet times alike. Adopting a regional perspective makes it possible to grasp at least some of these discrepancies, and to describe and analyse penal practices in the variety of their historical and local forms. I have tried, as much as possible, to address both the local dimension and the developments of the whole system simultaneously, but while in some chapters a combination of the two optics prevails, in others, one of the perspectives dominates. The in-depth cases are generally based on the Western Siberian archival materials, but accounts from other regions were also included as illustrations. This regional approach also highlights how Russian and Soviet penal and repressive policies were inextricably connected to colonial expansion into Siberia. Western Siberia was at the core of crucial events and processes that defined the shape of the repressive system: the development of transport, mass peasant migration of the last decades before 1917, the mass captivity of prisoners of war during World War I, and the tumult and violence of the revolution and the civil war. Some of the key sites of Stalinist industrialization that relied on forced labour were also located there. These transformations continuously changed the face of Western Siberian sites of repression.

Although the focus here is on continuities and ruptures between the imperial and the Soviet periods, I also sought to include, where possible, discussions of relevant global developments of repressive policies. Recent contributions in the global history of convict labour and penal transportation, on which I build these reflections, have shown that the uses of displacement and labour as punishment around the world and through the centuries had strong similarities.[6] To put it simply, penal practices globally were rarely driven only by the internal logic of punishment, but were shaped by a host of economic, political, and cultural factors. As made stark by Ann Laura Stoler, across very different historical contexts, "changes in sites of incarceration and the specific types of hard labour performed were rarely determined by the priority of punishment alone, nor by what was imagined to be commensurable with the severity of what was considered

---

6   Two edited volumes published in recent years can serve as entry points into this rich and sophisticated literature: Clare Anderson (ed.), *A Global History of Convicts and Penal Colonies* (London: Bloomsbury Academic, 2018); Christian G. De Vito and Alex Lichtenstein (eds), *Global Convict Labour* (Leiden, Boston, MA: Brill, 2015).

a crime".[7] These observations appear particularly pertinent for the Russian and Soviet cases. Considering how widespread the use of extrajudicial measures of repression was in tsarist Russia and especially in the Soviet Union, it is crucial to include in the analysis not only the displacement and forced labour of convicts, in other words, of those who received a court sentence, but also of those who never were convicted, but had to endure repression nevertheless. Such an inclusive, wide-angle approach is also crucial to understand why these repressive arrangements have had such a long-running impact on society in Russia.

The starting point for this investigation is the last third of the nineteenth century. Chapter 1 focuses on the long-running practice of exile and central officials' attempts to create alternatives to it by launching a prison reform. The centrality of exile and its persistence must be understood within the wider setting of Russian colonial expansion to Siberia, political struggles, and the absence of full-scale judicial and police reform. Incarceration thus emerged as a potent alternative to exile, contributing to the fragmentation and complexity of the imperial penal system. Chapter 2 follows the transformations of the penal system as it was put under pressure, first by growing social unrest and the tsarist authorities' responses to it, and then by the burdens of World War I. Already during the tsarist period, wartime needs spurred a greater reliance on the concentrated, centrally organized, and increasingly exploitative use of convict labour on large-scale infrastructural projects. Chapter 3 offers an analysis of two wildly different, albeit almost coeval, systems of camps: prisoner-of-war camps during World War I and the early revolutionary camps as they took shape in Western Siberia. This short but impactful period heralded the spread of mass internment, another crucial element of the future repressive architecture. Early Soviet penal experiments and their consequences are at the heart of Chapter 4. During the 1920s, the camps for political dissenters established by the secret police provided just one among many forms of confinement and use of forced labour. Examining the abandoned alternatives helps to understand the state of the penal system on the eve of Stalin's offensive in the first Five-Year Plan. Chapter 5 focuses on the establishment of the large-scale repressive system of settlements for deported peasants in the 1930s Soviet Union, which lay at the foundation of the Gulag along with the forced labour camps. Tracing the developments of the special settlements system makes clear the extreme interconnectedness between the free and

7   Ann Laura Stoler, "Epilogue – In Carceral Motion: Disposals of Life and Labour", in Anderson (ed.), *A Global History*, pp. 371–80, 372.

unfree spheres of labour and the extensive reliance on forced labour both in rural and urban contexts.

Chronological overview

As the narrative of this book spans over seven decades of Russian history, a brief chronological sketch might be helpful for the non-specialist reader. The history of forced labour and forced displacement as the dual pillars of the Russian punitive policies begins before the creation of the first Gulag camps, indeed long before the camps were established in Russia at all. With this book, I seek to integrate this history within the larger narrative not simply as a prelude to the behemoth system of the Soviet camps, but as a rich and contradictory story in its own right.

The point of departure of this analysis is the penal system of the Russian empire of the last third of the nineteenth century, in which the traditional penal practices of exile and hard labour as punishments for the most danger-ous crimes coexisted with prisons and other carceral institutions. Consistent attempts to reform and "modernize" the penal system started during the reign of the tsar Alexander II (ruled 1855–1881) and continued under his successors. Known as "the Liberator" for abolishing serfdom (1861), Alexander II encouraged a wide range of reforms that transformed crucial aspects of social life. The prison reform was in gestation for decades before it was initiated in 1879; although initial plans for it were ambitious, the immediate impact was very moderate. Due to political change and lack of budget and qualified prison staff, this reform faltered and did not lead to immediate expansive changes in the practices of punishment. Nevertheless, it was taking place in a society that was rapidly changing: judicial reform, financial reform, the *zemstvo* reform of local government, reforms of middle and higher education, in addition to the abolition of serfdom, contributed to changes in the socio-political landscape of the empire. However, the fundamental aspect of imperial governance, the absolute power of the tsar, remained untouched. Discontent grew, and revolutionaries resorted to spectacular acts of violence against high-ranking administrators, and even the tsar himself, hoping to radicalize the masses with such propaganda by the deed.

After several failed assassination attempts, in March 1881 Alexander II was killed in a bombing. As his son Alexander III (ruled 1881–1894) as-sumed the throne, he thwarted the political reforms. In an attempt to subdue the revolutionaries, Alexander III introduced a state of emergency in August 1881. Although it was intended as a temporary measure, in some regions it remained in force for decades, endorsing the local authorities in their attempts to repress the revolutionary movement and allowing them to persecute those suspected of being a threat to public order extrajudicially. These attempts to undermine the revolutionary movement were far from successful, and the heir of Alexander III, tsar Nicholas II (ruled 1894–1917), was faced with an intensifying social and political unrest. Strikes by industrial workers, dissent from the educated layers of society, and discontent among the peasants plagued the reign of the last Romanov. Aspiring to be a strong autocratic ruler, Nicholas consistently refused to reform the empire's political order until he was forced to do so during the 1905 revolution. This revolution, which exposed the empire's deep social problems, was marked by mass support for its radical causes. In the aftermath of the revolution, the tsarist government exiled, imprisoned, and sentenced to hard labour thousands of revolutionaries. Conditions in the penal system, which had improved over the decades of long prison reform, rapidly deteriorated, leading to rising mortality in both prisons and transit jails.

The last Romanovs were also preoccupied with consolidating Russia's colonial expansion to the east. A forceful drive towards centralization and russification defined the imperial policies towards Siberia during the reigns of Alexander III and Nicholas II. Central administrators saw the Trans-Siberian Railroad as the definitive solution to Siberian problems with infrastructure and the ultimate means to solidify imperial presence. Construction started in 1891, and once the first stretches became operable in 1901, this new opportunity spurred peasant migration to Siberia, with as many as 10 million migrants resettling within a span of ten years. The gradual integration of Siberia into the Russian empire had an effect on penal policies, as it transformed the way imperial administrators viewed Siberia within the empire: the growth of connectivity and population density facilitated flights of exiles and undermined the harsh character of the punishment.

The 1917 February revolution brought to an end the reign of Nicholas II. In March, he was forced to abdicate in favour of his brother Mikhail, who refused the throne. With the future of Russian governance insecure, a provisional government was created. The politics of the Provisional Government, which ruled Russia between February and October 1917, was characterized by liberal aspirations that were undermined by the lack of control over enforcement of the new legal acts. The Provisional Government abolished the exile and katorga.[8] In a country torn apart by war and revolution, some

---

8   Katorga was the second harshest punishment after the death penalty. It implied full loss of rights (civil death), lifelong exile, and hard labour terms of up to 25 years.

regions remained cut off from the central government for years, and the penal system practically disintegrated.

As the Bolsheviks came to power in October 1917, they sought to underline that the creation of the first proletarian state brought about a fundamental departure from the tsarist policies in all aspects of political and social life. The immediate post-revolutionary period was marked by the coexistence of the coercive policies of war communism and the start of intensive experimentation with noncustodial types of punishment. At the same time, in their fight against political dissent, the Soviet security police (the Cheka) used concentration camps among other tools of terror. Following the death of Vladimir Lenin in early 1924, intense internal struggles for power changed the face of the Bolshevik party. Joseph Stalin emerged victorious, having decimated any opposition within the party towards the end of the 1920s. He abandoned the New Economic Policy, which was introduced in 1921 as a measure to alleviate the economic challenges prompted by war and revolution. Instead, the Soviet economy was organized through ambitious Five-Year Plans. Implementation of the first of these plans (1928–1932) profoundly transformed not only the economy of the Soviet Union, but also its repressive system, launching the building of sprawling network of camps and other punitive institutions.

1   A Threatening Geography: Shifting Usages of Forced Displacement and Convict Labour, 1879–1905

Abstract

This chapter analyses how exile and forced labour became inextricably connected in the evolution of penal and repressive policies and practices in the Russian empire. In doing so, it also sets the backdrop for the long-term history of exile and forced labour in the Russian empire and the Soviet Union. The chapter comprises an overview of the early histories of exile and forced labour in local Russian policies and practices, an examination of the Russian case of exile in the wider context of convict transportation practised by maritime empires, and a discussion of exile's longevity. It also offers an innovative analysis of imperial "prison reform" – attempts to introduce modern penitentiaries – highlighting tensions that stemmed from the effort to adapt Western European penological narratives to Russian realities.

Keywords: exile, katorga, prison reform, convict transportation, Russian empire

Vast expanses of Siberia and the Far East, stretching from the Ural Mountains in the west to the Pacific Ocean in the east, have been a persistent source of imperial anxieties for officials in Moscow and Saint Petersburg. Securing the migration and resettlement of ethnic Slavs in Siberia became one of their central preoccupations vis-à-vis the region after the first military ventures into Siberia at the end of the sixteenth century.[1] At the

---

1   For a brief but helpful introduction to the topic of Russian settler colonialism, see Alexander Morrison, "Russian Settler Colonialism", in Edward Cavanagh and Lorenzo Veracini (eds), *The Routledge Handbook of the History of Settler Colonialism* (Abingdon: Routledge, 2016), pp. 313–26.

Popova, Zhanna: *Coerced Labour, Forced Displacement, and the Soviet Gulag, 1880s-1930s*. Amsterdam: Amsterdam University Press, 2024
DOI: 10.5117/9789048560356_CH01

same time, the state was concerned with preserving the taxable population within its borders, seeking to control the movement of peasants. The system of serfdom that was gradually established in the sixteenth and seventeenth centuries effectively tied peasants to the land. As migration constituted flight from serfdom and was discouraged, up until the abolition of serfdom in 1861, the state had to rely on alternatives to peasant migration. One such alternative was exile, which implied the expulsion of wrongdoers from European Russia and their forced settlement in Siberia. Although this practice had arguable impact on the growth of the ethnically Russian population in Siberia, it persisted for multiple centuries. Indeed, it is impossible to write a history of the Russian imperial penal system without paying close attention to Siberia.

I seek to highlight the complex and dynamic transformations of the imperial penal system in the decades before the 1917 revolution. The focus here is on the two most notorious, and most enduring, imperial punishments: exile and katorga, the punitive regime that combined forced displacement with forced labour and was intended for the most dangerous offenders. Both had existed for centuries, and continuously evoked critiques of central and local officials alike, yet remained at the foundation of the imperial penal system. Exile, incarceration, and katorga were only some of the parts of a complex and differentiated penal system in the Russian empire, which included other institutions of confinement, corporal punishment, fines, and other punishments.

The goal of this chapter is not to give a comprehensive picture of the penal system prior to the 1905 revolution, but to focus on the early usages of forced displacement and convict labour by analysing the persistence of exile to Siberia and state officials' attempts to create alternatives to it. The prison reform was aimed at modernizing the prisons and putting confinement, rather than forced displacement, at the core of the penal system. Crucially, as I discuss below, the use of exile and katorga was governed not only by the traditional goals associated with punishment and crime control, such as retribution or deterrence, but from the earliest instances was defined by a variety of statist goals that over more than three centuries of its existence included the colonization of borderlands, infrastructure construction, the extraction of resources, control of the mobility of subaltern groups, and the repression of political dissenters. The fact that the Russian penal system was heavily impacted by statist goals that took precedence over the considerations of crime control is one of its definitive long-running features.

Early history of exile and katorga

The first uses of exile in Russia date back to early modern times. During the sixteenth century, exiles were sent to practically everywhere in Muscovy, including monasteries in Yaroslavl and Uglich, the Caucasus and other southern borderlands, the Far North and the Urals. The earliest accounts of exile to Siberia date back to the end of the sixteenth century, and towards the end of the seventeenth century, it emerged as the dominant destination of exile. The primary goals of early exile were, on the one hand, retribution for crimes and, on the other, expulsion of criminals from European Russia. Crimes punished by exile included forging money, robbery and theft, bootlegging and illegal trade in tobacco (as the state ran monopolies on both alcohol and tobacco), and begging, although the list changed regularly.[2] Exile was a tangible manifestation of the state's power over individuals and territories: already the 1649 Code (*Sobornoe Ulozhenie*) stated that criminals had to be "lashed and exiled to wherever the sovereign orders".[3] Andrew Gentes has called exile "the transmission belt linking the sovereign's punitive vengeance to the state's utilitarian exploitation", highlighting the economic considerations that defined the shape of exile from its inception.[4] The concrete practical aspects of exercising this power, however, were a continuous source of strain for the authorities. As Nancy Kollmann has emphasized, a tension between attempts at centralization and the challenges of imperial governance characterized the early modern Russian state.[5] One of the most prominent, and most persistent, tensions that riddled the system related to the distribution of exiles. Vast Eastern Siberia was supposed to profit the most from the presence of exiles due to the sparsity of its (Slavic) population. It was not, however, the destination of the majority of exiles: Western Siberia, the more densely populated and economically developed region between the Ural Mountains and the Yenisei River, received more exiles than its eastern neighbour. The Western Siberian authorities responsible for settling the exiles faced a shortage of available arable land and suitable service roles to which exiles could be assigned as

2   L.M. Dameshek and A.V. Remnev (eds), *Sibir' v sostave Rossiiskoi imperii* (Moscow: Novoe literaturnoe obozrenie, 2007), p. 271.
3   M.N. Tikhomirov and P.P. Epifanov (eds), *Sobornoe ulozhenie 1649 goda* (Moscow: Izadatel'stvo Moskovskogo gosudarstvennogo universiteta, 1961), p. 139.
4   Andrew A. Gentes, *Exile to Siberia, 1590–1822: Corporeal Commodification and Administrative Systematization in Russia* (Basingstoke, New York: Palgrave Macmillan, 2008), p. 57.
5   Nancy Shields Kollmann, *Crime and Punishment in Early Modern Russia* (Cambridge, New York: Cambridge University Press, 2012), p. 4.

early as in 1698.[6] This discrepancy between the aspirations of colonization and the practical realities of exile persisted, with varying acuity, throughout the whole existence of the exile system. Almost two centuries later, in 1876, in his report to the tsar, the governor-general of Western Siberia still evoked problems with finding land for exiles and insisted that more exiles had to be directed towards Eastern Siberia, as it still had available land, unlike the region he governed.[7]

Regardless of such complaints, directing exiles towards particular regions was the prerogative of the autocrat. During the reign of Peter I (1682–1725), a new type of punishment, katorga, was created. It became the first precedent of the coordinated use of forced labour of convicts in tsarist Russia. Katorga (the name stemming from the Greek word for "galley"), intended as the second harshest punishment after the death penalty, emerged in 1696 as Peter assigned runaway state servitors and exiles to work at the naval shipyard in the southern town of Azov. Their families were ordered to follow them, in an attempt to expand not only the labour force, but also the Russian population in these borderland territories newly conquered from the Ottoman empire.[8] According to Brian Boeck, the "aborted imperial initiative" of Azov prompted two crucial changes in the state's punitive policy: it created new alternatives to Siberia as the principal destination of exile, Azov being the first of them, and it marked the shift of focus from exile exclusively towards its combination with forced labour.[9] The Azov enterprise failed to achieve its imperial goals: a cession of the town and surrounding territories to the Ottoman empire followed the disastrous 1711 military campaign. But katorga survived the colony where it was first implemented, as throughout his reign, Peter used convict labour on projects like the construction of his new capital, Saint Petersburg, or at the Baltic fortress of Rogervik.

With the creation of katorga, the fundamental dyad of the Russian repressive system – namely forced labour combined with forced displacement – emerged in its initial form. In the centuries to come, punishments combining these two elements tended to be the most severe and generally served not only the typical goals of retribution, deterrence, and, later, rehabilitation,

6   *Ibid.*, p. 248.
7   Russian State Historical Archive in Saint Petersburg (*Rossiiskii gosudarstvennyi istoricheskii arkhiv*, hereafter RGIA), *Vsepoddaneishii otchet general-gubernatora Zapadnoi Sibiri za 1876 g.*, p. 38.
8   Brian J. Boeck, "When Peter I Was Forced to Settle for Less: Coerced Labor and Resistance in a Failed Russian Colony (1695–1711)", *The Journal of Modern History*, 80:3 (2008), pp. 485–514.
9   *Ibid.*, pp. 511–14.

but also wider statist goals of colonization and mobilization of labour. The pursuit of these goals, which were often connected to remote geographical locations, presented significant logistical and administrative challenges for the state actors from early on. Already in Azov, exiled workers and their families were locked up in jail instead of being put to work, as the ships they were supposed to be labouring on sat idle.[10] In the nineteenth and early twentieth centuries, putting convicts and exiles to work in distant destinations proved to be a challenge that the officials and local authorities were not always able to surmount, and when it was achieved, it often was at the high cost of convicts' lives. Administrative disarray had ambivalent consequences. On the one hand, it compounded the suffering of exiles and prisoners, cost them their health and often their lives, and multiplied crime within the penal system due to the lack of oversight. On the other, the chaos also made the system laxer, facilitating escapes, an informal economy, and, later, the emergence of a strong prison and camp subculture.

Although katorga was far from disappearing after the death of Peter I, his successors tended to rely more heavily on exile as a means of forced colonization. One of the main laws that shaped the practice of exile was passed by the Senate on 13 December 1760.[11] This law granted landowners the power to exile "unruly" peasants to the region of Nerchinsk in Eastern Siberia. Other categories of peasants, including those owned by monasteries and the state, could also be exiled. Thievery and alcoholism were named as the main reasons for exile. The goals of social control can explain the delegation of this right to the landlords, but not the destination of exile. As noted by the Soviet historian A.D. Kolesnikov, this law was passed in response to the growing financial needs of the state. In order to satisfy these needs, the government sought to increase the volume of silver mining at the state-owned Nerchinsk mines by increasing the number of forced labourers there.[12] Thus the landowners received the power to punish a particular category of wrongdoers: healthy peasants below forty-five years of age. These were overwhelmingly men, and if they had families, the law encouraged landowners to banish their wives and children as well, with monetary compensation from the government provided. This law established the legal foundation for the two-fold coercion of the peasant population

10 *Ibid.*, p. 500.

11 *Polnoe sobranie zakonov Rossiiskoi Imperii. S 1649 goda. Tom XV. S 1758 po 28 iunia 1762* (Saint Petersburg, 1830), no. 11166 (13 December 1760), p. 582.

12 A.D. Kolesnikov, "Ssylka i zaselenie Sibiri", in L.M. Goriushkin (ed.), *Ssylka i katorga v Sibiri (XVIII-nachalo XX v.)* (Novosibirsk: Izdatel'stvo "Nauka", 1975), pp. 38–59, 42–44.

that combined displacement with forced labour for the state, while at the same time further privileging landowners, since the decision to banish a peasant remained dependent purely on their will, extending their power over the peasants in the domain of punishment. Kolesnikov remarked that this early nexus of exile and labour coercion was a response to the labour shortage at state enterprises. It was also a way to facilitate the fulfilment of "state interest in the population (*zaselenie*)" of Siberia, as proclaimed by the law. However, serf owners often disregarded state interest and tended to exile peasants who were infirm, unable to work, and much older than forty-five, preserving the more valuable young workers for their own estates. This practice must have been widespread, as another law was promulgated in 1787 to reinforce the initial conditions of exile.[13]

An attempt to populate the Baraba steppe in the south of Western Siberia with exiled settlers is illustrative of these aspirations of internal colonization and use of coerced labour for the state's benefit. The Baraba steppe, known for its hostile marshes riddled with mosquitoes and gadflies, was at the time a sparsely populated region important for the connectivity of Siberia. Exiles, runaway state servitors and soldiers were forcibly relocated there: some of the settlers had to establish agriculture, while others worked to build and maintain the road that ran through the steppe. Initiated under the rule of Empress Elizaveta Petrovna in 1760, this project lasted until 1765, and cost thousands of settlers their lives.[14]

Exile proved to be an unreliable tool of colonization not only because of the shortcomings of its administrators, but also due to the agency of exiles who used the fact that policing in Siberia barely existed outside of urban centres to ran away en masse. It is impossible to gauge the number of runaway exiles prior to the nineteenth century, but they must have been extremely significant. To combat the escaping and to make controlling the exiles more transparent, a gruesome practice of branding was introduced. In some cases, it was accompanied by other types of bodily mutilation, such as the severing of ears and hands. Katorga convicts typically were branded with the letters "KAT" on their cheeks and forehead, a practice which was only abolished in 1863 during the major reform of corporal punishment.

By the beginning of the nineteenth century, exile to Siberia had already been used as a punishment for more than two centuries. While for thousands

---

13   *Polnoe sobranie zakonov Rossiiskoi Imperii, s 1649 goda. Tom XXII. 1784–1788* (Saint Petersburg, 1830), no. 16602 (31 December 1787), pp. 973–74.

14   Aleksandr Salomon, *Ssylka v Sibir'. Ocherk eia istorii i sovremennago polozheniia* (Saint Petersburg: Tipografiia S.-Peterburgskoi Tiur'my, 1900), p. 15.

of exiles who had to undertake long and exhausting journeys it was a feared ordeal that could end with injury or death, for the state officials it represented first and foremost a logistical challenge. Transit relied on multiple regional agencies to secure the exiles' long passage towards their destinations, and the absence of a unified agency to coordinate and control their movement made the system utterly inefficient. Corruption of the local administration exacerbated these structural problems.[15]

The first consistent attempts to reform the practice of exile are associated with Mikhail Speransky, initially a prominent reformer at the court of Alexander I. Speransky fell into disfavour, was banished from Saint Petersburg, and was eventually appointed governor-general of Siberia in 1819. Influenced by the ideals of the Enlightenment, Speransky envisioned a systematic overhaul of Siberia's governance, and restructuring of the exile system was part of this project. In preparation for his project of exile reform, Speransky toured some of the main sites of exile and katorga and ordered an investigation of their condition.[16] This endeavour uncovered the lamentable condition of exiles and katorga convicts and the failures of organization of their labour. Sceptical of the role of exiles in the colonization of Siberia, Speransky wrote in private correspondence that the number of exiles in Siberia was so small that they were barely a "drop in the sea", but he took seriously the challenge of using them for the state's benefit.[17] His elaborate projects, approved by the tsar in July 1822, codified and updated existing regulations regarding exile and katorga. In addition to the systematization of legislation, these projects aimed at making exiles more productive by categorizing them in an intricate system, which was supposed to guide their employment on state projects, including industries and road building.[18] These reforms encouraged the creation of a system of transit jails with a view to reducing mortality and flight during the long transit to Siberia.[19] They also limited the maximum duration of exile to twenty years, while previously it was de facto for life.

15 Andrew Gentes, "Roads to Oblivion: Siberian Exile and the Struggle between State and Society in Russia, 1593–1917" (Ph.D. dissertation, Brown University, 2002), pp. 173–74.
16 Dameshek and Remnev, *Sibir' v sostave Rossiiskoi imperii*, p. 277.
17 Salomon, *Ssylka v Sibir'*, p. 17.
18 Gentes, *Roads to Oblivion*, pp. 190–96.
19 Prior to the implementation of these regulations, exiles walked to Siberia on foot all year round. They walked in groups under surveillance and stayed overnight in villages along the way, in private houses or in the open air. Extreme temperatures both in summer and in winter, inadequate clothing, infectious diseases, dehydration, and lack of food made these journeys extremely dangerous.

These substantial changes, however, proved hard to implement. Money dedicated to the construction of transit jails was often stolen by local authorities, and making exiles work, including potential labour for the state, hinged on efficient local administration. Forcing exiles and convicts to work was further complicated as the traditional forced labour sites in Western Siberia were abandoned due to the exhaustion of old mines. According to Russian historians Lev Dameshek and Anatolii Remnev, only the development of gold mining during the nineteenth century created some need for the labour of exiles. They also underlined that among exiles who were able to find work, many laboured as hired workers for the local peasants.[20]

Resistant to reform, the exile system attracted growing critique. Concerns were raised regarding its punitive capacity and its influence on the local population of Siberia. Wilhelm Rupert, governor-general of Eastern Siberia between 1837 and 1847, advocated for a harsher stance towards exiles and called for the transfer of responsibility over them from civil to military authorities and the subsequent implementation of strict military discipline.[21] Such transfer did not materialize, and neither did early suggestions to use confinement as a substitute to exile. By the mid-nineteenth century, the crisis of exile was admitted by a wide range of state actors. Its logistics remained complex, underfunded, and inefficient, and attempts of reform were inadequate considering the rapid growth in the number of exiles. During the second half of the eighteenth century, an estimated 60,000 people were exiled, while between 1807 and 1851, as many as 282,963 people were sent to Siberia.[22] In 1888, central authorities estimated that during the first eighty years of the nineteenth century, more than 670,000 people were exiled, thus putting the estimate of those exiled between 1851 and 1881 at around 387,000.[23] Failures of administration compounded the suffering of exiles, for whom transit was often the most gruesome part of the punishment, although this appears to have been unintended on the part of the authorities.[24] The system continued to rely strongly on the cooperation of local officials, who in many cases had neither the capacity nor the will to secure the settlement

---

20 Dameshek and Remnev, *Sibir' v sostave Rossiiskoi imperii*, pp. 278–79.

21 *Ibid.*, p. 280.

22 *Ibid.*, pp. 275 and 279.

23 RGIA, f. 1149, op. 10 (D.Z.), d. 60, l. 11 (1888). When referring to archival documents, I use the taxonomy common for Russian archives: *fond–opis'–delo–list*. "Fond" is a collection; "opis'" is a list of files; "delo" is a file; and "list" is a page.

24 Daniel Beer, "Penal Deportation to Siberia and the Limits of State Power, 1801–81", *Kritika: Explorations in Russian and Eurasian History*, 16:3 (2015), pp. 621–50.

of exiles.[25] Despite the attempts at reform, exile remained in use both as a judicial punishment and as an administrative measure.

Development of the Russian penal system and the centrality of forced displacement to it can only be understood in conjunction with wider imperial policies. Exile was an embodiment of the asymmetric political and administrative relation between Siberia and the metropole. Unlike the overseas colonies of the Western European maritime empires, Siberia and the Far East were part of the same vast landmass as the European part of Russia. This contiguity contributed to ambiguous perceptions of Siberia's position within the empire: while some observers considered it a distant and foreign Asiatic colony, others highlighted the centuries-long peasant migrations and conceived of it as a frontier where the Russian culture and way of life could be spread.[26] Central authorities were also ambivalent towards the region, oscillating between the desire to better integrate it within the empire, develop its economic potential, and create a class of competent local administrators, and the fear that too much political or economic autonomy would lead the locals to contest the tsarist power. Fear of the secession of Siberia loomed large. Throughout the nineteenth century, approaches to this dilemma differed: during the reign of Alexander I, Mikhail Speransky overhauled the governance of Siberia, persecuting corrupt officials and dividing the vast region into two administrative entities, Western and Eastern Siberia, each headed by a governor-general. His goal was to create a legal and administrative framework that would allow the region to develop efficiently and would minimize corruption.[27] Under Nicholas I, the First Siberian Committee leaned in the other direction, making "a conscious decision to keep Siberia backward and underdeveloped as the best way of bringing about the firm unification and complete amalgamation of Siberia with central Russia".[28] Officials under Alexander II saw the task of governing Siberia as part of the state-building process of a single, united Russia and sought to overcome Siberia's administrative separateness.[29] This

---

25 Zhanna Popova, "Exile as Imperial Practice: Western Siberia and the Russian Empire, 1879–1900", *International Review of Social History*, 63:S26 (August 2018), pp. 131–50.

26 Mark Bassin, "Inventing Siberia: Visions of the Russian East in the Early Nineteenth Century", *The American Historical Review*, 96:3 (1991), pp. 763–94, 766.

27 Marc Raeff, *Michael Speransky: Statesman of Imperial Russia 1772–1839* (Dordrecht: Springer, 1957), pp. 260–65.

28 Steven G. Marks, *Road to Power: The Trans-Siberian Railroad and the Colonization of Asian Russia, 1850–1917* (Ithaca, NY: Cornell University Press, 1991), p. 49.

29 S.G. Svatikov, *Rossiia i Sibir': (k istorii sibirskogo oblastnichestva v XIX v.)* (Prague: Izd. Obshchestva Sibiriakov, 1929), p. 76.

process accelerated under Alexander III, and by 1887, "the very name Siberia was no longer used as an administrative term", as Western and Eastern Siberia were subdivided into several smaller governorates (*gubernii*).[30] At the end of the nineteenth century, policies shifted towards the economic and social integration of the region, and the development of transport and education, rather than penal colonization, to become the chief tools of the russification of Siberia.[31]

Legislative framework

The gulf between legislation and practice in the domain of punishment was wide, but even a brief sketch of the legal framework that regulated punishments in the late Romanov empire helps to grasp the conceptions, aspirations, and ambitions of the state officials when it came to reforming the penal system. In the second half of the nineteenth century, punishments of all subjects of the tsar were defined by the Criminal Code of 1845. It reflected the social structure of the empire during the existence of serfdom. It implied two separate "ladders of punishment" for the privileged and unprivileged estates, and proposed an intricate system that included twelve types (and thirty-eight degrees) of common punishment, not to count the special punishments such as eternal expulsion outside the empire or confinement in a monastery.[32] Some of these punishments, like the workhouses, never became widespread, and were ultimately abandoned.[33] Serfs were punished

---

30 Marks, *Road to Power*, p. 58.

31 Anatolii Remnev, "'Vdvinut' Rossiiu v Sibir'. Imperiia i russkaia kolonizatsiia vtoroi poloviny XIX – nachala XX vv.", *Ab Imperio*, 3 (2003), pp. 135–58.

32 "Ladder" in this context signifies a ranking of punishments, starting with those for the gravest crimes down to the lightest infractions. These twelve types were: (1) death penalty; (2) exile to katorga; (3) exile to resettlement (*ssylka na poselenie*) in Siberia; (4) exile to resettlement in Transcaucasia; (5) exile "for life" (*ssylka na zhit'ye*) to Siberia; (6) exile "for life" to other distant regions; (7) incarceration in "corrective arrest divisions" (*ispravitelnye arestantskie otdeleniia*); (8) incarceration in prison; (9) incarceration in strongholds; (10) short-term arrest; (11) reprimand (*vygovor*) in court; (12) fine. Numbers (2)–(4) also implied civil death, or the loss of all estate rights and property. Moreover, additional corporal punishment was frequently used against lower-class offenders. The existence of multiple degrees further complicated this system of punishment, although in practice degrees could not always be respected. The plurality of places of confinement also contributed to the confusion: arrest, for example, could be spent in one of five different types of carceral institution. See more on the 1845 Criminal Code in Nikolai Tagantsev, *Russkoe ugolovnoe pravo*, vol. 2 (Saint Petersburg: Gos. Tip., 1902), pp. 960–67.

33 Apparently, by the time the workhouses were abolished, there were only four in the empire: in Simbirsk, Kostroma, Tver, and Kazan. See: *Polnoe sobranie zakonov Rossiiskoi Imperii. Sobranie*

at their landlords' discretion for a large number of offences and crimes. Rural and urban communities (*obshchestva* and *meshchanstva*) could also administratively exile their members, as is discussed in more detail below. The establishment of adequate policing and a criminal justice system in the rural areas became a continuous challenge for the imperial authorities in the decades after the abolition of serfdom, and administrative exile was used to alleviate these weaknesses.

As socio-political change gathered pace following the Crimean War (1853–1856), the 1845 Criminal Code rapidly became obsolete. Notably, the emancipation of serfs in 1861 changed the legal status of peasants, scrapping the possibility of exile at the landlord's will, although communities retained their power to exile their members. Over the course of the second half of the nineteenth century, several legal acts updated some aspects of the criminal justice system, although a profound restructuring of the system was not realized, as exile and katorga remained the main punishments for the most serious crimes up until the fall of the Russian empire in 1917. The reform of prison administration, introduction of compulsory labour in prisons, and further attempts to abolish exile are particularly relevant within the framework of this study and thus are discussed in more detail below. The level of practical implementation of these legal acts, especially in the regions, still remains to be investigated in detail, as existing works on the topic have generally focused on materials from the central archives.[34]

On 17 April 1863, a law curbed the use of corporal punishment, both as a separate and as an additional punishment. This flattened out the distinctions in the execution of punishment between the privileged and unprivileged estates. Prior to 1863, corporal punishment was one of the dominant punitive practices in the Russian empire. Despite the fact that Empress Elizaveta Petrovna suspended the death penalty for common criminals in 1754, thus legally making katorga the gravest punishment, officials admitted later that punishment by knout constituted a qualified death penalty.[35] Knout was abolished by Nicholas I in 1845, and the 1863 reform further limited the use of corporal punishment, although it failed to completely abolish

---

tret'e. Tom IV. 1884 (Saint Petersburg, 1887), no. 2172 (24 April 1884), p. 261.

34 Two central English-language volumes investigating the mid-nineteenth-century punishments are Bruce F. Adams, *The Politics of Punishment: Prison Reform in Russia, 1863–1917* (DeKalb: Northern Illinois University Press, 1996) and Abby M. Schrader, *Languages of the Lash: Corporal Punishment and Identity in Imperial Russia* (DeKalb: Northern Illinois University Press, 2002).

35 A knout was a type of heavy whip, somewhat similar to a scourge; it had many varieties, some of which had wires and other metal parts. For knout as de facto death penalty, see: RGIA, f. 1151, op. 15, d. 196, l. 2.

it. The lash (*plet'*) was abolished as a separate punishment and as a part of punishment for those sentenced to katorga and exile, but it was still used as a disciplinary punishment for those who were already serving their katorga and exile terms. For the wrongdoings that convicts committed while serving their term, they could be punished by up to hundred lashes. Birching, a much lighter punishment than lashing or knouting, was abolished as a part of punishment for those sentenced to imprisonment, but was still used against male exiles and katorga convicts up until February 1917.[36] From early on, imperial officials argued for preserving corporal punishment for these convicts by underlining the fact that they were subjected to civil death and therefore there were no other punishments left to persecute those of them who reoffended.[37] The most severe types of corporal punishment for convicts (the lash, sticks, and running the gauntlet) were only abolished on 3 June 1903.[38] Corporal punishment gradually left the punitive repertoire, but its continued use against katorga convicts and exiles effectively put them outside of the general system of criminal justice.

On 11 December 1879, another law saw the creation of the Main Prison Administration, and thus initiated prison reform, while on 11 June 1885 the distinction between katorga labour in mines, strongholds, and plants was abolished.[39] This distinction was de facto obsolete, as only katorga labour in the mines was still practised, and this law simply regularized the existing situation. An important law was published on 6 January 1886 and introduced obligatory labour for prisoners. This law and its ramifications are discussed below in the section dedicated to convicts' forced labour. Finally, in June 1900 exile to Siberia was curbed.[40] This attempt to limit exile did not have long-lasting results, as the persecution of political dissenters following the 1905 revolution meant that thousands were sent to Siberia as exiles and hard labourers. Nevertheless, this reform and discussions surrounding it marked an attempt to depart from forced displacement as one of the main punishments in the empire, and highlighted the alternatives that were proposed to this punitive practice. A closer look at these unrealized alternatives provides an opportunity to better understand the reasons for the tenacity of forced displacement as one of the main punishments in the Russian empire.

---

36   Mikhail Isaev, *Osnovy penitentsiarnoi politiki* (Moscow: Gosizdat, 1926), p. 87.

37   Schrader, *Languages of the Lash*, p. 211.

38   RGIA, f. 1151, op. 15, d. 196, l. 2.

39   *Polnoe sobranie zakonov Rossiiskoi Imperii. Sobranie tret'e. Tom VI. 1886* (Saint Petersburg, 1888), no. 3447 (6 January 1886), pp. 8–11.

40   *Polnoe sobranie zakonov Rossiiskoi Imperii. Sobranie tret'e. Tom XX. 1900* (Saint Petersburg, 1902), no. 18777 (10 June 1900), pp. 630–36 and no. 18839 (12 June 1900), pp. 757–58.

On the legal level, the tsarist authorities started to move away from the traditional retributive punishments like corporal punishment. This movement was slow and uneasy and did not lead to a profound restructuring of the penal system: it updated some of its parts, while others, like exile, remained resistant to change. At the same time, new legislation offered a modernized vision of forced convict labour and sought to re-conceptualize it as a productive and re-educating process rather than harsh retributive punishment.

Usages of exile

By the end of the nineteenth century, exile was a complex and con-flicted system, a long-running penal tradition that persisted despite the consistent complaints of local authorities and the critiques of progres-sive officials from the capitals and outside observers.[41] This section provides an analysis of the goals and usages of exile. I argue that exile's polyvalence contributed to its longevity despite the fact that it did not perform adequately to achieve its intended goals of controlling crime and colonizing Siberia. This multiplicity of goals also led to a proliferation of different categories of exiles. By the end of the nineteenth century, nine categories existed, all differing in the degrees of deprivation of rights. I will discuss here in detail the three largest of them: administrative exiles, judicial exiles, and katorga convicts.[42] Although these categories de jure implied significantly different conditions for exiles, according to contemporary observers, most of those subject to them were equally destitute.[43] This conflation of different groups started already during transit: administrative exiles, who did not commit any crimes, had to travel the whole way to Siberia together with convicts, staying in transit prisons and experiencing the same gruelling journey on foot and, later, on boats and barges.

41 For the range of critical opinions regarding exile in the nineteenth century, see A.D. Margolis, *Tiur'ma i ssylka v imperatorskoi Rossii. Issledovaniia i arkhivnye nakhodki* (Moscow: Lanterna VITA, 1995), pp. 13–28.
42 There were eight categories of exiles in the narrow sense: (1) administrative exiles; (2) judicially exiled; (3) exiled settlers; (4) "settled workers" (exiled vagrants); (5) exiled for life (*soslannye na zhit'e*); (6) political exiles; (7) exiled for up to five years and under police surveillance; (8) criminal convicts from the Grand Duchy of Finland who chose exile instead of incarceration. In addition, katorga convicts constituted a separate category.
43 Salomon, *Ssylka v Sibir'*, pp. 109–11.

We are most familiar with exile in tsarist Russia thanks to the narratives of political exiles, who often belonged to the privileged estates.[44] Prior to the 1905 revolution, however, they represented only a minuscule fraction of exiles, and even after 1905, only accounted for around 10 per cent of the overall number.[45] Before 1905, the largest cohort of political exiles were the Poles exiled after the 1863 Uprising.[46] In its routine application, exile was overwhelmingly an instrument of repression against subaltern groups, above all peasants and the urban poor. Their perspective is elusive, as most of them were illiterate and did not leave any records of their exile experience. Although the official sources are of little help in grasping these experiences, they do help to de-centralize the narratives of political exiles and explore the usages of judicial and administrative exile against the wider population, and elucidate the usages of forced displacement beyond the aim of political repression which has been long a focus of militants, observers, and researchers alike.[47]

Exile to Siberia was part of the criminal justice system, but it would be reductive to understand it only as punishment. Judicial exile undoubtedly had the traditional punitive goals of retribution and distancing the wrongdoers socially and geographically. There are no consistent statistics that could help estimate its impact as a tool of crime control in the European part of Russia, but numerous authors have stated that it led to a rise in crime in Siberia itself, in part due to the weakness of local policing and lack of oversight. Katorga was the most extreme form of this retribution and forced isolation: during their terms of hard labour, convicts worked and lived at separate penal sites and were held in shackles. Upon their release, such convicts were expected to live in Siberia as members of a separate exile estate, which effectively prevented their return to society. Backbreaking labour and the harshness of climatic and economic conditions in Siberia

---

44 Sarah J. Young has discussed this double marginalization of convicts and exiles from the unprivileged estates: Sarah J. Young, "Knowing Russia's Convicts: The Other in Narratives of Imprisonment and Exile of the Late Imperial Era", *Europe-Asia Studies*, 65:9 (2013), pp. 1700–15.

45 Sarah Badcock sought to recover voices of exiles of unprivileged background in the post-1905 period in her 2016 book: Sarah Badcock, *A Prison without Walls? Eastern Siberian Exile in the Last Years of Tsarism* (Oxford: Oxford University Press, 2016).

46 According to different estimates, between 34,000 and 70,000 Poles were exiled to various locations in the empire, perhaps around half of them to Siberia. See Andrew A. Gentes, *The Mass Deportation of Poles to Siberia, 1863–1880* (Cham: Springer International, 2017), pp. 78–79.

47 For a recent English-language account of exile as a tool of political repression, see Daniel Beer, *The House of the Dead: Siberian Exile under the Tsars* (London: Penguin Books, 2017). For a wider history of modern political imprisonment, see Padraic Kenney, *Dance in Chains: Political Imprisonment in the Modern World* (New York: Oxford University Press, 2017).

destroyed the health of many of these convicts, leaving them unable to survive as settlers upon release. In this chaotic, ruthless, and exploitative system convicts frequently turned from villains into victims.[48]

Non-judicial exile can be understood as a delegation of power over forced displacement to communities. Exile by serf owners disappeared with the abolition of serfdom in 1861, but exile by rural and urban communities (*ob-shchestva* and *meshchanstva*) remained. This resilience can at least partially be explained by the fact that policing and criminal justice institutions were weakly developed in the rural areas, and state agents had fairly little control over the deployment of punishment there. The desire to prevent popular mob justice by allowing communities to exile suspected criminals also played a certain role.[49] Crime control was thus partially delegated to communities by granting them the possibility to expel their undesired members to Western Siberia. Two modalities of such expulsion existed. First, communities had the right to refuse to accept back their members who were convicted but had served their terms, which was called "the right of non-acceptance" (*pravo nepriiatiia*). When these expelled community members tried to return to European Russia after serving their term within the penal system, communities could prevent them from doing so. Such administrative exile became de facto a second, non-judicial punishment. Second, communities had "the right of expulsion" (*pravo udaleniia*), which could be used against the most troublesome and unruly community members, including suspected arsonists and horse thieves, the most disruptive criminals in the countryside. In either case, the procedure was rather uncomplicated: a two-thirds vote of the community assembly in favour of the expulsion and approval by the provincial administration were needed, and the communities had to cover the costs of exile.[50] On paper, such administrative exiles faced the least severe limitations of rights, but in practice they bore the burden of uprooting and the necessity to start a new life without any resources, which often pushed them towards destitution and crime. As with convicts, their families were also expected to "voluntarily" follow them into exile. Once exiled, they were free to move in Siberia, but prohibited from travelling back to the European part of Russia for at least five or, later, three years. A variety of reasons independent of the gravity of crime or the degree of guilt

48   Sarah Badcock, "From Villains to Victims: Experiencing Illness in Siberian Exile", *Europe-Asia Studies*, 65:9 (November 2013), pp. 1716–36.

49   For more on rural crime and policing, see Stephen P. Frank, *Crime, Cultural Conflict, and Justice in Rural Russia, 1856–1914* (Berkeley: University of California Press, 1999). For the discussion of administrative exile, see especially pp. 236–42.

50   *Ibid.*, p. 236.

guided the communities in their decision to exile their members, including the convict's family connections and the land situation in the community, as it was possible to redistribute the land of the exile to other members.[51] Moreover, wealthier peasants bribed the village heads to have their poorer neighbours exiled and thus to avoid being conscripted into the army, as exiles were counted towards the communal conscription quotas.[52]

At the end of nineteenth century, non-judicial exile continued to be widely used. According to official statistics, in the years 1887–1898, 52.3 per cent of all exiles, or 52,611 people, were exiled in this manner. Out of this number, 26,391 were exiled according to the right of non-acceptance, while another 20,834 were banished due to the right of expulsion.[53] When it came to this last measure, for example, rural communities were responsible for expelling around 1,700 members yearly, while urban communities exiled only 300 people per year during this period, reflecting the overwhelmingly rural character of the country.[54] For an earlier period (1867–1876), approximately 40 per cent of the total number of administrative exiles were the families of the exiled.[55] Considering that in the following two decades there were no major reforms of administrative exile, it is possible to assume that a similar proportion was maintained towards the end of the century.

This prevalence of administrative exile distinguished the Russian case from other systems of convict transportation, where judicial deportation dominated. At the end of the nineteenth century, according to the head of the Main Prison Administration (*Glavnoe Tiuremnoe Upravlenie*, or the GTU), the governmental agency responsible for managing the penal system, half of the approximately 300,000 exiles present in Siberia were administratively, rather than judicially, exiled.[56] One of the harshest punishments that existed in the empire was in half of the cases used against people who did not commit any crimes. Legal distinctions between the judicial and administrative exiles were supposed to improve the situation of the latter. Often, these distinctions were rooted in imperial imagination that did not translate into a difference of conditions for exiles themselves. For instance, central authorities considered exile to Western Siberia less punitive than that to

---

51 *Zhurnaly vysochaishe uchrezhdennoi Komissii o meropriiatiakh po otmene ssylki. Zasedaniia 3 iunia, 9 i 16 dekabria 1899 g., 10 ianvaria i 7 fevralia 1900 g.* (Saint Petersburg, 1900), p. 35.
52 Gentes, *Exile to Siberia*, p. 139.
53 Salomon, *Ssylka v Sibir'*, p. 133.
54 *Zhurnaly vysochaishe uchrezhdennoi Komissii*, p. 56.
55 K.V.N., "Ssylka po prigovoram krestianskikh i meshchanskikh obshchestv", *Russkaia rech*, 3 (1881), pp. 49–78, 51–52.
56 Salomon, *Ssylka v Sibir'*, p. 335.

Eastern Siberia, thus creating a hierarchy in the geography of punishment where the degree of punishment was defined by the physical distance from the metropole. Administrative exiles, considered the least dangerous, were sent to Western Siberia, unless they asked to be exiled further east. Realities of exile, the long and arduous journey, the hardships of uprooting and displacement, and the stigma associated with exile status flattened out such intended distinctions. Families of exiles who followed them to Siberia were a particularly vulnerable group. Although the state recognized the wives and children of katorga convicts and exiles as innocent, and tried to alleviate their plight, their condition remained extremely difficult, especially in Eastern Siberia.[57] As Sarah Badcock has remarked, the position of these families showed that "categories of free and forced, convict and innocent, punished and unpunished, were profoundly blurred when face to face with the realities of daily life".[58]

By law, administrative exiles became members of communities in Siberia, even though the locals routinely opposed this practice by complaining to regional and central authorities. Exiles were granted land and expected to settle down and thus contribute to the colonization of Siberia, turning from unruly offenders and criminals into industrious peasants. This signals that in theory, exile was not devoid of reformatory aspirations. Colonization thus served not only the statist goals, but also became a measure of the successful rehabilitation of criminals. In practice, sustainable settlements remained elusive, not only because of economic difficulties or mass escapes. Another reason was the rarity of women among the exiles. Women were crucial labourers on the family plot, as farms were unsustainable with solitary workers, and obviously necessary for the biological reproduction of the colonists. But their role among the exiles in Siberia was not limited to purely pragmatic considerations. Women became symbolically central to the enterprise of penal colonization: officials emphasized their role as civilizing, domesticating agents capable of restraining the destructive forces of the dangerous and unstable single male exiles.[59]

The scarcity of resources and stable exiled settlers was exacerbated by the scarcity of land. This led to an experiment that was unique in the late imperial policy of exile. In 1888, Tobolsk authorities realized that they could not ascribe exile to communities anymore, as there was no arable

57 Abby M. Schrader, "Unruly Felons and Civilizing Wives: Cultivating Marriage in the Siberian Exile System, 1822–1860", *Slavic Review* 66:2 (2007), pp. 230–56.
58 Badcock, "From Villains to Victims", p. 1734.
59 Schrader, "Unruly Felons".

land available within existing settlements. In an attempt to distribute the incoming exiles, central authorities ordered the creation of twenty-two new settlements destined exclusively for exiles. Only fourteen of these settlements ended up being actually populated.[60] Ten years later, the head of the Main Prison Administration looked in detail into the condition of exiles in these settlements and found that only eight settlements still existed, and among the exiles who were sent there between 1889 and 1899, the overwhelming majority (1,234 out of 1,378) left immediately upon arrival.[61] This was one of the rare, if not unique, attempts to create separate penal settlements in pre-Soviet times, and it failed completely: as exiles fled en masse, the local authorities did not have any means to stop them, neither by force nor by attracting them back with opportunities.

In the exile system, unintended consequences proliferated. A type of exile called "exilic placement" (*ssylka na vodvorenie*) existed as a punishment only for one single type of crime, namely vagabondage. This type of exile can be understood as an attempt to control subaltern mobility with forced displacement.[62] In the early nineteenth century, imperial authorities continued to consider vagabondage a serious crime that challenged state and societal order. As Adele Lindenmeyr has underlined, "Russian law strove to maintain a tightly ordered society in which every man and woman had a master and an assigned place of residence".[63] Unlike their Western European counterparts, Russian imperial authorities opted for exile rather than imprisonment as the chief punishment for this infraction.[64] In the

60   Salomon, *Ssylka v Sibir'*, pp. 160–61.

61   *Zhurnaly vysochaishe uchrezhdennoi Komissii*, p. 60.

62   Ample literature exists on the Western European attempts to control the vagrant poor. Michel Foucault extensively discussed this confinement of the poor in his *Discipline and Punish: The Birth of the Prison* (New York: Vintage Books, 1995 [1977]). The emergence of workhouses in Great Britain, the Netherlands, and the German lands was associated with the drive to criminalize the mobility of the lower classes. For a brief introduction to the literature on the topic, see Thomas Mathiesen, *Prison on Trial* (Winchester, Portland, OR: Waterside Press, 2006 [1990]), pp. 18–19, and for an analysis of these interconnections in early modern continental Europe, see, for instance, Pieter Spierenburg, *The Prison Experience: Disciplinary Institutions and Their Inmates in Early Modern Europe* (Amsterdam: Amsterdam University Press: 2007 [1991]), pp. 41–86.

63   Adele Lindenmeyr, *Poverty Is Not a Vice: Charity, Society, and the State in Imperial Russia* (Princeton, NJ: Princeton University Press, 1996), p. 37.

64   For more on fugitives in Siberia, see Abby M. Schrader, "Branding the Exile as 'Other': Corporal Punishment and the Construction of Boundaries in Mid-Nineteenth-Century Russia", in David L. Hoffmann and Yanni Kotsonis (eds), *Russian Modernity: Politics, Knowledge, Practices* (Houndmills, New York: Macmillan, 2000), pp. 19–40, 26–29, and Andrew A. Gentes, "Vagabondage and the Tsarist Siberian Exile System: Power and Resistance in the Penal Landscape", *Central Asian Survey*, 30:3–4 (2011), pp. 407–21.

first half of the nineteenth century, runaway serfs, deserters, and young men escaping military recruitment were considered particularly prone to becoming vagabonds. By the last third of the nineteenth century, despite the abolition of serfdom and loosening of the conscription laws, vagabonds remained numerous, especially in Siberia. This punishment turned out to have acquired a more subversive dynamic. According to official reports, a significant share of the vagabonds were actually runaway katorga convicts who demonstrated an intricate knowledge of the judicial system and pretended to "not remember their kin" (*rodstva nepomniashchii*), as the juridical formula of the time stated, in order to conceal their identity as convicts. This allowed them to avoid severe disciplinary punishments associated with running away from katorga, as well as to receive lighter punishment in case they committed new crimes. Numbers of such exiles were not negligible: in the 1880s, around 1,450 people per year were subjected to this type of exile.[65] It was eventually substituted with exile to the island of Sakhalin and, according to a report from 1899, this led to an instant reduction in the number of vagabonds.[66] Only during the discussions in preparation of the 1900 exile reform were workhouses and forced labour discussed as an alternative punishment for vagabonds, beggars, idlers, and petty thieves.[67]

Over the course of exile's long existence, its goals were gradually updated and redefined. In the second half of the nineteenth century, central officials planned it as a place of retribution and rehabilitation, a tool of crime control and colonization, but achieving these goals was continuously undermined by the discrepancies between the officials' visions and the realities of exile. These lofty aspirations hinged on efficient local bureaucracy, the development of rural policing to control the exiles, and sufficient funding for the settlements, all of which were absent. Although the initial experience of exile was characterized by violent state intervention and subsequent uprooting and displacement, experience of life in Siberia typically meant abandonment, rather than control.

The failed abolition

The Russian empire was not alone in relying on exile as a tool of colonial expansion, crime control, and labour mobilization. Western European

65 RGIA, f. 1149, op. 10 (D.Z.), d. 60, l. 7 (1888).
66 *Zhurnaly vysochaishe uchrezhdennoi Komissii*, pp. 21–22.
67 *Ibid.*, p. 4.

colonial empires used convict transportation for a variety of similar goals over centuries. Starting with the Portuguese who first sent convicts to work at the port of Ceuta in 1415, and until 1938, when the last convicts were deported to French Guiana, convict transportation, often combined with forced labour, was a mainstay of imperial ventures throughout the globe.[68] Clare Anderson and Hamish Maxwell-Stewart have attributed this longevity of transportation to four interrelated factors. First, the destiny of convicts, judged guilty and thus deserving punishment, had attracted little attention from elites and society at large, thus allowing governments to use and abuse convicts freely. Second, convict transportation offered officials flexibility, as it created a relatively cheap and expendable pool of coerced workers who could be directed towards the destinations where free labourers would not settle. Third, it served as a tool of both metropolitan and colonial policing. Finally, administrators perceived transportation as a cheaper alternative to the construction of new prison buildings.[69]

By the second half of the nineteenth century, however, most colonial empires had ceased transportation to overseas territories. One notable exception was France. The French experimented with transportation at least since the early eighteenth century, sending convicts to a variety of locations including Algeria, but struggled to find a stable destination for convicts. Only by the mid-nineteenth century did the principal destinations of transportation, French Guiana and New Caledonia, emerge. It is estimated that between 1854 and 1938, nearly 100,000 political and common law prisoners were banished to these two locations.[70] The French turned to penal transportation comparatively late, just as the British began to stop sending convicts to Australia. This late shift prompted critique from the international penological community, as many considered transportation a decidedly outdated punishment. This emergent community comprising jurists, prison officials, penologists, and representatives of governmental agencies sought to professionalize the domain of punishment. They discussed and compared various punitive measures at the International Prison Congresses, first convened in 1872.[71] Russian delegates were in the

68   Anderson, *A Global History*.

69   Clare Anderson and Hamish Maxwell-Stewart, "Convict Labour and the Western Empires, 1415–1954", in Robert Aldrich and Kirsten McKenzie (eds), *The Routledge History of Western Empires* (London, New York: Routledge, 2014), pp. 102–18.

70   Christian G. De Vito and Alex Lichtenstein, "Writing a Global History of Convict Labour", in De Vito and Lichtenstein (eds), *Global Convict Labour*, pp. 1–45, 22.

71   For more on these Congresses, and especially on the gradual exclusion of the non-Western participating countries, see: Nir Shafir, "The International Congress as Scientific and Diplomatic

core group of the participants and consistently took part in the Congresses, while the 1890 Congress took place in Saint Petersburg. At these Congresses, debates regarding transportation included the question whether it belonged to the "rational" penal repertoire at all.[72] In search of justification, French officials argued that transportation was inherently rehabilitative, as outdoor labour and a promise of a new life in the colonies prompted the convicts to change their criminal behaviour. As Briony Neilson has underlined, these arguments aroused the curiosity of foreign observers: scepticism towards the rehabilitative capacity of the penitentiary was growing at the time, and some state officials, notably from Italy and Belgium, envisioned transportation both as a cheaper and more efficient alternative to the construction of new prisons.[73] Debates surrounding the French case, however, also shone a light on the inherent paradox of penal colonization, as "the success of colonial settlement inevitably meant the obsolescence of its penal function".[74] Arguments and controversies that emerged during the International Prison Congresses were echoed in internal Russian discussions regarding exile. In 1874, for example, the Russian Minister of Transport Communications Konstantin Possiet directly referred to the British and French experiences with exile, and underlined the lack of reformatory potential of exile to Siberia because of weak surveillance and control over the lives of exiled settlers. According to him, and in line with the interventionist penological logic, criminals needed to be viewed as sick people, and their "healing" had to happen through careful professional intervention in urban prisons.[75]

In the global scholarship on convict transportation the question whether the Russian imperial case can be analysed together with the overseas empires has been subject to debate: for example, in the chapter quoted above, Anderson and Maxwell-Stewart exclude it from their analysis due to the overland, rather than maritime, nature of the Russian empire, but in the more recent volume on global convict transportation, the Russian case is included.[76] The fact that the colony and the metropole constituted a single

---

Technology: Global Intellectual Exchange in the International Prison Congress, 1860–90", *Journal of Global History*, 9:1 (March 2014), pp. 72–93.

72   *Ve Congrès Pénitentiaire International (Paris – 1895)*, vol. 3: Rapports de la Première Section (Melun: Imprimerie administrative, 1896), p. 101.

73   Briony Neilson, "The Paradox of Penal Colonization: Debates of Convict Transportation at the International Prison Congresses 1872–1895", *French History and Civilization*, 6 (2015), pp. 198–211, 201.

74   *Ibid.*, p. 210.

75   RGIA, f. 1149, op. 10 (D.Z.), d. 60, l. 67.

76   Anderson, *A Global History*; Anderson and Maxwell-Stewart, "Convict Labour and the Western Empires".

landmass undoubtedly created some specificities in the imperial policies overall, especially when it came to economic and political development. Siberia was part of the same polity and, as discussed above, over centuries Russian authorities had ambivalent and even conflicting policies towards the region, pursuing ruthless resource extraction along with attempts to integrate Siberia within the empire socially, politically, and economically. Nevertheless, exile in tsarist Russia shared marked similarities with the overseas transportation of the maritime colonial empires because of its role in the underlying processes of imperial expansion.

The four factors distinguished by Anderson and Maxwell-Stewart are a productive starting point for an analysis of the longevity of the Russian practice of exile. In this case as well, the destiny of convicts and administrative exiles evoked little interest in society until the second half of the nineteenth century. The pivotal point was the publication in 1861–1862 of a semi-autobiographical novel *The House of the Dead* by Fyodor Dostoevsky. This was one of the earliest literary accounts of katorga and exile, followed by a host of fiction and non-fiction works that pictured the grim realities of exiles and convicts. The authors included former convicts, like Dostoevsky himself, local Siberian authors, journalists and writers from the capitals, and international observers.[77] Officials of the GTU also offered accounts of their visits to the sites of exile and katorga, including rather critical ones.[78] Public discussions spurred the drive towards reform within the government, but ultimately failed to stop the use of exile.

Using the labour of exiles at state-run projects was a priority of the central authorities in the eighteenth century, as the experiments of Peter I and his successors show. During the nineteenth century, however, the focus shifted

---

77   For more on exile to Siberia in Russian literature, see Harriet Murav, "'Vo Glubine Sibirskikh Rud': Siberia and the Myth of Exile", in Galya Diment and Yuri Slezkine (eds), *Between Heaven and Hell: The Myth of Siberia in Russian Culture* (New York: Palgrave Macmillan, 1993), pp. 95–112. For international reactions to the narratives of Siberian exile, see Ben Phillips, *Siberian Exile and the Invention of Revolutionary Russia, 1825–1917: Exiles, Émigrés and the International Reception of Russian radicalism* (New York: Routledge, 2022).

78   Among them: Dmitrii Dril', *Ssylka i katorga v Rossii* (Saint Petersburg: Tipografiia Pravitel'stvuiushchego Senata, 1898) and Dmitrii Dril', *Ssylka vo Frantsii i v Rossii: Iz lichnykh nabliudenii vo vremia poezdki v Novuiu Kaledoniiu, na o. Sakhalin, v Priamurskii krai i Sibir'* (Saint Petersburg: Izdanie L.F. Panteleeva, 1899); P.K. Gran, *Katorga v Sibiri. Izvlecheniia iz otcheta o sluzhebnoi poezdke Nachal'nika Glavnogo Upravleniia P. K. Grana v Sibir' v 1913 godu* (Saint Petersburg: Tipo-litografiia S.-Peterburgskoi Odinochnoi Tiur'my, 1913); S.S. Khrulev, "*Katorga v Sibiri: Otchet nachal'nika Glavnogo tiuremnogo upravleniia S.S. Khruleva o sluzhebnoi poezdke v 1909 v Irkutskuiu guberniiu i Zabaikalskuiu oblast'*" Supplement to *Tiuremnyi vestnik*, no. 8–9 (1910); Salomon, *Ssylka v Sibir'*; and Aleksandr Salomon, "O. Sakhalin (Iz otcheta byvshego nachal'nika glavnogo tiuremnogo upravleniia A.P. Salomona)", *Tiuremnyi vestnik*, 1 (1901), pp. 20–53.

from using the labour of exiles towards organizing the forced labour of prison inmates. Exiles, with the exception of katorga convicts, were generally not forced to work. The meagre governmental allowances they were paid were not sufficient to survive. Agriculture, road construction, mining, and river transport offered some seasonal and short-term jobs, but for most exiles, forced displacement entailed prolonged periods of unemployment. By the beginning of the twentieth century, as free migration to Siberia gained pace, finding work for the growing number of exiles in Siberia continued to be a challenge. Political exiles, many of whom were professionals, students, and skilled workers, were often only able to find unstable unskilled jobs. White-collar work and industrial occupations were available in Siberian towns and cities, but virtually non-existent in the rural areas. Political exiles were ascribed residence far from urban centres, and leaving the countryside to find employment required them to petition regional governors, and not all of these petitions were satisfied. Some exiles took up teaching and scientific work, but these opportunities were rare. Finding secure employment in exile was elusive, and most exiles from unprivileged backgrounds either directly faced hunger and destitution, or lived in their constant fear.[79]

Siberian exile was perceived as a cheaper alternative to the construction of penitentiaries: the financial argument was used to stifle exile reform proposals at least since Speransky. In 1871–1873, during the preparation of the prison reform, a Ministry of Justice committee headed by Eduard Frish, charged with updating the Criminal Code for the post-emancipation realities, also made suggestions to abandon the use of exile as punishment in favour of incarceration (but reserved its use for cases relating to communal self-governance).[80] These propositions were refused, as prompt construction of new prison buildings was considered too expensive, and exile continued to coexist in the imperial punitive repertoire along with the modernizing system of penitentiaries.[81] An official of the Ministry of Finance who reviewed the renewed exile reform projects in 1888 again argued against them, underlining that not only the construction, but also the maintenance of prison buildings was prohibitively expensive.[82] Curiously, during these 1888 discussions, officials of the Ministry of Interior tried to counter-argue that these new penitentiaries would be constructed in a

79   Badcock, *A Prison without Walls*, pp. 107–30.
80   For more on the workings of the Frish committee, see Adams, *The Politics of Punishment*, pp. 77–78. Adams argued that Frish "lived and worked in a legal world distant from the realities of prison administration", which also did not contribute to the success of his projects.
81   RGIA, f. 1149, op. 10 (D.Z.), d. 60, l. 11–12 (1888).
82   *Ibid.*, l. 14.

"caserne-like fashion", hinting at a cheaper, camp-like militarized alternative to traditional prisons, where collective confinement and collective work would be favoured. These suggestions were not realized, but they signify the aspirations to move away not only from exile, but also classic modern prisons towards carceral institutions that would be cheaper, more flexible, and more responsive to state construction goals. Whether exile was actually cheaper to maintain is debatable, because the transit of exiles and katorga convicts could be very costly, especially in the case of distant destinations like the island of Sakhalin in the Far East, which became one of the principal katorga sites in the second half of the nineteenth century.

Exile's capacity to serve as a tool of policing was perceived as controversial. Prominent Siberian regionalist (*oblastnik*) activist Nikolai Iadrintsev was among the most convincing voices to criticize exile's impact on criminality in Siberia.[83] As the wave of critique rose, even central officials openly admitted that exile as a tool of policing had failed. Estimating the impact of exile on crime in the European part of Russia is not possible, but in Siberia, marginalized, impoverished exiles often resorted to begging, theft, robbery, and murder. The negative effect of exile on crime in Siberia was one of the key arguments in the discussions surrounding its abolition. In 1899, according to data from the GTU, although exiles constituted only 5.4 per cent of the total population of Siberia, they accounted for 70 per cent of its prison inmates.[84]

At the very end of the nineteenth century, another governmental committee charged with exile reform was organized. Its proclaimed goal was radical, as the tsar required it to solve the "exile question" definitively and prepare its abolition. The fundamental paradox of the incompatibility of sending convicts to a region as a means of both punishment and colonization featured prominently in these discussions. Free peasant migration to Siberia and the development of railroads were said to undermine the punitive effect of exile, while the presence of exiles, in its turn, was identified as thwarting the economic and social development of the region. However, when the reform of exile was at last finalized in 1900, it was far more moderate than abolition. As discussions of a new criminal code were on the way, the reform of exile was shaped as a temporary measure until the adoption of the new code, which would offer further updates regarding exile. The 1903 Criminal

---

83   Nikolai Iadrintsev, *Sibir' kak koloniia* (Saint Petersburg: Tipografiia M.M. Stasiulevicha, 1882), pp. 104–222.

84   "Po povodu predstoiashchego preobrazovaniia katorgi i ssylki", *Tiuremnyi vestnik*, 6 (1899), pp. 246–53, 249.

Code ultimately did not have the comprehensive character it was intended to have, and reform regulations remained in force until the end of the empire. As Russian historian Aleksandr Margolis has underlined, this reform was profound, but long overdue.[85] Two laws of June 1900 curbed several varieties of exile that accounted for the largest number of displaced: judicial exile for most crimes was substituted with incarceration in the corrective divisions (*ispravitel'nye arestantskie otdeleniia*), and administrative exile was limited as well.[86] Judicial exile remained in force for religious and political offences.

Although the katorga system remained untouched by the reform, in the discussions the subject was approached again and again. The traditional katorga sites in Nerchinsk (Eastern Siberia) and Sakhalin, the members of the committee suggested, needed to be transformed, and exile to Sakhalin had to be limited. Katorga, according to their plans, would turn into a more mobile enterprise that would be more responsive to the needs of the "state and public construction".[87] These proposals were not realized, but they make it clear that the ideas of reorganizing katorga and binding forced labourers to infrastructural projects were circulating among governmental officials long before they were widely put into practice at the beginning of World War I.

Modernizing the penal system

At the beginning of the 1860s, the Ministry of the Interior required regional governors (*nachal'niki gubernii*) to collect information about the condition in prisons. Submitted findings revealed the same problems in prisons throughout the empire: overpopulation, lack of separation of inmates, and failure to organize their labour.[88] Inmates were all crammed in giant common cells: those under investigation were held together with suspects on trial and convicts; teenagers and women inmates were rarely separated from others.[89] This survey spurred the Ministry of the Interior to systematically consider the conditions of Russian prisons. While an agenda of re-education and concerns about the ability of individual prisoners to reform had not

85 Margolis, *Tiur'ma i ssylka*, p. 25.
86 *Polnoe sobranie zakonov Rossiiskoi Imperii. Sobranie tret'e. Tom XX. 1900* (Saint Petersburg, 1902), no. 18777 (10 June 1900), pp. 630–36 and no. 18839 (12 June 1900), pp. 757–58.
87 *Zhurnaly vysochaishe uchrezhdennoi Komissii*, p. 3.
88 *Materialy po voprosu o preobrazovanii tiuremnoi chasti v Rossii. Izdany Ministerstvom Vnutrennikh Del po svedeniiam, dostavlennym ot Nachal'nikov Gubernii* (Saint Petersburg: Tipografiia Ministerstva Vnutrennikh Del, 1865), p. i.
89 *Ibid.*, p. 3.

yet come into the focus of the prison administrators, they were bothered by the fact the prisons served as breeding grounds for disease and disorder.

Incarceration was a constitutive part of the imperial penal system, but not the dominant punishment against the offenders deemed most dangerous. While imperial exile has rightfully attracted the unrelenting interest of researchers in the recent years, contemporary critical historiography of the imperial prison reform remains underdeveloped. For this book, the history of confinement in Russia is only relevant insofar as it intersected with coerced labour and forced displacement. In the long run, confinement tended to be reserved to convicts, while forced labour and displacement were often used extrajudicially against much wider groups of population. What makes confinement in the last third of the nineteenth century of particular interest to the current study are the attempts to establish prisons as an alternative to katorga and exile. Although the process of prison reform that started in 1879 was slow, irregular, and conflicted, analysing it puts into relief long-running tendencies, especially the drive towards the centralization of the prison administration and the conceptualization of convict labour as a tool of individual and societal transformation. In this section, I will briefly discuss the main changes spurred by the Russian prison reform and highlight some of its specificities in order to provide an institutional context to the developments in the domain of forced labour of convicts that I will discuss further.

In the first half of the nineteenth century, confinement in the empire was extremely diverse, with a variety of forms and functions. Incarceration was part of the katorga: these convicts were held in special central prisons, strongholds, or fortresses for years before being exiled. Before 1845, regular prisons were generally intended for offenders under investigation, and were often refurbished out of wine cellars, army barracks, or other buildings deemed suitable. Another type were transit prisons, where exiles and convicts were held before being transferred to other locations. Conditions there were harrowing, often with up to two hundred people locked up in a single giant cell. Spatial segregation prescribed by law was hardly ever enforced, opening up possibilities for all kinds of abuses and making inmates vulnerable to infectious diseases. There were other places of confinement, including monasteries, where both the clergy and the laymen could be held. This practice was particularly common during the reign of Nicholas I.[90] Smaller regional (*uezd* and *guberniia*) prisons were

---

90   A. Joy Demoskoff, "Penance and Punishment: Monastic Incarceration in Imperial Russia" (Ph.D. dissertation, University of Alberta, 2016).

often run by a philanthropic society called the Russian Prison Aid Society (*Popechitel'noe obshchestvo o tiur'makh*). This charitable organization of gentry was established in 1819 in Saint Petersburg, and over the following decades it opened regional dependencies as well. This association, created according to the plans of English Quaker Walter Venning, had transnational roots and shared similarities with the contemporary prison philanthropic groups in Western Europe and America.[91] The founders of the Prison Aid Society underlined that the goal of the state was to dispense justice and put criminals in prisons, while they saw their mission in offering mercy to these inmates.[92] Proclaimed charity was not the only goal of this association. According to Adele Lindenmeyr, Nicholas I directly charged the Saint Petersburg section of the Prison Aid Society with taking beggars off the streets of the capital.[93] Loosely coordinated and lacking an agenda, the Prison Aid Society was rarely able to improve conditions in individual prisons and did not have any ambitions vis-à-vis the prison system as a whole. Once the discussions of prison reform had started in the 1860s, it was the Department of Executive Police of the Ministry of Internal Affairs, rather than the Prison Aid Society, that became the main base for the creation of a unified prison administration agency.

Various periodizations have been suggested for the advance of prison reform globally, and for Western Europe, a certain consensus exists that the shift towards incarceration took place between 1740 and 1840. As sensibilities of elites changed, the spectacles of punishment became increasingly revulsive, and instead, criminals started to be hidden away in intricately designed prison buildings, where isolation, disciplinary regime, and forced labour were expected to reform them into industrious individuals ready to return to the capitalist society.[94] More recent research has widened the scope of research on prison reform by studying the spread of confinement as the dominant punishment beyond Western Europe and its offshoots, re-evaluating this periodization by including global developments of the second half of the nineteenth century, and expanding the focus to include not only the disciplinary measures used by prison administrators, but also the agency of inmates.[95]

---

91 Adams, *The Politics of Punishment*, pp. 40–42.
92 *Ibid.*, p. 42.
93 Lindenmeyr, *Poverty Is Not a Vice*, p. 40.
94 The most influential historical narrative of this transition is offered in Foucault, *Discipline and Punish*.
95 Mary Gibson, "Global Perspectives on the Birth of the Prison", *The American Historical Review*, 116:4 (October 2011), pp. 1040–63.

Penitentiaries became symbols of prestige and hallmarks of civilization, and governments sought to adopt and adapt them to modernize their penal systems. Russian imperial officials, like other elites across the world from Latin America to Asia, found the ideal of the penitentiary extremely appealing.[96] In Russia, as I will discuss in the following section, experimental prisons were created in the capitals to showcase their transformative and disciplining potential. Several commissions were organized throughout the 1870s to discuss and prepare prison reform. These commissions initially discussed a possible full-scale modernization of the imperial penal legislation. American historian Bruce F. Adams studied in great detail these discussions, as well as political and personal controversies that surrounded the protracted elaboration of prison reform at the highest levels of the tsarist state apparatus, including the interdepartmental rivalries that complicated the management of the prison system.[97] Like in Peru, China, and Japan, where the creation of penitentiaries was part of a wider project of liberal reform, in the Russian empire the shift towards imprisonment, which started already with the limitation of corporal punishment in 1863, began during the liberal reforms of Alexander II.[98] The prison reform in the narrow sense, however, only took place in 1879, when the general policies swerved away from liberalism once again. Plans for a fundamental legal reform of the penal system were abandoned, but the idea of reorganizing "the prison affairs along more rational foundations", meaning a Western-European-inspired system of penitentiaries, lingered.[99] On the most immediate level, the prison reform consisted in the creation within the Ministry of Internal Affairs an agency dedicated to prison management: the Main Prison Administration (*Glavnoe Tiuremnoe Upravlenie*, or the GTU). Vested with executive power to manage and transform prisons, it came into existence and functioned in the context of growing social unrest, organized political resistance to tsarism, and the development of modern terrorist groups that targeted state officials at all levels, from prison wardens to the tsar himself.

The overarching goal of the Main Prison Administration was a fundamental overhaul of the system of places of confinement and the creation of a centralized and standardized prison system. Ambitious as it was, this goal implied profound changes on all levels of prison management, from the

---

96   Frank Dikötter and Ian Brown (eds), *Cultures of Confinement: A History of the Prison in Africa, Asia, and Latin America* (London: Hurst, 2007).

97   Adams, *The Politics of Punishment*, pp. 65–120.

98   Gibson, "Global Perspectives on the Birth of the Prison", p. 1057.

99   *Tiuremnoe preobrazovanie. I. Ispravitel'nyi dom, zakliuchenie v kreposti i tiur'ma* (Saint Petersburg, 1905), p. 9.

way individual prisons were run to the general principles of administration. The main directions of the GTU's work in the first decades of its existence included the collection of information about prisons and prison populations all over the empire, the elaboration and dissemination of norms and standards, the construction of new prison buildings, research into and the publication of materials on contemporary penology, as well as the integration of emergent Russian prison professionals into the international penological community.

Guided by the rather amorphous idea of rational prison governance, GTU officials sought to translate it into practice by attempting to standardize prison conditions and regulate every aspect of the inmates' day-to-day life through norms regarding clothing, ratios, working conditions, and hours. However, their control over the fulfilment of these regulations was initially weak and only slowly grew stronger with the introduction of prison inspection and other mechanisms of oversight, as well as a gradual professionalization of the prison staff. Beyond a handful of prisons in the capitals, the impact of the reform on prison conditions was delayed.

Like other proponents of modern prisons globally, GTU officials saw prison buildings as the main tool for solving the crucial issues of internment. Prison architecture itself was expected to have a transformative impact on inmates.[100] Removing convicts from society and isolating them in cells was expected to contribute to the criminals' moral rebirth. With architecturally correct, well-planned buildings, prisons could function with fewer guards, convict labour would be easier to organize, and the sanitary and hygienic conditions would be easier to control.[101] Construction of new prison buildings also helped to solve the pressing issue of overpopulation. Although symbolically it was at the heart of the reform, in practice construction was constantly thwarted by the lack of funds. Before the creation of the GTU, repairs of prison buildings were consistently underfunded, and at least in the first five years of its existence, almost three quarters of its whole construction budget had to be spent on repairs and renovations of existing prisons.[102]

As much as prison officials strove to make the convicts invisible to the wider society by hiding them behind the thick prison walls, within these

100 Robin Evans, *The Fabrication of Virtue: English Prison Architecture, 1750–1840* (Cambridge: Cambridge University Press, 1982).

101 *Obzor desiatiletnei deiiatel'nosti Glavnogo Tiuremnago Upravleniia. 1879–1889* (Saint Petersburg: Tipografiia Ministerstva Vnutrennikh Del, 1889), p. 27.

102 More precisely, 3,589,626 rubles out of the overall budget of 5,028,231 rubles. *Tiuremnoe preobrazovanie*, p. 37.

walls, inmates had to be as visible as possible. This was not only a matter of surveillance, although providing sufficient guards was always on the agenda. It was the matter of knowing the prison population. The initial shock of central officials as they discovered the lamentable condition of prisons in the 1860s transformed into the desire to make the inmate population more legible through the collection, aggregation, and analysis of data.[103] The centralized collection of prison statistics was one of the first major endeavours of the Main Prison Administration, which also sought to produce an image of an orderly, well-studied prison system by producing yearly reports of its activities.

The GTU also pursued the goal of the professionalization of the prison staff. The creation of a periodical dedicated to prison affairs was a step in this direction: *The Prison Herald* (*Tiuremnyi vestnik*) was printed monthly from 1893. Every issue consisted of an official and an unofficial section. Laws, circulars, and all sorts of state documents concerning prison affairs constituted the official section; in the unofficial section, a reader could find book reviews, articles penned by jurists and prison wardens, reports of international congresses and visits abroad, as well as letters from the readers. The unofficial section offers an insight into the gradual conceptualization of what forced convict labour meant in the Russian empire and, as I will discuss in the following sections, offered some examples of how it was instituted in different prisons.

Penal reforms in the nineteenth century highlight not only the transfer of ideas and practices, but also contradictions between the locally developed penal practices, like, in the Russian case, exile and katorga, and modern notions and practices inspired by the Western European prison systems. Abby M. Schrader has underlined that despite the clear desire of officials to rely on "organic historical development" when they elaborated the reform of corporal punishment in the 1850s, they nevertheless incorporated Western European laws as they decided who should be punished through physical pain, and who should be spared.[104] At the same time, traditional punishments continued to be seen as viable and adequate penal practices due to their "organic" roots despite the apparent collapse of the system. In other words, fully abandoning the traditional punishments was never a goal on the state level, but Western European laws and penal institutions formed an important

---

103 On the concept of legibility, see James C. Scott, *Seeing Like a State: How Certain Schemes to Improve the Human Condition Have Failed* (New Haven, CT, London: Yale University Press, 1998).
104 Abby M. Schrader, "The Languages of the Lash: The Russian Autocracy and the Reform of Corporal Punishment, 1817–1893" (Ph.D. thesis, University of Pennsylvania, 1996), p. 237.

frame of reference for officials, especially those inclined towards reform. In 1906 still, a prison official blamed the tension between the "historical" and the "rational" currents of penological thought for undermining any consistent efforts to modernize the penal system.[105] The degree to which Western European penitentiary ideas were actually incorporated in late Russian imperial prison governance in practice is debatable, especially for the regional prisons, but it is clear that on the level of the central officialdom some creative appropriation continuously took place.

The prison reform was long and conflicted, but it did eventually change the face of imperial prisons. By the beginning of the twentieth century, the condition of inmates had improved, and overall prisoner mortality reduced.[106] A uniform and centralized prison system, however, never materialized: prisons remained a sphere of conflict and cooperation between the Ministry of Internal Affairs and the Ministry of Justice. On the eve of the 1917 revolution, the GTU – which in 1895 had been transferred from the Ministry of Internal Affairs to the Ministry of Justice – on the regional level still needed the assistance of the local institutions of the Ministry of Internal Affairs in securing the day-to-day functioning of the prisons, especially when it came to guarding inmates during extramural labour. While such an arrangement functioned under normal circumstances, in the crisis of revolution and civil war it undermined the GTU's capacity to run prisons.[107]

Modalities of convict labour

In one form or another, the forced labour of convicts was a mainstay of the Russian penal system well before the nineteenth century. As part of katorga, hard penal labour had been used at state-run sites, such as silver and lead mines and naval construction shipyards, at least since the Petrine times. This was typically backbreaking retributive labour which was guided by the desire to punish the offenders deemed most dangerous while using

105 Nikolai Luchinskii, "Arestantskie raboty vo Frantsii i v Rossii", *Tiuremnyi vestnik*, 1 (1906), pp. 39–56, 49.
106 Stephen G. Wheatcroft, "The Crisis of the Late Tsarist Penal System", in Stephen G. Wheatcroft (ed.), *Challenging Traditional Views of Russian History* (London: Palgrave Macmillan, 2002), pp. 27–54.
107 M. Dzhekobson [Michael Jakobson] and M.B. Smirnov, "Sistema mest zakliucheniia v RSFSR i SSSR. 1917–1930", in M.B. Smirnov (ed.), *Sistema ispravitel'no-trudovykh ligerei v SSSR* (Moscow: Zven'ia, 1998), pp. 10–24, electronic version available at: http://old.memo.ru/history/nkvd/gulag/, last accessed 6 June 2022.

their labour for the state's benefit. The harshness of this labour was also intended as a deterrent for potential wrongdoers. In workhouses (*rabotnye* or *rabochie doma*) and houses of correction (*smiritel'nye doma*), beggars, idlers, and other criminalized poor also had to work. In other places of confinement, inmates' labour was used episodically for prison maintenance and also for extramural works such as canalization, snow shovelling, or road construction.

While the use of convict labour with statist goals had emerged already in the early eighteenth century, throughout the nineteenth century, most inmates did not work, and no coordinated efforts existed to implement convict labour countrywide until the 1870s, when forced labour began to be discussed as part of the prison reform. The 1880s marked the emergence of a new conception of forced labour of convicts in the empire, one that was strongly associated with the Western European and American ideas of prison as a modern disciplining institution aimed at the re-education of criminals. In this section, I discuss the elaboration of this complex agenda that placed convict labour at the heart of the convict's rehabilitation, his (or, rarely, her) return to society, and reducing crime in society overall. Although implementation of this agenda was quite limited, it had long-running consequences. It established convict labour as an acceptable, and indeed desired, state-controlled instrument for the transformation of individual prisoners and for society overall by reducing crime in the long run.

The experimentation with prison workshops aimed at disciplining and re-educating convicts started in the main cities of the empire in the 1860s.[108] These attempts were connected with two high-ranking officials who would play pivotal roles in the development of the prison reform in Russia: Count Vladimir Sollogub and Mikhail Galkin-Vraskoi. Both travelled extensively to research Western European prison systems, and both were eager to implement their freshly acquired penological knowledge in practice.[109] They tapped into the pool of contemporary penological thought to find ideas and practices adaptable to the Russian terrain, and these efforts first resulted in two rather short-lived prison experiments, one in Moscow and the other in Saint Petersburg. Sollogub, who would in the 1870s head a commission that elaborated the blueprint of the prison reform, starting from 1866 was

108 For a discussion of central prisons in the Ottoman empire, see: Ufuk Adak, "Central Prisons (Hapishane-i Umumi) in Istanbul and Izmir in the Late Ottoman Empire: In-Between Ideal and Reality," *Journal of the Ottoman and Turkish Studies Association* 4, no. 1 (2017): 73–94.
109 Galkin-Vraskoi's report of his tour through the prisons of Switzerland, France, and Belgium was published as Mikhail Galkin, *Materialy k izucheniiu tiuremnogo voprosa* (Saint Petersburg: Tipografiia Vtorogo otdeleniia sobstvennoi E.I.V. kantseliarii, 1868).

responsible for the Moscow corrective workhouse.[110] Galkin-Vraskoi, the future head of the Main Prison Administration, ran the Saint Petersburg prison in 1867–1868. These two institutions shared similar principles of organization that were clearly inspired by the contemporary Western European urban prisons. They were intended to showcase the rehabilitative and disciplining power of the modern prison and combined some of the most fashionable penological innovations of the time: the remunerated artisanal labour of convicts, prison vegetable gardens, and the night-time separation of inmates.[111] Both institutions were considered successful and opened up career opportunities for Sollogub and especially for Galkin-Vraskoi, but these successes turned out to be hard to replicate outside of the carefully managed and well-funded central prisons.

In addition to prison, another disciplinary institution based on coerced labour proved extremely appealing: the famous Mettray colony for juvenile delinquents. Mikhail Galkin-Vraskoi visited it during his Western European research trip.[112] Located next to Tours in the Loire valley, Mettray was perhaps the most famous penal colony in France, and an object of fascination for international observers.[113] Ambitions for the forceful re-education of delinquents at Mettray were so intricate and far-reaching that Michel Foucault stated that the opening of this penal colony in 1840 marked the completion of the modern carceral system. According to Foucault, Mettray was "the disciplinary form at its most extreme, the model in which are concentrated all the coercive technologies of behaviour".[114] Galkin-Vraskoi clearly was captivated by the disciplinary techniques practised in Mettray, and adapted them to the Russian context. In 1870, he became the governor of Saratov region, and in 1873 with the help of donations he opened an "instructive-corrective house" (uchebno-ispravitel'nyi dom), which ran according to some of the principles he observed in the Mettray colony. The major difference was that Mettray was only for boys, while in Saratov both boys and girls were interned. Young inmates had to stay in the colony for at least one year: according to Galkin-Vraskoi, shorter terms were not enough for the full disciplining effect, while such longer internment allowed the detainees to work through the

110 Adams, The Politics of Punishment, pp. 65–77.
111 V.B. Lebedev and E.V. Stepanova, "V.A. Sollogub i ego eksperimenty v oblasti organizatsii truda arestantov", Vestnik instituta: Prestuplenie, nakazanie, ispravlenie, 23:3 (2013), pp. 82–87.
112 Galkin, Materialy k izucheniiu tiuremnogo voprosa, pp. 129–42.
113 For a recent social history of the Mettray colony that focuses on the agency of inmates, see Stephen A. Toth, Mettray: A History of France's Most Venerated Carceral Institution (Ithaca, NY: Cornell University Press, 2019).
114 Foucault, Discipline and Punish, p. 293.

whole cycle of agricultural production. The colony was intended for children and adolescents between five and sixteen, but most inmates, according to Vraskoi, were teenagers of thirteen or fourteen who were detained for theft. Like in Mettray, they had to obey a strict schedule and performed artisanal and agricultural work. The range of works was gender-specific: boys were taught the trades of shoemaking, carpentry, and locksmithing, and girls were to study knitting, sewing, and performing household chores, ostensibly preparing them for domestic service. In summer, all laboured in the vegetable garden and in the fields.[115] As in Mettray, the model of school was also mobilized in Saratov as an additional tool of discipline: children were taught to read, write, and count, and studied the scriptures.

The destiny of the Saratov colony after Galkin-Vraskoi's departure from the post of governor is unknown, but other cases suggest that the early organization of convict labour was a fragile enterprise. For instance, prison wardens in the densely populated Kingdom of Poland successfully ran prison workshops, but in the 1860s, as prison overpopulation grew more acute, they were forced to transform workshops into cells and living quarters for the prison personnel.[116]

Convict labour slowly became more widespread after the law that introduced obligatory labour for convicts in the Russian empire was promulgated on 6 January 1886.[117] According to the law, the establishment of facilities for convict labour was the responsibility of the local prison wardens. The law forced large groups of inmates to work: katorga convicts, the judicially and administratively exiled (while awaiting exile and during transit), as well as those incarcerated for theft, fraud, and begging. Those incarcerated for other crimes also had to work, but could choose the preferred type of labour among those available in the place of confinement where they were held (it is unclear how this functioned in practice, as I could not find any descriptions of such arrangements). Labour both inside and outside prisons was allowed, although women and vagabonds were not allowed to perform extramural

115 These descriptions are based on a short biographical monograph on Galkin-Vraskoi written by local Saratov historian: Sergei Zubov, *M.N. Galkin-Vraskoi – nachal'nik Glavnogo Tiuremnogo upravleniia Rossiiskoi Imperii (1879 – 1896 gg.)* (Saratov: Izdatel'stvo Saratovskogo Gosudarstvennogo Universiteta, 2007), pp. 16–17. I was unfortunately unable to consult documents on the functioning of the juvenile colony that are held in the Saratov regional archives, but it would be extremely interesting to get a more in-depth look into the workings of this early imperial carceral experiment.

116 *Obzor desiatiletnei deiiatel'nosti*, p. 7.

117 *Polnoe sobranie zakonov Rossiiskoi Imperii. Sobranie tret'e. Tom VI* (Saint Petersburg, 1888), no. 3447, pp. 8–11.

labour. Convicts were remunerated: various categories of inmates received between 6/10 (for inmates who worked voluntarily) and 1/10 (for the katorga inmates) of the wages of free labourers for similar work. The rest of the money was split in half between the state and the prison. The law defined the maximum duration of the workday to be eleven hours, and prescribed that all convicts, including the katorga ones (who previously worked without any days off), had a right to one day of rest per week plus other holidays according to their religion. Such a strong focus on remuneration as means of rehabilitation, as well as the close attention to regulating convicts' work times demonstrate that the officials responsible for the preparation of the law were aware of the Western European discussions and sought to mobilize the ideal of orderly industrial work to discipline the wrongdoers. This ambitious plan, however, collided with the prison realities.

Articles in *The Prison Herald* and the internal documentation of the Main Prison Administration suggest that implementation of this law was slow and inconsistent across the regions. Reliance on local prison wardens proved to be a stumbling block, as there was, unsurprisingly, no uniformity in competences and managerial capacities of wardens across the country. The law failed to mention any particularities regarding the forms of labour to use, or any repercussions for the wardens in case they failed to comply. In the following years, the Main Prison Administration released dozens of circulars in order to clarify the precise guidelines for the organization of convicts' labour. These circulars, however, remained recommendations at best. The first department within the GTU to coordinate the issues of convict labour was created only at the end of 1902.[118]

Discussions in the professional press regarding convict labour revolved around two fundamental questions: What are the functions of convict labour, and how should it be organized to balance the rehabilitative and the punitive aspects of incarceration? Officials of the Main Prison Administration proclaimed three main goals of convict labour. Balancing between the strictness of the regime and the severity of the punishment was one of them. The other two were the creation of a moral influence on the inmate by removing corrupting idleness, and funding the convict's life immediately upon release by paying out the accumulated wages earned during the period of incarceration.[119]

118 *Kratkii ocherk meropriiatii v oblasti tiremnago dela v Rossii za period s 1900 po 1905 god, sostav-lennyi dlia VII Mezhdunarodnogo tiuremnogo kongressa v Budapeshte Nachal'nikom Glavnogo Tiuremnogo Upravleniia A.M. Stremoukhovym* (Saint Petersburg: Tipografiia S.-Peterburgskoi tiur'my, 1905), p. 15.
119 *Obzor desiatiletnei deiiatel'nosti*, p. 100.

Unfortunately, reports from the local prison wardens with concrete examples of convict labour were far less common in the press than the theoretical reflections of jurists, publicists, and central officials, but in combination with archival documents, they do allow us to sketch the range of works that convicts were forced to perform. The basic, and crucial, distinction was whether the inmates worked inside or outside the prison building. For intramural work, wardens could employ the inmates at prison maintenance work, such as laundry or cleaning, but also the construction of new prison buildings. Maintenance work was generally unqualified, but could also imply manufacture, for instance, when it came to sewing prison uniforms. Wardens could also organize work that required little equipment and special competences, such as basket weaving or making brushes. Another possibility would be work on the prison's vegetable garden, or in a separately organized agricultural colony. Finally, the most complex option among the intramural forms of work were artisanal workshops where production was oriented towards local markets; such workshops could also fulfil orders from local entrepreneurs. Outside of the prison walls, convicts could work for the needs of the town where the prison was located, digging ditches, clearing snow, emptying sewers, or transporting timber or clay. They also could be hired out to local peasants or entrepreneurs. Towards the end of the century, as discussed in more detail in the following chapter, they started to be employed at larger state-run infrastructural projects, such as road construction.

Although convict labour was presented as a way to simultaneously solve two major problems of prison administration, namely funding prisons and rehabilitating the inmates, in practice a contradiction between these two goals emerged from early on. The ideal of industrial wage labour as the blueprint for the organization of convict labour was extremely appealing to high-ranking officials. Prisons, as institutions "directed towards the future", also would be serving as schools of capitalism, where convicts could be disciplined to comply with an industrial working schedule, taught a trade, and then released into society ready to labour as free workers.[120] Despite the trend towards centralization of the prison administration, when it came to convict labour, in the 1880s the GTU officials promoted small, decentralized workshops that were well inscribed in local conditions. According to the central officials, productive labour, even if it was unqualified, and remuneration were the main tools of rehabilitation, as they allowed the convicts to

---

120 Dmitrii Dril', "Tiuremnyia raboty, ikh znachenie i organizatsiia", *Tiuremnyi vestnik*, 1 (1902), pp. 23–47, 29.

appreciate the fruits of their labour and helped them to abandon crime in favour of a life of industry.

These compelling capitalist dreams, however, were less appealing to the local prison wardens who faced the immediate problems of setting up convict labour. The first host of complications arose straight away, as workshops were expensive to establish, and required the inmates to learn a trade, which was often impossible due to the lack of instructors and the fact that most inmates only served short terms, making them unable to complete any consistent training.[121] Another set of concerns emerged by the 1900s, as doctors noted that intramural labour was not ideal from the sanitary and hygienic perspective, and did not offer the benefits of outdoor physical labour such as physically strengthening the "soft" bodies of idle convicts and improving their resistance to disease.[122] Eventually, by the early 1900s, the ideal of prison workshops had been abandoned, and artisanal labour became simply one among many modalities of convict labour, rather than the ultimate tool of rehabilitation. At the first all-Russian convention dedicated to the issues of convict labour, held in March 1902, participants issued a resolution saying that prison workshops were unsustainable outside of large industrial centres (mentioning in particular Saint Petersburg, Moscow, Warsaw, and Odesa), and extramural work should be encouraged instead. They recommended agricultural colonies and land-improvement work such as digging canals and ditches, as well as the use of convict labour for state projects, as the best options.[123] This resolution marks the death of the GTU's ambitious project of rehabilitation of convicts through artisanal labour and shows how the appealing Western European blueprints of modern urban prisons collided with the realities of an overwhelmingly rural empire. Although extramural labour was not supported by an elaborate narrative of rehabilitation and education through artisanal labour, it offered to state officials an opportunity to match the availability of convicts with the necessity of developing and maintaining infrastructure. As the following decades showed, the wide use of extramural labour, compared to the maintenance of prison workshops, was also relatively resistant to the challenges created by war and political ruptures.

121 N. Luchinskii, "Raboty, dostupnye dlia vsekh arestantov", *Tiuremnyi vestnik*, 12 (1909), pp. 1171–82, 1172.
122 N. Gur'ev, "Sanitarnoe sostoianie nashikh tiurem", *Tiuremnyi vestnik*, 1 (1910), pp. 65–85, 74–75.
123 *Kratkii ocherk meropriiatii*, pp. 15–16.

Extramural labour

Initially, GTU officials considered that extramural labour did not harbour
sufficient potential to balance the punitive and the rehabilitative aspects
of forced labour: labour on the streets of towns "presented too many temp-
tations and facilitated relations with the outside world", which, clearly,
undermined the punitive character of incarceration.[124] This meant not only
escapes, but also casual contacts outside of prison walls. In the 1880s and
early 1890s GTU officials recommended such labour only as a temporary
measure until the construction of new prison buildings with workshops
would be concluded.[125] Road construction outside of cities was more punitive,
as locations were more secluded, labour more taxing, and escapes, perhaps,
more complicated, but such work was harder to organize, ostensibly because
it necessitated cooperation between multiple state agencies and required
more guards.[126] As I will discuss in the following chapter, coordinated
infrastructural projects using convict labour became more common shortly
before World War I and turned truly widespread in the wartime conditions.

For GTU officials, another drawback of extramural labour was its lack
of reformatory impact. With the exception of agricultural production and
hiring convicts to entrepreneurs, which will be discussed separately, such
labour was rarely productive, which contradicted their idealized conception
of convict labour that prepared the inmates for the industrial labour market.
However, small-scale extramural labour such as cleaning the streets or
digging ditches had several undeniable practical advantages: it was relatively
easy to organize with the help of municipal officials, offered a profit, and
did not require any particular skills – neither in the prison staff nor in the
inmates – making it attractive for local wardens. Almost ten years after the
introduction of the obligatory convict labour, the GTU praised the steady
growth of profit earned from it in the period between 1886 and 1895, but
admitted that extramural work brought more profit than either intramural
workshops or prison maintenance work.[127] In another ten years, more than
half of all profit was generated by extramural labour.[128]

In the years immediately following the introduction of obligatory convict
labour, GTU officials were so focused on prison workshops and the alleged

---

124 *Obzor desiatiletnei deiiatel'nosti*, p. 106.
125 *Ibid.*, p. 105.
126 *Ibid.*, p. 106.
127 *Otchtet po Glavnomu tiuremnomu upravleniiu za 1895 god* (Saint Petersburg: Tipografiia
S.-Peterburgskoi tiur'my, 1897), pp. 91–94.
128 Luchinskii, "Raboty, dostupnye dlia vsekh arestantov", p. 1173.

reformative potential of artisanal labour that convicts' agricultural labour was discussed only episodically. As agriculture was the most common occupation in the empire, it was unsurprising that prison administrators did eventually opt for this type of forced labour. Already in 1874, Mikhail Galkin-Vraskoi discussed the disciplining effects of agricultural labour on the underage inmates at his Saratov colony, as the number of new offences committed decreased in spring and summer, when the children were forced to work on the land.[129] A warden of a small prison in Smolensk region, P. Vikharev, in 1895 reported to *The Prison Herald* that for his prison, located in a semi-urban area, agricultural labour and the production of goods targeted at peasants (such as basket weaving and the making of bast shoes) were the only way of making profit. He also explicitly addressed the meaning of forced labour for convicts themselves: as most inmates were peasants, he suggested, they were not only familiar with such work, thus making additional training unnecessary, but also found it inherently useful and were therefore more motivated.[130]

The most ambitious attempt to use agricultural labour as a means of rehabilitation of convicts was the project of modernizing katorga. By the mid-nineteenth century, the katorga system was in crisis. On the one hand, such hard labour was initially devoid of any rehabilitative aspirations or even regard for convicts' lives, and these premises were increasingly contradicting the dominant ideas about punishment and its rehabilitative potential. On the other hand, as vividly described by ethnographer Sergei Maksimov, who travelled to Siberia in 1860–1861, by the 1860s, traditional katorga sites in Eastern Siberia were in utter decay, partly because of mismanagement and partly because the silver and lead mines where convicts were supposed to work were exhausted.[131] A solution to this crisis was offered, however, not in the form of profound reform or the abolition of this punitive regime. Instead, katorga was reimagined with a more rehabilitative potential as a tool for the forced colonization of the easternmost location in the empire: the island of Sakhalin.[132]

The Sakhalin experiment went hand in hand with the prison reform on the mainland. High hopes were placed on Sakhalin as the new penal colony where the katorga regime would be restructured and updated in

129 Zubov, *M.N. Galkin-Vraskoi*, p. 17.
130 P. Vikharev, "Arestantskie raboty", *Tiuremnyi vestnik*, 8 (1895), pp. 430–32.
131 S.V. Maksimov, *Sibir' i katorga*, 3 vols. (Saint Petersburg: Tipografiia A. Transhelia, 1871), vol. 3, pp. 274–377; D.G. Tal'berg, "Ssylka na Sakhalin", *Vestnik Evropy*, 5 (1879), pp. 218–51, 219–21.
132 The law that created the Sakhalin penal colony dated from 18 April 1869: *Polnoe sobranie zakonov Rossiiskoi Imperii. Sobranie vtoroe. Tom 44* (Saint Petersburg, 1869), no. 46984, pp. 330–33.

accordance with the needs of a modernizing empire. Officials, engineers, agronomists, and other researchers toured the island in the 1860s and 1870s, collecting information and preparing a planned colonial and penitentiary intervention.[133] Starting in 1869 and until 1905, thousands of convicts were transported to Sakhalin, where they were expected to mine coal, build roads, and transform the desolate island into a flourishing province by the means of agriculture. Early on, two farms were installed to explore the potential of forced agricultural labour, and convicts and their families grew vegetables and cold-resistant grains there. Only the farm in the southern part of the island was considered economically viable, but in both cases work at the farms seemed to have succeeded in shaping exiles into settlers, as many continued living in the region after their katorga term ended.[134] Despite the agenda of re-educating the convicts, the retributive aspects of katorga were not abandoned on Sakhalin: its remoteness and hard labour in mines were expected to be punitive enough to deter crime on the mainland.[135] Observers and officials were, however, overly optimistic about the potential of the island in terms of agriculture and resource extraction. In practice, climatic conditions on the island made agricultural labour extremely taxing, and its results precarious. Achieving self-sufficiency on the island proved impossible. In its 1899 report, the GTU finally admitted that "Sakhalin's climate cannot be considered fully suitable for farming and favourable for the development and prosperity of an agricultural colony".[136]

Ultimately, it was not the logistical difficulties, scientific miscalculations, administrative chaos, or extreme destitution of penal settlers that pushed the state to abandon this ambitious colonial project. The head of the GTU, Aleksandr Salomon, who visited Sakhalin in 1898, admitted all these shortcomings and remarked that the island's penal colonies were in a much worse condition than the most unorganized places of confinement in the European part of Russia, but still asserted that the state would not cease its efforts on Sakhalin after having spent 20 million rubles on it since

---

133 For an analysis of this imperial effort, see: Sharyl M. Corrado, "The 'End of the Earth': Sakhalin Island in the Russian Imperial Imagination, 1849–1906" (Ph.D. dissertation, University of Illinois at Urbana-Champaign, 2010).

134 *Ibid.*, pp. 46–47.

135 *Ibid.*, p. 55.

136 *Otchet po Glavnomu tiuremnomu upravleniiu za 1899 god* (Saint Petersburg: Tipografiia S.-Peterburgskoi tiur'my, 1901), p. 105.

1879.[137] The penal colonization of Sakhalin only ended when Russia had to cede the island to Japan as it found itself on the losing side of the 1904–1905 Russo-Japanese war.

The Sakhalin experiment was not simply a katorga colony installed in a new destination, but a symbolic attempt to create a penal colony for a modernizing empire, a colony that could transform both the territories and the convicts. The reconceptualization of penal colonization and extramural labour of convicts, including agricultural labour, as part of the global penitentiary reform can be understood as an attempt to integrate traditional Russian punishments, known for their severity and deadliness, into the canon of modern penology. Instead of discardable labouring bodies whose only prospect was to die working for the benefit of the sovereign, on the discursive level the katorga convicts were promised rehabilitation and teased with a hope of becoming productive agricultural settlers capable of changing the face of the most distant borderlands of the empire. On the ground, however, this discursive change did not translate into an improvement of conditions for exiled convicts: reports of starvation, extreme poverty, and widespread prostitution, as well as brutal corporal punishment and bodily mutilation on Sakhalin proliferated.[138]

Like the attempts to modernize the traditional punishment of katorga in the Far East, the incorporation of convicts into the industrializing economy of the western part of Russia was riddled with trouble. Hiring workers out to local entrepreneurs was controversial from the standpoint of labour law and security alike, as in this case convicts often became intermixed with free workers. One case in particular initiated long discussions between the representatives of three ministries: Finance, Justice, and Internal Affairs. In 1897, a sawmill owner in the governorate of Livonia wanted to hire convicts to transport timber, but was faced with opposition by the local factory inspector, who argued that convicts could not be hired out to factories, as they did not have legal rights to sign work contracts, and the regular labour legislation did not apply to them, effectively scrapping their labour rights. Representatives of the Ministry of Finance and Ministry of Internal Affairs supported this conclusion, and also argued against hiring convicts to factories.[139] The GTU, by then part of the Ministry of Justice, insisted that convicts could work at factories without contracts, as they were hired

137 Aleksandr Salomon, "Rech' Nachal'nika glavnogo tiuremnogo upravleniia ha o. Sakhalin", *Tiuremnyi vestnik*, 1 (1899), pp. 9–11, 10.

138 Corrado, "The 'End of the Earth'", p. 108.

139 RGIA, f. 20, op. 13a, d. 92, ll. 2–3.

out collectively (*otdany v arendu*) by the prison wardens. Finally, in 1903, the Ministry of Finance allowed it, but only if the complete separation of convicts from free workers could be secured.[140] The labour rights of convicts, or rather their absence, remained under the control of the prison administration.

A focus on the extramural labour of convicts reveals the dynamics between forced displacement and forced labour on the micro level. Before the establishment of large-scale infrastructural projects that relied on the involvement of the central state apparatus, tensions surrounding extramural labour first evolved on the level of separate penal sites and involved the short-range displacement of convicts. The mobility of inmates appears here as both desirable and problematic. Prison wardens relied on extramural labour as a more readily available source of profit in comparison to the investments needed for the creation of in-prison workshops. At the same time, extramural labour did not comply with the central officials' idealized vision of modern prison. It undermined the drive to separate prisoners from society and hide them away in the specialized buildings, making the borders of prison sites more permeable than higher prison officials were comfortable with, at least initially. Outside observers were also suspicious of inmates leaving the prison. A factory inspector from Kharkiv (then Kharkov) reported in 1899: "As I visited the Kharkov sugar refinery, I witnessed in practice convict labour at factories for the first time. Around one hundred convicts worked at the refinery, completely mixing in among the general mass of workers. The plan of the refinery building was so complex, and sundry rooms for production so numerous, that oversight by the prison guards could only be fictitious. [...] I will not talk about the distressing impression produced by the presence of convicts and guards armed with sabres (*shashkas*) among the free workers".[141]

While prison workshops were perceived as laboratories for industrial workers, where convicts could learn a trade and produce marketable goods under the strict control of guards and wardens, extramural labour, even at actual industrial establishments, offered less control over the inmates and, consequently, less transformative potential. For some inmates, this could mean a greater possibility of escape, while for others, it led to more intense exploitation due to the nature of such labour, as it was often extremely taxing physically and combined with walking long stretches from and back to prison.

140 *Ibid.*, l. 35.
141 *Ibid.*, l. 22.

Conclusion

Nineteenth-century histories of punishment in the Russian empire are marked by the coexistence of a plethora of forms of forced labour, confinement, and displacement, and their combinations. Exile has largely developed as a punitive facet of the process of colonization of Siberia. Inspired by Western European examples, imperial officials and penologists faced considerable difficulties in translating the ideals of confinement and rehabilitative labour into Russian realities. Prisons and exile continued to exist side by side and, with the harsher punishment of katorga, overlap within the carceral trajectories of the convicts deemed most dangerous. By the beginning of the twentieth century, no single type of convict labour came to dominate in the prison system, but extramural labour in all its forms remained more widespread than labour in workshops. The imperial Russian variant of prison reform led to the construction of new prison buildings and the introduction of obligatory prison labour, but the efforts to build a centralized network of standardized prisons bore limited results, and prisons failed to fully replace exile.

A plurality of different types of punishment, underpinned by different conceptions of reformability and standards of rehabilitation, persisted within the penal system. Progressive prison officials formulated ambitious plans of reforming the criminals through strict interventions, the central one being forced labour. The reformation of offenders, according to the desires of authorities, implied their profound transformation: a thief or an arsonist was supposed to turn into a disciplined, industrious inmate remunerated for his labour, who was then expected to join the ranks of docile, productive urban workers. However, despite attempts to establish artisanal labour in prison workshops as the main framework of convict labour, a wide range of types of convict labour emerged, guided by the concerns of profitability and prison management, rather than this ambitious dream of reformation. At the same time, exile and katorga remained largely unchanged, and although their use was limited, their role as the most severe imperial punishments was preserved.

2   Under Pressure: Revolution, Repression, and War in the Russian Empire, 1905–1917

Abstract

This chapter analyses the developments that contributed to the destabilization of the imperial penal-repressive system on the eve of the 1917 revolutions. First, it discusses the variety of coercive regimes against the subaltern populations and the inability of the central authorities to adequately address subaltern crime, especially in the countryside. Second, the chapter highlights how the tsarist authorities responded to rising political militantism by rehabilitating specific punishments (katorga and exile) that were supposed to be substituted by incarceration in penitentiaries. Finally, it offers a close analysis of how the central officials' idea of "reformatory" artisanal labour in prison workshops failed in practice. It stresses that the shift towards extramural convict labour on large-scale projects of infrastructural construction was already underway in the late imperial era.

Keywords: Russian empire, extramural labour, convict labour, World War I

In the years preceding the 1917 revolutions, the penal system was continuously put under strain amid the growing social and political unrest. The central tension here played out as various groups (industrial workers, educated elites, ethnic minorities, and peasants) sought to challenge the autocracy and its coercive regimes, while the tsar and state officials tried, but failed to find, adequate responses to these challenges. Suppression of the 1905 revolution partially reverted the trends of the penal system's development in the previous decades, and marked the government's growing reliance on exile and katorga as means of political repression. Although the years 1907–1913 provided a welcome peaceful interlude, the beginning of

Popova, Zhanna: *Coerced Labour, Forced Displacement, and the Soviet Gulag, 1880s-1930s*. Amsterdam: Amsterdam University Press, 2024
DOI: 10.5117/9789048560356_CH02

World War I created new challenges for the penal system, as the labour of convicts was mobilized for the war effort all over the country.

In the decades before 1917, the Russian government sought to reinforce the economic and military might of the empire without compromising absolute autocracy. The tsar proved unable to anticipate the advent of mass politics and to incorporate the masses into political life, even by autocratic means, which ultimately exacerbated social tensions. He was unwilling to provide any kind of political representation, and only the revolution of 1905 forced him to make some half-hearted concessions. Laura Engelstein has underlined that "the regime's reluctance to disperse the mechanisms of social discipline weakened, however, in the last years of imperial rule, as the growing complexity of the modern sector and the spread of education and technology strengthened the professional cohort and multiplied the kinds of social problems with which such mechanisms contend".[1] The professional cohort was a vocal group which called for deep social and political transformation and challenged autocratic power. Some professionals opted for radical political dissent, while others envisioned less violent means of achieving transformation and looked for possibilities to reform the existing order. Many became pivotal figures in the emergence and development of new scientific agendas and research techniques in psychiatry, statistics, criminology, and other disciplines.[2] These professionals, including penologists, conceptualized society and individuals as objects to be acted upon, malleable and transformable through their intervention.

This interventionist logic and the aspirations of "progressive" social transformation were, in some cases, adopted by state actors. In the case of penal policies, this translated into the state's acceptance of the disciplines of criminology and penology. As shown in the previous chapter, prison administrators took part in elaborating new visions of convict labour and creatively interpreted the legal acts. Even in the aftermath of the 1905–1907 whirlpool of war and revolution, many central and local administrators

---

1   Laura Engelstein, "Combined Underdevelopment: Discipline and the Law in Imperial and Soviet Russia", *The American Historical Review*, 98:2 (1993), pp. 338–53, 348.

2   On the emergence of the social sciences in the Russian empire, see Daniel Beer, *Renovating Russia: The Human Sciences and the Fate of Liberal Modernity, 1880–1930* (Ithaca, NY: Cornell University Press, 2008). On the emergence of military statistics and its role in governance, see Peter Holquist, "To Count, to Extract, and to Exterminate: Population Statistics and Population Politics in Late Imperial and Soviet Russia", in Ronald Grigor Suny and Terry Martin (eds), *A State of Nations: Empire and Nation-Making in the Age of Lenin and Stalin* (New York, Oxford: Oxford University Press, 2001), pp. 111–44. On the interventionist logic, see David L. Hoffmann, *Cultivating the Masses: Modern State Practices and Soviet Socialism, 1914–1939* (Ithaca, NY: Cornell University Press, 2011).

did not give up on the attempt to build a centralized "modern" prison system. They tapped into the transnationally produced pool of penological knowledge, learned from local situations, and imagined a penal system based on the rationalist understanding of crime and punishment which could overcome the multitude of regional contexts and would, through manual labour, be a means of rehabilitating convicts. Such a system never materialized, but these ideals continued to shape the penal system.

As discussed in the previous chapter, progressive prison administrators aspired to create a penal system that would not only serve as a way of delivering retribution for crimes and deter potential lawbreakers, but would also impact the whole of society by reducing criminality. The 1905 revolution and the repression of political activists that followed undermined the efforts of improving prison conditions and reducing inmate mortality.[3] After 1905, prison administrators were faced with the fact that the same punishments they considered obsolete, namely exile and katorga, were being instrumentalized by the central authorities in their fight against political dissenters. The reformatory endeavour was underfunded and slow-paced, and ultimately could not build a prison system that would be capable of facing the crisis without slipping back into overcrowding, with its numerous negative implications, including increased prisoner mortality. This tension between attempts to deliver modern prison reform on the one hand, and repressive instrumentalization on the other, placed a strain on the penal system, which, along with other factors, ultimately led to its increasing fragility and eventual collapse after the February 1917 revolution.

Apart from being embedded within this interventionist logic of societal progress, penal policies were also a part of the state's attempts to face the challenges created by the advance of capitalism globally and the rise of political discontent domestically. What is characteristic of this period is not only that the state employed new tactics to discipline and control its subjects, but also that the society itself underwent a profound militarization, having been continuously mobilized over the course of many years, first during the Russo-Japanese war and the 1905 revolution, then World War I, the 1917 revolution and the numerous conflicts that came to be referred to as the Civil War.[4] This militarization and its repercussions in terms of forced labour are discussed in the final section of this chapter. This chapter

---

3   On the crisis of the condition of prisons prompted by the 1905 revolution, see Wheatcroft, "The Crisis of the Late Tsarist Penal System".

4   Peter Holquist, "Violent Russia, Deadly Marxism? Russia in the Epoch of Violence, 1905–21", *Kritika: Explorations in Russian and Eurasian History*, 4:3 (2003), pp. 627–52, 639.

thus reviews the processes that contributed to the increasing fragility of the prison system, and demonstrates the search for alternatives to incarceration as the dominant penal practice as the situation in the Russian empire destabilized.

Coercive regimes and the deployment of punishment

Coercive regime, in this context, is understood as the array of limiting and restrictive legal and administrative measures that were used by state officials in order to establish and maintain control over the population, and over subaltern groups in particular. This coercion could be warranted, such as in the case of punishing criminals, or it could be intended to reduce the freedom (especially the freedom of movement and the freedom to choose an occupation) of the subaltern.

Up until World War I, coercion by the old regime had been diminishing in some aspects of social life. This slow and inconsistent development started with the abolition of serfdom in 1861. The emancipation did free serfs from bondage, but it did not grant them full political rights. Their freedom of movement, as well as their capacity to use the reformed legal system, remained constrained. At the same time, local peasant institutions continued to function "as the lowest rungs within the state's administrative apparatus".[5] Only the Witte-Stolypin reforms of 1890–1906 started to open up property rights and the right of free movement to wider populations.[6] This process was neither rapid nor straightforward, and the case of the passportization reforms illustrates how slow the pace of change was.

The passport regime was part of the coercive repertoire directed against subaltern groups, especially those in Central Russia. Passports served a double goal: not only were they used to ascribe people to certain places of residence, but also to levy taxes (*podati*). The passport regime limited freedom of movement: it did not allow peasants to leave their place of residence without special permission. Iterations of this regime implied different degrees of freedom of movement for the inhabitants of Siberia, the Caucasus, Finland, Poland, the Baltic governances, the

---

5   Frank, *Crime, Cultural Conflict, and Justice*, p. 6.
6   M.A. Davydov, *Dvadtsat' let do Velikoi voiny: Rossiiskaya modernizatsiya Vitte–Stolypina* (Saint Petersburg: Aleteiia, 2016).

Jewish population, Kalmyks, and the Roma.[7] Minister of Finance Sergei Witte and Minister of the Interior Ivan Durnovo were responsible for the preparation of the reform of the passport regime as early as 1893. They labelled this regime the "heritage of serfdom" and sought to simplify it by eliminating these numerous differentiations. However, their project did not opt for any radical measures against the passport regime, and after corrections by members of the state council the reform became even more moderate.

The new passport regime that came into effect on 1 January 1895 continued to reinforce the distinction between the privileged groups of the population and those obliged to pay taxes (*podatnye*). The nobles, bureaucrats, merchants, and other privileged groups could freely choose their place of residence. Peasants and urban dwellers ascribed to communities (*obshchestva*), on the contrary, still needed special permission to move.[8] Until 1897, the passport also remained a fiscal document: it lost this role only when fees for residence permits were abolished. The regime of residence permits, apart from heavily controlling the movement of peasants and unprivileged urban dwellers, was also connected to administrative exile, as the police could, after investigating the condition of a person without a valid residence permit, exile this individual.[9] A more radical reform of the passport regime was approved only in 1905, and was introduced in 1906: passports came to be used exclusively as identity documents; they had no expiry date and were not required for relocation.[10]

While the methods of coercion slowly became less straightforward, analysis of some critical situations reveals that the violent suppression of dissent remained the modus operandi of the tsar's officials. Reactions to political dissent among the educated groups was one example of repression. In the case of peasant rebellions, violence against dissent was coupled with deep contempt towards the peasants. The suppression of the 1902 peasant rebellion in the Poltava and Kharkiv *guberniias* provides a telling example. The governor of Kharkiv, prince I.M. Obolensky, not only used the military to suppress the uprising and put more than a thousand peasants on trial, but personally lashed the uprising's leaders. His strong-handed response won him praise from the central government, while the governor of Poltava,

---

7   B.V. Anan'ich, R.Sh. Ganelin, B.B. Dubentsov, V.S. Diakin, and S.I. Potolov, *Krizis samoderzhaviia v Rossii, 1895–1917* (Leningrad: Nauka, 1984), p. 49.

8   Anan'ich *et al.*, *Krisis samoderzhaviia*, pp. 52–54.

9   V.M. Gessen, *Iskliuchitel'noe polozhenie* (Saint Petersburg: Pravo, 1908), p. 49.

10   *Ibid.*, p. 68.

whose attempts to punish the rebels were not deemed sufficiently diligent, was demoted shortly afterwards.[11] The recurrent use of the military and extrajudicial repressive measures was another source of tension that strained the penal system.

Despite attempts by the central authorities to modernize the criminal justice system, a comprehensive actualization of laws was never accomplished. By 1905, the Criminal Code of 1845 was considered archaic and inefficient to manage criminality in the rapidly changing society, but it remained in force for the prosecution of the majority of common crimes. Work on the new code started in 1881, but the 1903 Criminal Code (*Ulozhenie o nakazaniiakh 1903 goda*), intended to simplify and update the system of punishments, was not implemented fully: only the chapters concerning crimes against the state and religious crimes were enacted.[12]

By 1905, the judicial system relied on incarceration, rather than exile, as the main type of punishment even for the more serious crimes. However, incarceration did not necessarily mean prison (*tiur'ma*) in the strict sense: a person could also be incarcerated in a katorga prison, a corrective house (*ispravitel'nyi dom*), a stronghold (*krepost'*), or an arrest house (*arestnyi dom*). The following sections discuss in more detail two of the carceral institutions: regular prisons, where convicts could be incarcerated for terms ranging from two weeks to one year, and, especially, katorga prisons, where convicts were incarcerated for terms of four to fifteen years. This focus is dictated by the goal of tracing tensions and developments in the domain of forced labour, as the places of confinement that held convicts for shorter terms had typically failed to create forced labour facilities.

Subaltern crime and the politics of criminalization

In the overwhelmingly agrarian realm that was the Romanov empire, most convicts were peasants. Understanding crime and punishment in the rural areas of the empire is, therefore, crucial for an overview of late imperial penal practices. The main intention of this chapter is to elucidate the tensions that shaped the penal system of the late Russian empire, and here I address the cultural conflict over the definition of crime and punishment in the rural areas that continuously fed these tensions. This conflict emerged after the

---

11   Anan'ich *et al.*, *Krisis samoderzhaviia*, pp. 60–61.
12   *Polnoe sobranie zakonov Rossiiskoi Imperii. The Third Series*, vol. 23 (Saint Petersburg, 1903), no. 22704 (22 March), pp. 175–261.

emancipation of the serfs, and became particularly acute by the beginning of the twentieth century.

The peasants and the elite, or to be more precise, the "legislators from the capitals",[13] had a differing understanding of what did or did not represent crime, how certain crimes had to be punished, and what the fulfilment of justice signified. The power to define crime, however, remained in the hands of the elite, and while the peasants did seek justice at the complex and sometimes confusing mix of judicial and administrative rural institutions, they would also turn to direct interpersonal violence, the organization of posses, and mob justice.[14] One example of such diverging understandings of crime and punishment concerned wood poaching: peasants considered it to be a very light crime when it was committed on the lands of a landlord or the state. However, if the poacher stole from another peasant, the situation became more complicated: the punishment for this crime then depended on whether the perpetrator knew whose land he was on.[15] Such a relative understanding of crime went even further; in the view of peasants, stealing from the poor constituted a serious crime, while stealing from the rich required a lesser punishment. The time of day when the crime was committed could also play a role in how peasants judged it: in some regions, crimes committed during daytime were considered more shameless and thus required a harsher punishment, while in other regions it was, on the contrary, night-time crimes that were considered premeditated and therefore demanded more severe prosecution.[16] Unsurprisingly, such region-specific, relative, and customary definitions of crime represented a considerable challenge for the local agents of the state, for whom the countryside remained "violent" and "lawless".

State agents' attempts to impose formal legal consciousness on the peasants constituted only one side of the conflict. When confronted with the legal framework, peasants often felt that it did not sufficiently protect them from the crimes they considered to be the most devastating: horse theft, robbery, and arson. These were rural crimes par excellence, yet it was extremely hard to punish horse theft and arson within the judicial system, as the evidence against the perpetrators was usually elusive.[17] Estimates suggest that only

13   I borrow this expression from George L. Yaney, *The Urge to Mobilize: Agrarian Reform in Russia, 1861–1930* (Urbana: University of Illinois Press, 1982).

14   Frank, *Crime, Cultural Conflict, and Justice*, p. 2.

15   Cathy Frierson, "Crime and Punishment in the Russian Village: Rural Concepts of Criminality at the End of the Nineteenth Century", *Slavic Review*, 46:1 (1987), pp. 55–69, 58.

16   *Ibid.*, p. 60.

17   Frank, *Crime, Cultural Conflict, and Justice*, p. 59. Rural areas accounted for 91.7 per cent of recorded incidents of arson. For more on arson, see Cathy A. Frierson, *All Russia Is Burning!*

one in ten horse thieves were ultimately arrested.[18] And even when horse thieves were captured, they often used their skills to escape, especially when engaging in extramural work.[19] For the overwhelming majority of peasant households, a loss of their main source of draft power (horses) was devastating. While peasants were alarmed about the instability that thieves brought to communities, "protection by the regular rural police and prosecution through the courts, however, proved sporadic at best".[20] It was not uncommon for peasants to seek to protect their horses themselves, and in order to do so, they "chose seemingly paradoxical extralegal measures of either community punishment of an apprehended thief or accommodation with horse thieves".[21] In other words, they either organized posses or tried to reach arrangements with the band of horse thieves by offering them money for the stolen horses.

The lack of policing at the village level and the extremely low professionalism of rural policemen were major reasons for the state's inability to exert social control in the countryside. By the beginning of the twentieth century, "the Department of Police reported a total complement of 47,866 (political police, port and river patrolmen, and some office personnel included) to handle a population of nearly 127,000,000".[22] This number does not create an impression of a heavily policed country, but the presence – or rather the lack thereof – of the police force in the rural areas is even more striking. There were only 1,582 constables and 6,874 sergeants to police a rural population of almost 90 million.[23] In other words, routine law enforcement outside of the cities had not significantly changed since the abolition of serfdom, and remained in the hands of the peasants.[24] Vigilante and mob violence were the most desperate measures of such peasant justice, and administrative

A Cultural History of Fire and Arson in Late Imperial Russia (Seattle: University of Washington Press, 2002).

18   Christine D. Worobec, "Horse Thieves and Peasant Justice in Post-Emancipation Imperial Russia", *Journal of Social History*, 21:2 (1987), pp. 281–93, footnote 26 on p. 284.

19   In 1913, the Main Prison Administration issued a circular demonstrating that they, at last, had become alerted to this problem. This circular stated that horse thieves were particularly prone to escape, and banned such convicts from extramural works. State Archive of the Russian Federation, Moscow (*Gosudarstvennyi arkhiv Rossiiskoi Federatsii*, hereafter GARF), f. 122, op. 8, d. 1, l. 64.

20   Frank, *Crime, Cultural Conflict, and Justice*, p. 13.

21   Worobec, "Horse Thieves", p. 285.

22   Neil Weissman, "Regular Police in Tsarist Russia, 1900–1914", *The Russian Review*, 44:1 (1985), pp. 45–68, 47.

23   *Ibid.*, p. 49.

24   *Ibid.*, p. 50.

exile was another. While the law of 10 June 1900 abolished the right of urban communities (*meshchanstva*) to exile their members, it preserved, in an attempt to prevent mob justice, such a possibility for rural communities. The exile theoretically had to remain under police surveillance for five years, and only after this term was over could they move somewhere else, but not to the region from which they had been exiled.[25]

As the political and social situation in the empire remained continuously unstable, the police were also less engaged with the routine policing of the countryside. As the police were increasingly redirected towards controlling the political situation and such activities as repressing rebellions, searching for illegal revolutionary publications, and surveillance of the "politically unreliable", they had less and less time and fewer resources to perform their regular duties and persecute robbers, arsonists, or horse and cattle thieves.[26]

The deployment of punishment in rural areas thus continued to be a source of tension. Social control in the countryside, and the prosecution of crime in particular, eluded the state. Prosecution largely remained the business of the peasants themselves, and this created an ever-widening gap between the popular and elite representations of punishment that guided prison reform. The weakness of policing of the rural regions of the empire and the inability (or unwillingness) of the state to adequately punish the crimes that were considered the most serious in the peasant world also contributed to the persistence of exile.

Dissent, state of exception, and exile

The assassination of Alexander II in March 1881 shook the political elites and had a deep impact on the socio-political organization of the empire.[27] The ruling elite was facing a deep crisis already prior to this. The state sought to elaborate new instruments to fight political dissent. Political terrorism carried out by radical groups like Land and Freedom (*Zemlia i volia*) and the People's Will (*Narodnaia Volia*), and the unwillingness of the regular courts to be instrumentalized in the fight against political dissent, prompted the state to seek extrajudicial measures.[28]

25   Gessen, *Iskliuchitel'noe polozhenie*, p. 48.
26   Frank, *Crime, Cultural Conflict, and Justice*, p. 81.
27   P.A. Zaionchkovskii, *Krizis samoderzhaviia na rubezhe 1870–1880-kh godov* (Moscow: Izdatel'stvo Moskovskogo universiteta, 1964), pp. 58–123.
28   Jonathan W. Daly, "On the Significance of Emergency Legislation in Late Imperial Russia", *Slavic Review*, 54:3 (1995), pp. 602–29, 606–8.

On 14 August 1881, five months after the death of his father, Alexander III issued the "Decree on Measures for the Preservation of the State Order and Public Peace", which, as with all legal acts validated by the emperor, had the full force of law and effectively introduced a state of emergency.[29] Jonathan Daly suggests that the tsarist government took the time to introduce this measure because it already possessed the administrative power it deemed sufficient. It was initially supposed to be temporary, yet in many regions of the empire it remained in power for decades. Daly has also underlined that from the very beginning, this decree directly "acquired the characteristics of a measure neither temporary nor exceptional".[30] The decree granted the administrative authorities – in most regions, governors general, governors, and city heads (*gradonachal'niki*) – with extensive extra-legal powers to prevent and punish political dissent. These nominally temporary measures gradually undermined the due process of the law.

One of the most prominent instruments of this repression was forced displacement, which took two forms: on the one hand was banishment (*vysylka*), i.e. the displacement of people from certain regions, and on the other was exile (*ssylka*), i.e. displacement to certain regions. Banishment was associated with a state of emergency: only under such conditions and with the agreement of a special committee that reunited representatives of the Ministry of the Interior and the Ministry of Justice, could local administrative authorities expel certain individuals. According to a 14 August 1881 decree, two types of delinquents could be banished: the first were those people deemed "politically unreliable" and the second were those considered morally corrupt and nefarious with regard to the "public peace".

Administrative exile occupied an extremely important place in imperial legislation, regardless of the introduction of the state of emergency; indeed, contemporary observers remarked that it was employed in such a wide variety of cases that it belonged to the regular, rather than emergency, repertoire of police action.[31] It was also tightly connected with police surveillance: exile could be administered for the term of one to five years, and the exiled person was supposed to remain under police surveillance throughout this time.[32] Considering that, as stated above, the regular police force was limited, it is unclear to what extent such surveillance was implemented.

29   *Polnoe sobranie zakonov Rossiiskoi Imperii. Sobranie tret'e. Tom I* (Saint Petersburg, 1881), no. 350 (14 August 1881), p. 261.
30   Daly, "On the Significance", p. 612.
31   Gessen, *Iskliuchitel'noe polozhenie*, p. 39.
32   *Ibid.*, p. 41.

During the 1905 revolution, tsarist authorities relied on the martial courts and the military suppression of the rebellion. Along with the use of the extrajudicial measures warranted by the state of exception, the use of army detachments to suppress the peasant rebellions, workers' protests, and soldier uprisings, and the use of military justice in the struggle against political militants, became the key instruments of repression in the course and especially in the aftermath of the 1905 revolution. However, as Jonathan Daly has suggested, prior to 1906, the tsarist authorities, when compared to their Western European counterparts, used the death penalty and harsher punishments such as katorga relatively sparingly, and even the peak of repression in 1906–1908 was considerably less violent than the repression against the Paris Commune.[33]

Political dissenters were exiled from all over the empire, but the areas from which the most exiles were deported were the urban industrial centres and the borderlands: Ukraine and the Donbass area, Poland, Saint Petersburg and the areas around it, Povolzhye, the Caucasus, and the Baltic region.[34] Militants deemed most dangerous were exiled to Siberia, but the geography of administrative exile after the 1905–1907 revolution was not limited to it.[35] Other dreaded distant destinations included some areas of Kazakhstan and the Russian north, namely the regions of Arkhangelsk, Vologda, Vyatka, and Olonets. During World War I, however, exile to European Russia effectively stopped.[36] Most importantly, unlike other regions, Siberia already had a

33 Jonathan W. Daly, "Criminal Punishment and Europeanization in Late Imperial Russia", *Jahrbücher für Geschichte Osteuropas*, 48:3 (2000), pp. 341–62, 347.

34 N.N. Shcherbakov, "Chislennost' i sostav politicheskikh ssyl'nykh Sibiri (1907–1917 gg.)", in *Ssyl'nye revoliutsionery v Sibiri*, vol. 1 (Irkutsk: Irkustkii Gosudarstvennyi universitet, 1973), p. 227 and p. 240.

35 Political exiles to Siberia, unsurprisingly, constitute the best-studied group among Russian convicts and exiles. Even the exiles themselves started to analyse their condition and gather statistics about their social and political composition. During the early Soviet period, the Society of Political Exiles and Hard Labourers was active both in Moscow and Siberia. It collected the testimonies of former exiles and published a magazine called *Katorga i Ssylka*, which, despite its clear ideological preoccupation, can still be used as a resource on life in exile. For more on the society, see Sandra Pujals, "When Giants Walked the Earth: The Society of Former Political Prisoners and Exiles of the Soviet Union, 1921–1935" (Ph.D. dissertation, Georgetown University, 1999) and Marc Junge, *Die Gesellschaft ehemaliger politischer Zwangsarbeiter und Verbannter in der Sowjetunion: Gründung, Entwicklung und Liquidierung (1921–1935)* (Berlin: Akademie Verlag, 2009). Studies of exile blossomed in Siberia in the later years. Starting in 1973, a series of yearbooks on exiled revolutionaries was published, comprising more than twenty volumes (*Ssyl'nye revoliutsionery v Sibiri*).

36 E.Sh. Khaziakhmetov, *Sibirskaia politicheskaia ssylka, 1905–1917 gg: Oblik, organizatsii, revoliutsionnye sviazi* (Tomsk: Tomskii Gosudarstvennyi universitet, 1978), p. 3.

significant population of administrative exiles, those exiled judicially, and settlers who had served katorga terms. Fearing radicalization of the earlier exiles by the politically minded newcomers, the authorities started to exile political militants to new, more distant locations in Western Siberia, such as the Narym region, but it was nevertheless not uncommon for the different groups of exiles to interact.

The change in the social composition of political exiles in Siberia reflected the growth of mass political dissent: unlike in previous decades when the overwhelming majority of exiles belonged to the privileged estates, after 1905 the majority of exiles were of unprivileged origin. Estimates based on surveys of the exiles suggest that throughout the 1906–1917 period, between 49.7 and 67.6 per cent of exiles belonged to the peasant estate. However, only 8.4 per cent of exiles in 1906–1910, and less than 2 per cent in 1914–1917, were peasants by occupation. Workers by occupation, on the other hand, constituted 56.1 per cent in 1906–1910, 48.9 per cent in 1911–1914, and 55.7 per cent in 1914–1917.[37] Despite the switch to urban industrial labour, many of these first-generation workers maintained tight connections with the countryside. As Victoria Bonnell has underlined, there were three categories of workers in the bigger cities: "permanent urban workers with no ties whatsoever to the countryside, transitional workers with attenuated ties to the countryside, and semirural workers with ongoing ties to their native village".[38]

This change in demographic composition of exiles also shifted the distinction between "political" and "common" criminals. Until that moment, the status of "political prisoner" was largely reserved for people with a privileged background, but after 1905, for the first time, large groups of workers, soldiers, and peasants were prosecuted for political crimes. Although the state did not force them to work, many of the exiles, especially those coming from unprivileged estates, could rely on their own labour as their sole source of income. The socio-economic situation in Siberia differed significantly from that of the European parts of the empire, which meant that the structure of available jobs was also different. There were fewer industrial centres, and many exiles had to abandon their previous occupations as metal or textile workers, students, or printing workers, and take up lower-paid manual labour jobs instead.[39]

37 *Ibid.*, p. 21.
38 Victoria E. Bonnell, *Roots of Rebellion: Workers' Politics and Organizations in St. Petersburg and Moscow, 1900–1914* (Berkeley: University of California Press, 1983), p. 53.
39 Khaziakhmetov, *Sibirskaia politicheskaia ssylka*, p. 29.

The efforts to increase state control over punishments appear to have been insufficient to achieve the aspired degree of state control over convicts, and especially political prisoners. Political prisoners often used their networks of solidarity, money, and skills in order to escape exile or at least make their presence in Siberia politically useful. While in exile, revolutionaries dedicated their time to reading and writing, advancing revolutionary theory and attracting the attention of the public to their condition. The importance of this experience to the building of the Russian revolutionary movement was such that researchers have called exile villages "academies of sedition".[40]

Exile and katorga were losing their importance as punishments against common crimes, yet they became instrumentalized by the central government in their fight against political dissent. The government's reliance on the forced displacement of revolutionaries, however, produced a stark unintended effect. By the beginning of the twentieth century, exile and the prison experience were definitively identified as the crucible of a true Russian revolutionary. Exile and prison provided shared political experience for many militants, often radicalized those activists who were initially more moderate, and became a cause for revolutionary supporters, both in the Russian empire and internationally. As Padraic Kenney has shown, the imprisonment of political opponents in modern times has rarely achieved its desired goals, and the Russian imperial case is no exception.[41]

The advance of extramural prison labour

In the Russian empire, prison reform took shape as state administrators sought to increase their control not only over the deployment of punishment, but also over the bodies of those already serving their terms. Prison theoreticians imagined this transition in terms that concur with the Foucauldian paradigm of "the carceral", but the reality of this reform had a limited disciplining effect and proved to be ridden with tensions and inconsistencies that contributed to its ultimate failure.[42]

Incarceration (especially the quest for the maximum isolation of inmates) and forced labour in theory constituted the two pillars of this

---

40 Beer, *The House of the Dead*, p. 353.
41 Padraic Kenney, "'I Felt a Kind of Pleasure in Seeing Them Treat Us Brutally': The Emergence of the Political Prisoner, 1865–1910", *Comparative Studies in Society and History*, 54:4 (2012), pp. 863–89 and Kenney, *Dance in Chains*.
42 Michel Foucault, *Surveiller et punir* (Paris: Gallimard, 1975), pp. 300–315.

reform, and prison was the embodiment of this nexus between the two. Some of the instruments intended to make prison dominate the penal landscape were already formulated in the late 1870s. They included centralization of the prison system, the construction of new prison buildings that allowed the separation of convicts, and the improvement of prison conditions in terms of discipline and hygiene. Although isolation via incarceration was initially considered an instrument for the rehabilitation of criminals (inspired by the early nineteenth-century penological conceptions of the Pennsylvania prison system), by the 1870s, central prison administrators unanimously promoted forced labour as the main instrument.[43]

As discussed in the previous chapter, the implementation of these ideas proved challenging. Reliance on incarceration, rather than exile, as the chief type of punishment for common criminals truly came into action only after exile was curbed in 1900. Solitary confinement, or at least the night-time separation of prisoners, proved even less attainable.[44] These arrangements, which were inspired by the international experience and largely relied on the ideas of John Howard, a British prison reformer who remained highly influential in the Romanov empire long after his death, were still considered, despite persistent critique, to be the state-of-the-art in penological practices. The building of new prisons became one of the chief preoccupations of the Main Prison Administration immediately upon its creation in 1879, but the night-time separation of inmates remained an elusive goal: as late as 1903, during preparation of the reform of criminal legislation, the Ministry of Justice received an order from the state council to introduce night-time separation in katorga prisons and total separation outside working hours in the corrective houses.[45]

While the solitary confinement of all convicts remained unattainable, and overpopulation could be alleviated only until the 1905 revolution – which resulted in an avalanche of new convictions – some prison employees still attempted to improve prison conditions through modern science, and especially hygiene. Prisons becoming laboratories of hygienist experimentation was a global trend. Especially in colonial contexts, prison could become "a model for the ordering of society according to the dictates of medical science

---

43   In the Pennsylvania system, which originated in the 1820s in Philadelphia, solitary confinement was considered the primary method of rehabilitation and fighting recidivism.

44   Night-time separation of inmates was the main premise of the Auburn prison system, which replaced the Pennsylvania system in the US. Both systems were extensively discussed by the international penological community, but found little application in the Russian case.

45   *Tiuremnoe preobrazovanie*, p. 3.

and sanitation".[46] Transit prisons in particular remained one of the most problematic areas of the prison system. Convicts and exiles were continuously moved around, and the poor conditions in the transit prisons had repercussions in the whole system. The shortcomings became particularly dangerous in crisis. In 1907–1908, due to the extreme overpopulation, prisons were struck by an epidemic of typhoid fever, which spread easily because convicts were constantly moved around the country and held together in large cells during transit.[47] Medical professionals also took up the challenges of the Russian imperial prisons. The doctor employed at the Smolensk katorga prison, Eikhgol'ts, for instance, suggested that forced labour for inmates could be used in order to improve the quality of air in the cells and thus prevent the spread of tuberculosis (*bugorchatka*).[48] The chief of the GTU at the time, Sergei Khrulev, found Eikhgol'ts's suggestions so ingenious that he printed them in *The Prison Herald* and recommended them for application in all katorga prisons throughout the empire.[49] Eikhgol'ts invented a ventilation machine that could be put in motion through the manual force of convicts. According to him, this machine had multiple benefits: it could be produced cheaply in the prison workshops, did not require the construction of new prison facilities, and improved the physical condition of the inmates by making them work, as "by being physically inactive, an inmate also makes his whole organism inactive" and is therefore "unable to fight disease with the same intensity as when his whole organism is active thanks to physical labour".[50]

The career of convict labour in the Russian empire was rocky. Throughout much of the nineteenth century, the only institution where convicts were consistently forced to work was the katorga, where inmates had to perform back-breaking labour in mines and other dangerous sites for the benefit of the central government. As discussed in the first chapter, on 6 January 1886, Alexander III approved a law proposed by the state council, thus introducing obligatory labour for inmates of all prisons, except for those in remand. Due to the fact that the law provided no blueprints for its implementation, and charged the prison wardens with the task of introducing forced labour in

---

46   David Arnold, "The Colonial Prison: Power, Knowledge and Penology in Nineteenth-Century India", in David Arnold and David Hardiman (eds), *Subaltern Studies VIII: Essays in Honour of Ranajit Guha* (Delhi, Oxford: Oxford University Press, 1994), pp. 148–87, 179.

47   "Obzor preobrazovanii po tiuremnoi chasti pri novykh zakonodatelnykh ustanovleniiakh (1906–1912 g.g.)", *Tiuremnyi vestnik*, 10 (1912), pp. 1581–701, 1593.

48   Eikhgol'ts, "Fizicheskii trud, kak sredstvo dlia ulutscheniia sanitarnogo sostoianiia tiur'my", *Tiuremnyi vestnik*, 6–7 (1910), pp. 923–38.

49   *Ibid.*, p. 923.

50   *Ibid.*, p. 935.

prisons, the variety of organizational forms that emerged by the beginning of the twentieth century was impressive.

In particular, two main varieties became increasingly distinct in terms of the organization of convict labour: forced labour in regular prisons, and the labour of katorga convicts. The first variety included all those decentralized, localized types of convict labour that emerged from the practice of the prison wardens. The second encompassed convict labour on infrastructural projects generally coordinated from the centre of the empire. This section reviews in greater detail the localized types of convict labour, while the large-scale infrastructural projects are the subject of the next section. In both cases, the key development in the years before the revolution related to the fact that remuneration became central to the practice of forced labour.

As discussed in the previous chapter, at the onset of penal reform, officials of the GTU favoured the creation of workshops in prisons and the development of artisanal labour. As prisons were predominantly urban, these officials deemed such types of labour to be perfectly aligned with the development of an industrial economy: it allowed prison wardens to receive profit as they sold the goods produced by the convicts on the market, and it also allegedly facilitated the return of convicts to society, as they would be able to find a legal occupation with the skills they learned in prison. Agricultural colonies existed, but they were more often used for underage offenders and were not taken up widely as a viable alternative to intramural workshops. Considering that Russia at the time was an overwhelmingly peasant country, the central officials' encouragement of artisanal and industrial convict labour as the foundation of this reform hints at their reliance on the penological concepts developed in industrialized Western European countries.

Left to their own devices, prison wardens approached the issue of convict labour differently and with varying degrees of success. The GTU project of creating workshops was confronted with a constant lack of funding, the absence of sufficiently trained prison personnel, and the fact that the majority of prisoners were incarcerated only for a few months, which made it impossible for them to truly learn a trade. All of these obstacles, if eventually manageable for certain bigger *guberniia* prisons situated in the main towns of the regions, proved to be insurmountable for the smaller *uezd* prisons, which were located in the towns with a population of several thousand. On average, terms in the *uezd* prisons were around three months, while they were slightly longer for the *guberniia* and *oblast* prisons.[51] A letter submitted

---

51   B. Krzhivetskii, "Vnutrenniia arestantskie raboty i kustarnyi trud", *Tiuremnyi vestnik*, 5 (1913), pp. 839–71, 841.

by the warden of the Arkhangelsk prison, L. Parshenskii, to *The Prison Herald* demonstrates the extent to which the introduction of any type of prison labour hinged upon the outstanding personal initiative of the wardens. When Parshenskii took up his position as a warden, the convicts were only working occasionally, and generally performed short-term unqualified jobs. Establishing convict labour outside of the prisons, and especially hiring out the prisoners to local entrepreneurs, proved to be difficult due to, among other things, the contempt and suspicion of entrepreneurs towards the convicts.[52] The warden was finally able to hire out some of the prisoners to the local brick factory, and eventually other potential employers also showed their interest. In his letter, the only argument he used to encourage his fellow prison wardens to establish convict labour was the profit derived from the works.

Deriving profit became appealing even to some wardens responsible to the katorga prisons. When a critically minded young jurist, Mikhail Isaev, lamented the disarray of the katorga prisons throughout the empire, he singled out the Tobolsk katorga prison as the only one that had convict labour organized "in a partially satisfactory manner".[53] The Tobolsk prison administrators opted for the establishment of their own brick factory instead of hiring the prisoners out for work. In the case of the Tobolsk prison complex, which at the time consisted of two katorga prisons, a corrective arrest division (*ispravitel'noe arestantskoe otdelenie*), and a stronghold, creation of this factory pursued a two-fold goal: on the one hand, the brick factory was a site of convict labour, and on the other, the bricks it produced were used for the construction of more prison buildings to help alleviate the overpopulation. As they asked for additional funds for the construction of this factory in 1903, the Tobolsk governor and prison inspector referred to the experience of the first brick factory run by the prison, which by 1903 was already functioning for four years.[54]

In other prisons, however, katorga convicts could find themselves in a completely different situation. For instance, as late as in 1910, a report about the katorga convicts in Chernihiv (northern Ukraine) stated that despite their sentences, which implied hard labour and exile, they were still detained in local prisons that were insufficiently guarded.[55] Therefore, other inmates

---

52 L. Parshenskii, "Pis'mo v redaktsiiu", *Tiuremnyi vestnik*, 4 (1913), pp. 703–4.

53 M. Isaev, "Predstoiashshee preobrazovanie katorgi", *Pravo*, 6 (13 February 1911), pp. 321–32, 323.

54 GARF, f. 122, op. 8, d. 1338.

55 GARF, f. 122, op. 48, d. 1171, l. 2.

in these prisons had to perform the extramural works, despite the fact that they were sentenced to lighter punishment, while the katorga inmates would spend their days without any work.

The examples of success among large prisons, such as the one in Tobolsk, were championed in the professional press, yet they were of little use to the wardens of the smaller *uezd* prisons. The presence in such prisons of a large percentage of detainees on remand, who were not obliged to work, proved particularly problematic. V. Ignat'ev, a *Prison Herald* correspondent, suggested that the introduction of convict labour was only possible with changes to the legislation: according to him, prisoners on remand should be forced to work just like convicts, otherwise the installation of workshops would not make financial sense. He also reaffirmed the necessity to invest in the organization of labour: at least one horse and some equipment, along with a salary for the overseer, he stated, were the absolute minimum for such prisons. Ignat'ev's suggestions were not limited to the demand for resources and access to more imprisoned labourers. His article also demonstrated that he perceptively incorporated such progressive penological ideas as the importance of education for convicts and prison personnel: he suggested that the *uezd* prisons should be equipped with libraries.[56]

By the beginning of the twentieth century, the GTU had mostly stopped promoting intramural artisanal labour as the dominant occupation for convicts. During the 1902 conference of prison workers, for instance, the council stated that it should instead encourage the development of agricultural and ameliorative works, alongside construction works for public and state interest.[57] As the following section will demonstrate, as the state became more and more interested in using convict labour, it opted for the employment of katorga convicts, as the more localized, distributed, uncoordinated variety of prison labour had lost its importance.

Redefining hard labour in the imperial borderlands

The emergence of the second distinctive variety of convict labour, namely large-scale infrastructure projects, was related to the attempts to reshape one of the oldest forms of punishment in Russian empire: katorga. These

---

56   V. Ignat'ev, "Chto nuzhno dlia razvitiia arestantskikh rabot?", *Tiuremnyi vestnik*, 5 (1908), pp. 432–34.

57   Mikhail Isaev, "Predstoiashchee preobrazovanie katorgi (prodolzhenie)", *Pravo*, 7 (20 February 1911), pp. 393–404, 396.

attempts can be best understood through an analysis of the discussion surrounding the 1910 katorga reform project. Despite the fact that it was never implemented, this project highlights the tension between the reformatory desires of the progressive penologists, who placed productive labour at the centre of their projects to rehabilitate convicts, and the lingering practice of katorga as a purely punitive regime.

Before it was abolished by the Provisional Government in February 1917, katorga remained a peculiarly obsolete form of punishment. The first consistent governmental suggestions to reform katorga appeared only in 1910. The need for this reform was created by a double pressure: on the one hand, after the Russo-Japanese war, the largest site of this kind in the empire, the island of Sakhalin, could no longer be used; on the other hand, in the aftermath of the 1905 revolution, the number of katorga convicts skyrocketed, and the existing facilities could not contain them.[58] Forced labour as a part of katorga became increasingly hard to organize by the mid-nineteenth century, and instead of convict labour becoming a source of income for the state, the necessity to find work for the convicts at most of the Siberian sites became a burden for local authorities. At the old katorga site of Nerchinsk, for instance, many inmates were so sickly and undernourished that they could not perform the hard labour they were convicted to.[59] A contemporary observer remarked that the proclaimed goals of katorga, namely retribution for particularly dangerous crimes, deterrence, and, in line with the advances of modern penology, rehabilitation, remained largely unfulfilled.[60] Another goal of katorga was colonization through "eternal settlement", which was also largely unsuccessful for the same reasons as exile. As discussed in the first chapter, hardship and social displacement pushed many exiles to vagabondage and crime, and the virtual absence of policing capacity to control the movement of exiles enabled a large proportion to try to return to European Russia, or try their luck elsewhere.

This crisis of katorga, however, was not produced exclusively by the pressures of war and revolution: it had been in the making for many years. The traditional katorga sites of Eastern Siberia were in such a lamentable state that they attracted the continuous attention of the GTU, and several inspections carried out by its directors documented the deplorable

58   Isaev, "Predstoiashchee preobrazovanie katorgi", pp. 324–25.
59   Dril', *Ssylka i katorga v Rossii*, p. 4 and p. 8. For more on illness in exile and katorga, see Badcock, "From Villains to Victims".
60   Sergei Poznyshev, *K voprosu o preobrazovanii nashei katorgi* (Moscow: Pechatnia A.I. Snegirevoi, 1914), pp. 4–5.

conditions of these sites.[61] Already in early 1905, only 2,620 katorga convicts actually reached their intended katorga sites in Siberia, while another 3,504 convicts, destined to be incarcerated in Siberian katorga prisons, were instead held in regular prisons and transit prisons, where they generally were not forced to work.[62] In the years preceding the 1905 revolution, the number of those serving katorga terms was decreasing, in part due to the pre-term release of convicts on Sakhalin into settlements, and in part due to the manifesto of 11 August 1904, which gave the right to pre-term settlement to convicts in other locations.[63] However, as katorga became more and more instrumental to political repression in the following years, the central authorities had to face the extreme overpopulation of katorga sites and could no longer use Siberia as the main destination for such convicts. In 1908, at the height of political repression, only 6,143 out of 20,936 katorga convicts actually reached the Siberian prisons, while another 4,000 people had to be incarcerated in seven temporary katorga prisons in the European part of the empire.[64] These measures could not fully restore the strict regime: in 1909, more than 11,000 katorga convicts, or more than half of the total number, were still held in regular prisons, including the small *uezd* prisons.[65] By 1913, the number of katorga convicts grew to reach approximately 30,000 people, but Siberia still hosted only around 11,500 convicts, and just 800 of them were inmates of the Tobolsk prison. The temporary katorga prisons in European Russia, however, contained as many as 13,200 convicts, while the rest were confined in other places of incarceration throughout the empire.[66]

As the Russian authorities finally attempted to reform katorga, prison administrators buttressed this reform by referring to other cases of colonial convict transportation. During the preparation of this reform, *The Prison Herald* published an essay that looked into the history of hard labour and convict transportation legislation in various Western European contexts. The essay described French exile and hard labour, and referred to the British convict transportation experience in North America and Australia. The author sought to inscribe the imperial katorga within the global context

61 Khrulev, *Katorga v Sibiri* and Gran, *Katorga v Sibiri*.

62 *Otchet po Glavnomu tiuremnomu upravleniiu za 1905 god* (Saint Petersburg: Tipo-Litografiia S.-Peterburgskoi tiur'my, 1906), p. 18.

63 "Kratkaia ob'iasnitel'naia zapiska po proektu Ministra Iustitsii o preobrazovanii katorgi", *Tiuremnyi vestnik*, 12 (1915), pp. 1925–2018, 1983.

64 Isaev, "Predstoiashchee preobrazovanie katorgi", p. 324.

65 Luchinskii, "Raboty, dostupntye dlia vsekh arestantov", p. 1171.

66 "Kratkaia ob'iasnitel'naia zapiska", pp. 1983–84.

of colonial punishments and underlined that in the Siberian case as well, exile would stop once a colony becomes "sufficiently developed". Colonial transportation was not the only inspiration for the reform: the author of the document also refers at length to the experience of the early modern German Zuchthaus, as well as the prison system of the USA.[67]

The 1910 project of reform formulated two main changes to the katorga regime: first, it sought to eliminate exile as part of katorga, and second, it intended to introduce remuneration for hard labour for all katorga convicts. The project of this reform had the goal of making the country more uniform in terms of the distribution of penal institutions, and further affirming the centrality of incarceration and forced labour as instruments of convict rehabilitation. Katorga, as the harshest general punishment, represented a challenge for the reformers, as they struggled to retain its extreme punitive effect while simultaneously "rehabilitating" the convicts, at least in theory. Once again, solitary confinement was presented as a penological panacea: according to the project, convicts had to spend the first three to six months of their terms in solitary confinement.

In the context of late tsarist penal practices, "rehabilitation" (ispravlenie) meant a very specific process: first, a convict "on his way to rehabilitation" (ispravliaiushchiisia) would comply with the discipline within the prison walls; second, once settled outside the prison, the rehabilitated convict would abstain from crime. This was initially not a priority in the case of katorga convicts, but by the beginning of the twentieth century, the authorities sought to align katorga with more modern penological goals of rehabilitation and decrease of recidivism. Considering the length of katorga terms, the authorities used the possibility of gradual improvement of the conditions of prisoners, and reduction of their terms, as leverage to make them comply with the discipline. Eventually, after the decision of a special committee, the convicts deemed most reliable could be allowed to work and live outside the prison in the special barracks (vnetiuremnii razriad). They remained under surveillance, however, as the guard would lock these barracks during the night.

It was not uncommon, however, that living outside of the prison was a consequence of the deficiencies of the prison management, rather than a leverage of "rehabilitation". Reports from the Aleksandrovskaia katorga

---

67   The Zuchthaus, or house of correction, was an urban carceral institution that emerged in the early seventeenth century in the Netherlands (Rasphuis in Amsterdam) and across Germany. Intended as a place of disciplining the "work shy", prostitutes, vagrants, petty thieves, beggars, and other urban poor, the Zuchthaus combined hard forced labour with confinement.

prison (in the vicinity of Irkutsk) suggest that prior to 1909, for instance, the convicts were not forced to wear shackles, and many worked and lived outside of the prison without any surveillance, occasionally attacking the population of the neighbouring villages.[68] In 1900, as the use of exile for common criminals was limited, it remained a separate punishment only for religious and political crimes. However, while the flow of exiles had waned since the 1900 law, large groups of convicts were still forced to remain in Siberia in "eternal settlement", which remained part of the katorga regime. Decoupling exile and katorga was at the core of the project of katorga reform.[69]

"Eternal settlement", as the final stage of katorga, was neither as punitive nor as territorially expansive as the authorities intended it to be. Police forces in Siberia were scarce and were focused mostly on the surveillance of political exiles, while the settled convicts were neglected. Once released into settlement, katorga convicts were faced with the need to build a life in a condition of extreme penury in an unfamiliar, often hostile environment. As discussed above, a large number opted to abandon the settlement and either join groups of vagrants (*brodiagi*), mostly former exiles and convicts like themselves, or attempt to return to European Russia. In 1913, in the Irkutsk region (where most katorga convicts were sent to), for instance, out of 75,187 exiles and forced settlers, 32,075 had escaped, and another 20,186 had been granted permits to temporarily leave the settlement and had not yet returned.[70]

The 1910 project reflects the fact that the goals that the state had pursued with exile and katorga had been updated since the 1880s. Previously, the conceptual foundation of exile was the idea that the mere presence of exiled bodies, irrespective of their material wellbeing, was already an instrument of imperial expansion. The fact that this concentration of exiles and other convicts in Siberia created setbacks for the economic and social development of the region started to bother the authorities already in the early nineteenth century, but they took no actions against it until the beginning of the mass peasant migration to Siberia. The abolition of "eternal settlement" as part of katorga, however, did not mean that the ex-convicts could return to the places where they had lived before their conviction. They were still deemed dangerous, and were prescribed to live in the special areas in proximity to the prisons where they had served the first part of their punishment, had to

---

68 "Kratkaia ob'iasnitel'naia zapiska", pp. 1966–67.
69 *Ibid.*, p. 1987.
70 *Ibid.*, p. 1980.

remain under police surveillance, and were threatened with incarceration in case they left.[71]

The project of reform attracted significant interest, and while the idea of abolishing eternal settlement was generally approved of, several authors lamented the lack of attention given to the organization of convict labour in the project. Mikhail Isaev, one of the most radical critics of katorgii from within the community of legal professionals, suggested that katorga in Siberia should be completely abolished, and that this should be paired with the development of extramural works in European Russia.[72] He also stated that the GTU was withholding information about katorga labour, and that the intramural labour facilities at many katorga sites were so dilapidated that "sometimes the katorga transforms into 'katorga idleness (*katorzhnoe bezdelie*)'", which, according to him, was "something worse than hard labour (*katorzhnye raboty*)".[73] Observers from the Ministry of Justice underlined the organizational benefits of large-scale works for katorga convicts, as opposed to the traditional sites: according to one, N.N. Pasynkov, such large-scale works created an opportunity for convicts to over-fulfil the norms (*sverkhurochnye raboty*). The fact that this over-fulfilment was accompanied by elevated remuneration represented a "powerful stimulus for labour".[74]

Already at the end of the nineteenth century, experiments with the use of convict labour in the construction of infrastructure, particularly railway construction, appeared to the administrators to be more promising than the previously existing types of katorga labour. Dmitrii Dril', an official for the Ministry of Justice who inspected several katorga sites in 1896, remarked that the conditions of surveillance and the productivity of convict labour for railroad construction had improved in the previous years.[75] He visited construction sites in the Far East, next to Chita and Khabarovsk, and stated that the benefits of such work for convicts (remuneration for their work and extra hours, better food rations, and term reductions) led to much better discipline, despite the fact that the convicts had more opportunities to escape than in prisons. He attributed this to the motivation for convicts: eight

71   *Ibid.*, pp. 2011–13.

72   Isaev, "Predstoiashchee preobrazovanie katorgi (prodolzhenie)", p. 397.

73   *Ibid.*, p. 396.

74   This remuneration for katorga convicts, however, still only amounted to 30 per cent of the wage of wage workers. See: N.N. Pasynkov, "Doklad prichislennogo k Ministerstvu Iustitsii koll. sov. N.N. Pasynkova po voprosu 6-mu perechnia voprosov, postavlennykh na obsuzhdenie s'ezda", *Tiuremnyi vestnik*, 4 (1914), pp. 885–87, 886.

75   Dril', *Ssylka i katorga v Rossii*, pp. 37–40.

months of such labour counted for a whole year of incarceration, and the over-fulfilment of norms (*sverkhurochnye raboty*) was better remunerated.[76]

The project of katorga reform demonstrates an attempt to prescribe these measures not only at separate sites, but as a general framework, and to introduce higher remuneration for katorga labour. For the inmates of regular prisons, remuneration of up to 6/10 of the wage of a free worker was introduced by the 1886 law on obligatory convict labour. The same law capped the remuneration of katorga convicts at 1/10. The 1910 katorga reform project suggested progressive remuneration: those in solitary confinement should still labour for free, while convicts in the next two groups could receive from 1/10 to 6/10 of the wage of a free worker for the labour they performed.

To conclude, the project of reform proposed little more than the legal normalization of practices that already existed. The construction of katorga prisons in the European part of the empire was one such practice, and the absence of intramural works for convicts was another. The introduction of remuneration for katorga convicts was also already being experimented with as the prison authorities handpicked small groups of young healthy male convicts to perform extramural labour, but the extent to which this would have changed the general conditions of katorga if it had been introduced universally remains unclear.

What the project did not touch upon were the consequences of having served a katorga term. For the convict who survived the hard labour, poor conditions, and harsh climate, these consequences still constituted an additional, long-lasting part of the punishment. While the branding of katorga convicts had been abolished in 1845, the social consequences remained. Katorga convicts were stigmatized for life, and the 1910 project did little to change the situation. Those who served full terms and even those released on parole were still stripped of all civil rights (unless they benefited from royal amnesty), they could only settle in specially designated areas of the empire, and they remained under police surveillance.

This overview allows us to see, first, that the substance of the imperial agenda in Siberia continued to change. The authorities started to treat the development of the infrastructure of the region through forced labour, rather than the occupation of land through forced settlement, as their new goal. The construction of the Chita and Amur railroads serve as the most prominent examples of this change, but the Ministry of Justice also recommended the use of convict labour for melioration, road construction,

76   *Ibid.*, p. 39.

reclamation of marshland, the construction of dams and river locks, and other infrastructural endeavours, not only in Siberia but also in Turkestan and even European Russia.[77]

Despite the fact that the 1910 reform project was never implemented, forced convict labour for centrally coordinated infrastructural projects acquired further importance as World War I unfolded.

Convict labour for the war effort

In the imperial context, extramural convict labour acquired its ultimate importance, both conceptually and practically, during the course of World War I. Disappointment among prison administrators vis-à-vis the installation of workshops for convicts met the state's goals of substituting for labour shortage and providing for the front. The first attempts to use convict labour for the war effort dated back to 1906, when convicts were put to sewing army uniforms.[78]

Although the use of forced convict labour for the war effort was not limited to large-scale extramural projects, they acquired particular importance in the historical perspective: while the use of convict labour for such projects was mostly experimental prior to 1915, in the war situation it became the focal point of the work of the GTU and, ostensibly, served as a blueprint for the use of prisoner-of-war (POW) labour later in the war. The use of convict labour in the construction of infrastructure, as opposed to road maintenance works or other types of forced labour, started as an experiment long before World War I. These experiments were tightly connected to railroad building in the hinterlands of the Russian empire. In Siberia, this involved the construction of the last stretch of the Trans-Siberian Railway, the Amur Railroad in the Far East. Construction started in 1910, and convict labour was employed there right from the start of the works.[79] At first, this construction employed 2,500 inmates, and the number of labourers grew to reach 7,000 in 1911–1912, but dropped to 3,193 convicts as of 1 January 1913, and 2,448 convicts as of 1 January 1914.[80] The number of convicts working on these projects was shrinking, because as the construction progressed, there were fewer tasks

77 "Kratkaia ob'iasnitel'naia zapiska", p. 1988.
78 "Obzor preobrazovanii po tiuremnoi chasti", p. 1594.
79 "O primenenii v 1914–1915 gg. truda katorzhnykh k dorozhnomu stroitel'stvu v Sibiri", *Tiuremnyi vestnik*, 6–7 (1915), pp. 1347–57, 1347.
80 "Raboty arestantov na Amurskoi zheleznoi doroge v 1913 godu v predelakh Amurskoi oblasti", *Tiuremnyi vestnik*, 4 (1915), pp. 933–43, 933, and *Obzor Amurskoi oblasti za 1914 god* (Blagoveschensk: Amur. obl. stat. kom., 1915), p. 83.

for them to perform. Convicts were directed towards heavy labour, such as clearing land for railways, cutting rock for tunnels, and cutting wood. The works were performed throughout the whole year, in day and night shifts.[81] The Amur Railway construction was praised especially because of the low frequency of escapes and the low rate of the use of physical punishment against the convicts.[82] This might be explained by the fact that several military detachments were used to guard the convicts, and throughout 1913, for instance, the average number of soldier guards constituted up to 40 per cent of the number of convicts.[83]

At the onset of war, such high numbers became much harder for the military guards to maintain, and at the construction of the Arkhangelsk Railroad in 1915, escapes became a bigger issue, as there were only 151 guards for 1,599 detainees.[84] Arkhangelsk, a port in the Russian north, became crucial for the Russian government for the transport of military supplies from the allies, and the old single-way Vologda-Arkhangelsk Railway constructed in 1898 no longer sufficed. Construction of the railroad started in February 1915, and despite the initial plans to employ only 200 convicts, their number soon soared to 1,600 due to the absence of free labourers.[85] Convicts were sent to the construction of the Arkhangelsk Railroad not only from the Vologda katorga prison, which was the closest (750 km away), but also from as far away as Riga (1,600 km away) and Kharkiv (almost 2,000 km away).

This railroad expansion in the north continued during the war. Construction of the railroad line from Petrozavodsk to Murmansk was part of this project. Work on the line had begun before the war and initially employed free workers, but already at the end of 1914 they were substituted by incarcerated labourers. In this case, however, these were not Russian convicts, but German and Austro-Hungarian POWs.[86] Despite being situated beyond the Arctic Circle, Murmansk benefits from an ice-free port. Therefore, this railroad had strategic significance, as it would have allowed the Russian army to receive supplies from the allies. The project was attributed the highest priority, and large groups of POWs were forced to work there: from 1 June 1915 to 1 November 1916, 50,775 POW labourers were engaged in the

81   *Obzor Amurskoi oblasti za 1914 god*, pp. 84–85.

82   "Raboty arestantov", p. 942.

83   *Obzor Amurskoi oblasti za 1914 god*, p. 83.

84   Vladimir Gradusov, "Zheleznodorozhnye raboty arestantov", *Tiuremnyi vestnik*, 6–7 (1916), pp. 657–58, 662 and 671.

85   *Ibid.*, pp. 657–58.

86   Georg Wurzer, "Die Kriegsgefangenen der Mittelmächte in Rußland im Ersten Weltkrieg" (Ph.D. dissertation, Eberhard-Karls-Universität zu Tübingen, 2000), p. 335.

construction.[87] This railroad became a symbol of the suffering of POWs of the Central Powers in Russia: they had to endure not only the harsh climate and inadequate living conditions, but also the lack of medical help amidst a typhus epidemic.[88] The modalities of POW labour in Russia during World War I will be analysed in greater detail in the following chapter, but it is necessary here to highlight the continuum of the use of incarcerated labour during war conditions: both convicts and POWs were used in place of free labourers, and were generally forced to work as a low-skilled workforce on projects of military importance that attracted very few free labourers to begin with.

Endeavours such as the construction of the Arkhangelsk Railroad marked an important change in the organization of forced convict labour, as these large-scale infrastructure projects in the borderlands were co-ordinated and supervised by a central agency. The military conditions allowed the prison administration to put forward their previous experience in organizing forced labour, as the state became more desperate to use forced labourers. A special committee on forced labour was organized within the GTU in order to plan and distribute convict labourers to a variety of projects throughout the empire: railroads in the Amur region and around lake Baikal, a mountain road in the Usinsk region (bordering Mongolia), gold mining in His Imperial Majesty's Cabinet mines, coal mining in the Ural mountains, and dock work on the White Sea.[89] It is unclear whether there was more funding provided for the organization of such works, but it is clear that the war prompted inter-departmental cooperation – the Ministry of Agriculture and the Department of Road Construction, for instance, were now eager to employ convicts.[90] This allowed the GTU to boast levels of convict employment it had never been able to achieve: out of more than 140,000 convicts that were incarcerated as of 1 January 1916, up to 108,000 people were forced to work.[91]

Conclusion

Experiments with forced convict labour in the decades prior to World War I led to the emergence of two chief varieties of convict labour. The first

87   *Ibid.*, p. 336.
88   Rainkhard Nakhtigal' [Reinhard Nachtigal], *Murmanskaia zheleznaia doroga, 1915–1919 gody: Voennaia neobkhodimost i ekonomicheskie soobrazheniia* (Saint Petersburg: Nestor-Istoriia, 2011), pp. 154–78.
89   "Arestantskii trud na nuzhdy armii", *Tiuremnyi vestnik*, 5 (1916), pp. 519–23, 519–20.
90   *Ibid.*, p. 521, and Gradusov, "Zheleznodorozhnye raboty", p. 658.
91   "Arestantskii trud na nuzhdy armii", p. 519.

coupled imprisonment with forced labour, as convicts would be taken out for the day to work and perform sundry physically taxing tasks such as road maintenance, snow shovelling, or timber works in the vicinity of the prison. The second, connected to katorga labour, implied large-scale infrastructural projects sustained by the convict labour force. Such sites were often located in the hinterlands of the empire and demanded hard physical labour, such as clearing land for railway construction. Large groups of convicts were transported from various locations from all over the empire specifically in order to perform these tasks. Such use of convict labour was clearly inscribed within the dynamics of imperial expansion, as it was used by the tsarist government in its desperate attempts to reinforce control over the hinterlands amidst political and social crisis.

The first attempts to use mass convict labour for infrastructure construction had been made shortly before World War I, and gained momentum as it became clear that the war would be a protracted one. The experience of World War I crystallized the practices of mass convict labour and, more importantly, brought a greater reliance on coercion overall. The use of forced convict labour during the war corresponds to the larger trend of the militarization of Russian society during the war.[92] This meant not only the restructuring of society in order to facilitate the fulfilment of war needs, but also the spread of the militarized extrajudicial practices of punishment and discipline.

From the onset of the war, and especially as the war progressed and required ever more resources, the tsarist state started to apply new coercive tactics against the population, and the organization of convict labour was one of the laboratories for such tactics. Other tactics included, but were not limited to, grain requisitions, land confiscations, coercive workforce mobilization, and mass deportations, both punitive and "pre-emptive".[93] These practices partly shaped the Soviet policies that were to follow. As Joshua Sanborn has underlined, the often overlooked developments between

92   For an overview of this pan-European process, see Michael Geyer, "The Militarization of Europe, 1914–1945", in John R. Gillis (ed.), *The Militarization of the Western World* (New Brunswick, NJ: Rutgers University Press, 1989), pp. 65–102.

93   On the 1916 rebellion in Turkestan, provoked by the mobilization of labour among the locals, see in English Daniel Brower, "Kyrgyz Nomads and Russian Pioneers: Colonization and Ethnic Conflict in the Turkestan Revolt of 1916", *Jahrbücher für Geschichte Osteuropas*, 44:1 (1996), pp. 41–53, and in Russian, the collection of documents: T.V. Kotiukova (ed.), *Vosstanie 1916 goda v Turkestane: dokumental'nye svidetelstva obschei tragedii. Sbornik dokumentov i materialov* (Moscow: Mardzhani, 2016). On the deportations and confiscation of land from ethnic Germans in imperial Russia, see Eric Lohr, *Nationalizing the Russian Empire: The Campaign against Enemy Aliens during World War I* (Cambridge, MA: Harvard University Press, 2003).

October 1915 and the February revolution in 1917 in particular should not be neglected. He has stated that "the shock of defeat ushered in a period of 'remobilization' that saw significant innovation and transformation in many different arenas: in combat tactics, in strategic goals, in the growth of forced labor, and in the expansion of social surveillance by 'progressive' activists".[94] The Provisional Government, faced with the same challenges as the tsarist officials, replied with similar measures, despite their political differences: the grain requisitions and soldier conscriptions that heavily relied on state force continued after the February revolution.

Reliance on coercion and extrajudicial measures in some domains was neither new nor specific to the war situation, as the cases of pre-war control of the movement of peasants and tsarist court martials make clear. The war, however, made coercive tactics, from the deportation of "enemy aliens" to grain requisitions, considerably more pervasive, and instigated experimentation with new methods of labour control and resource mobilization that relied on coercion. This created a very particular context for the continuing war and the Russian Revolution, and the long-running impact of this experience on the nascent Soviet state has already been underlined.[95] Peter Holquist has demonstrated how the coercive policies in the domain of food supply first emerged at the beginning of World War I and were solidified during the 1917 revolution. According to him, "the Russian Revolution occurred at a critical moment in the world conflict, just as all combatants were seeking new, more intensive techniques for conducting the war".[96] State officials continuously returned to coercion and violence to acquire the resources they deemed necessary, including labour. This pattern continued and was reinforced during Soviet times. In order to spread and become persistent beyond the war situation, these wartime practices and institutions needed to be further supported and driven by an ideology and political organization.

World War I spurred innovation in another aspect of coercion, namely in the domain of internment. The camps for prisoners of war constituted the first large-scale system of mass confinement in Russia. The next chapter discusses camp advances in Western Siberia during World War I and in the early years after the revolution by comparing and contrasting the POW

94 Joshua A. Sanborn, *Imperial Apocalypse: The Great War and the Destruction of the Russian Empire* (Oxford, New York: Oxford University Press, 2014), p. 111.

95 Peter Holquist, "Tools for Revolution: Wartime Mobilization in State-Building, 1914–1921", *Ab Imperio*, 4 (2001), pp. 209–27 and Holquist, "Violent Russia, Deadly Marxism?".

96 Holquist, "Tools for Revolution", p. 220.

camps and the revolutionary concentration camps. These institutions of confinement were constructed as an attempt to solve the issues that emerged during the war and the revolution: the isolation of captive soldiers and political enemies and the coercion of labourers in an attempt to alleviate shortages within the labour force – both of which occurred on a mass scale.

3 Blueprints for the Gulag? The Advance of Mass Internment, 1914–1923

Abstract

This chapter discusses the spread of mass internment across the territories of the Russian empire spurred by World War I and the following civil wars. Relying on archival materials from Western Siberia, it analyses the development and impact of two carceral institutions: prisoner-of-war camps and revolutionary concentration camps. The chapter argues that an analysis of the emergence of the camps system in the Soviet Union needs to integrate the diverse regional experiences. This chapter also discusses the struggles of building a camp system, administrating individual camps, and the differentiations of camp population. It offers a fine-grained analysis of the functioning of several revolutionary camps in Western Siberia and the types of forced labour performed by inmates there.

Keywords: prisoners of war, POW camps, mass internment, Western Siberia, concentration camps, World War I

Austro-Hungarian prisoner of war Alexander Dworsky remembered:

> During our transport in the winter of 1914/1915 from the snowy Carpathian Mountains to Siberia we did not pay attention to the freezing-cold weather and were excited as children thinking about the 'camp' [...] We associated the 'camp' with 'settle down', 'lie' and 'rest', in short, with a place where a person can live well [...] When we passed through train stations along the way, we were curious to find out from prisoners, who had already been there, what their 'camp' was like. All of them answered in amazement that they had never been to a camp.[1]

---

1   Alexander Dworsky, "Im Lager", in Hans Weiland and Leopold Kern (eds), *In Feindeshand* (Vienna, 1931), p. 106, quoted and translated in: Alon Rachamimov, *POWs and the Great War: Captivity on the Eastern Front* (Oxford: Berg, 2002), p. 88.

Popova, Zhanna: *Coerced Labour, Forced Displacement, and the Soviet Gulag, 1880s-1930s.* Amsterdam: Amsterdam University Press, 2024
DOI: 10.5117/9789048560356_CH03

Dworsky's initial fascination with the camps, as well as his later disappointment, is illustrative of how many of his contemporaries envisioned the first mass internment camps. Camps were still perceived first and foremost as military facilities; concentration camps were a novelty and had not yet become the symbols of horror that they would be fewer than three decades later. The above quote also reflects the process of appropriation of the camps as instruments of mass internment in very distinct contexts. There already existed an "ideal type" of camp: regular lines of barracks surrounded by barbed wire, designed to contain thousands and even dozens of thousands of people at once. However, in the first two years of World War I, combatants on all sides were unprepared for the enormous influx of enemy captives, and the early places of internment were largely improvised.[2] The camps were installed gradually and could be adapted to a multitude of conditions. Their use at that early point was above all an attempt to handle large numbers of captives, although the belligerent countries had also used camps for interning "enemy aliens" and national minorities since the start of the war, and Russia was not an aberration in this respect.

This chapter explores two distinct types of encampment that emerged in the tumult of war and revolution: the prisoner-of-war (POW) camps and the revolutionary concentration camps. Within the span of less than ten years, these two types of camps profoundly transformed the carceral landscape in Russia. Both were crucial for the further development of techniques of internment, yet they had fairly little in common in terms of organization and incarcerated populations. They were installed by two different states – the Russian empire and Soviet Russia – and served different purposes. The system of the POW camps was vast and relied on a fairly developed military infrastructure, while the small and scattered post-revolutionary camps were used as a cheaper alternative to traditional prisons, many of which were destroyed during the revolutionary struggles. I analyse these camps together in order to trace the conditions that led to their emergence and to understand the carceral innovations that they brought about.

I seek to understand how these early camps emerged and functioned. I analyse both the legislation and, where possible, conditions in the camps, as the gaping differences between the two defined the internment experience. The forced labour of inmates, especially an analysis of its forms

---

2   On the Russian case, see Rachamimov, *POWs and the Great War*, pp. 88–93, and on the case of captive Russian soldiers in Germany, see Oksana Nagornaia, *Drugoi voennyi opyt: Rossiiskie voennoplennye Pervoi mirovoi voiny v Germanii (1914–1922)* (Moscow: Novyi Khronograf, 2010), pp. 100–101.

and functions, remains a red line throughout the chapter. The first part is dedicated to the earliest institutions of mass internment: the POW camps of World War I. The second part analyses the setup of the revolutionary camps in one region and the ways in which convict labour was used there. In the final part, the attempts to create a post-revolutionary penal system are discussed. This enables the pinpointing of several moments of carceral innovation which were later important for the creation of the Soviet system of labour camps.

POW camps during World War I

Mass internment was one of the darkest sides of twentieth-century history. Used as a tool of warfare and an instrument of repression against large swathes of people, it originated at the end of the nineteenth century in the colonial wars as the colonial administration struggled to subdue the local populations. As part of a wider repertoire of counterinsurgency action, concentration camps were used to intern indigenous populations in an attempt to "pacify" the countryside and crush guerrilla resistance. The first cases of civilian concentration date back to the Cuban war of independence (1895–1898), when the Spanish authorities interned non-combatants as part of the policy of *reconcentración*, aimed at cutting the Cuban insurgents off any local support and securing the whole island under martial law. In the following years, mass internment globally assumed a wide variety of constantly evolving forms that depended on the political, ideological, economic, and cultural specificities of the local conditions. Americans interned civilians in the Philippines after 1898 in the aftermath of the Spanish-American war. Similar methods of mass internment were used across colonial Africa: the British created a vast network of concentration camps during the Anglo-Boer war (1899–1902), and the Germans interned Ovaherero in German Southwest Africa.[3]

Death was a frequent consequence of such internment, as the inmates suffered from exposure, lack of hygiene, hunger and outright starvation, infectious diseases, and the overall lamentable conditions in the camps. The

---

3   For Boer combatants during the Anglo-Boer War, captivity could mean not only internment in a camp, but also deportation to the British colonies, including India, Ceylon, St. Helena, and Bermuda. As many as nine thousand prisoners of war were deported and interned in India: Isabel Hofmeyr, "South Africa's Indian Ocean: Boer Prisoners of War in India", *Social Dynamics*, 38:3 (2012), pp. 363–80.

mass death of Boer women and children caused an international outcry, and the mobilization of public opinion and intervention of activists pressured the British authorities to admit these wrongdoings and improve conditions in the camps. Such interventions proved to be a rare occurrence in other colonial settings. In the case of the Ovaherero, inmates were not only held under inhumane conditions, but also brutally exploited, marking the first case of the mass internment of civilians combined with forced labour.[4] In recent years, scholars have sought to draw connections between German imperialism and the Holocaust, and have more generally worked to incorporate the early history of concentrations camps within the global history of violence.[5] Historians have identified the structural similarities between these asymmetrical colonial conflicts that contributed to the recurrent use of concentration camps, such as counter-guerrilla warfare, the presence of local militias, and forced displacements.[6] Complementing this search for structural similarities, another global approach also highlights the global dimension of these early camps and traces the transfer of techniques of violence between empires.[7]

Mass civilian internment emerged in the colonial wars, but its use did not remain limited to the colonies for long. World War I was the pivotal point when the technologies of colonial warfare, including mass internment, were brought to Europe. The repression of civilian populations became a tool of total war, as civilians in Europe also became war victims. Mass internment, in the shape of transit camps for refugees, camps for ethnic minorities, and especially the POW camps, became widespread.[8] Distinctions in conditions

---

4   Klaus Mühlhahn, "The Dark Side of Globalization: The Concentration Camps in Republican China in Global Perspective', World History Connected, 6:1 (2009), https://worldhistoryconnected.press.uillinois.edu/6.1/muhlhahn.html, last accessed 4 April 2022; Klaus Mühlhahn, "The Concentration Camp in Global Historical Perspective", History Compass, 8:6 (4 June 2010), pp. 543–61; Sibylle Scheipers, "The Use of Camps in Colonial Warfare", The Journal of Imperial and Commonwealth History, 43:4 (8 August 2015), pp. 678–98; Iain R. Smith and Andreas Stucki, "The Colonial Development of Concentration Camps (1868–1902)", The Journal of Imperial and Commonwealth History, 39:3 (September 2011), pp. 417–37.

5   For an overview of the debates on German colonialism and the Holocaust, see Thomas Kühne, "Colonialism and the Holocaust: Continuities, Causations, and Complexities", Journal of Genocide Research, 15:3 (2013), pp. 339–62.

6   Andreas Stucki, "'Frequent Deaths': The Colonial Development of Concentration Camps Reconsidered, 1868–1974", Journal of Genocide Research, 20:3 (3 July 2018), pp. 305–26.

7   Jonas Kreienbaum, "Deadly Learning? Concentration Camps in Colonial Wars around 1900", in Volker Barth and Roland Cvetkovski (eds), Imperial Co-operation and Transfer, 1870–1930: Empires and Encounters (London: Bloomsbury Academic, 2015), pp. 219–36.

8   Peter Gatrell has underlined that for certain categories of refugee in the Russian empire during World War I, such as Lithuanians, conditions in the transit camps resembled significantly

between interned civilians and POWs were often blurred.[9] Until recently relatively understudied, the early history of civil mass internment as an instrument of total war is now a dynamic research area.[10]

In the Russian case, it was also World War I that brought mass internment into the country. Research on the early history of mass internment in Russia that incorporates both the wartime camps and the revolutionary institutions still largely needs to be done. Tellingly, Manz *et al.*'s volume on the global dimension of mass internment during World War I, referenced above, includes articles on several belligerent and neutral countries, including the Ottoman and the Habsburg empires, but not on the Russian empire. German-language scholarship offers rich insights into the history of POW camps and the conditions of POWs from the Central Powers in the Russian empire, and important research in English has also been done.[11] Attempts to trace the connection between these camps and the Soviet labour camps and Nazi camps have been made, but this topic does require more profound analysis.[12]

Mass internment also has been analysed as a measure against enemy aliens.[13] However, not all institutions of mass internment during and after World War I in Russia have been explored. Even the most basic facts about the early revolutionary concentration camps, another institution created during this decade of war and revolution, remain virtually unknown, partly due to their ephemeral character, extremely decentralized organization, strong regional varieties, and overall chaos of war and revolution that meant that few records survived. Central authorities encouraged the creation of such camps, but had little to no means of centralizing their administration, and the variations between different regions in terms of the conditions in the camps,

those in the POW camps: Peter Gatrell, *A Whole Empire Walking: Refugees in Russia during World War I* (Bloomington: Indiana University Press, 1999), pp. 160–62.

9   Stefan Manz, Panikos Panayi, and Matthew Stibbe (eds), *Internment during the First World War: A Mass Global Phenomenon* (Abingdon, New York: Routledge, 2019), p. 1.

10   *Ibid.*; Rotem Kowner and Iris Rachamimov (eds), *Out of Line, Out of Place: A Global and Local History of World War I Internments* (Ithaca, NY: Cornell University Press, 2022).

11   Hannes Leidinger and Verena Moritz, *Gefangenschaft, Revolution, Heimkehr: Die Bedeutung der Kriegsgefangenenproblematik für die Geschichte des Kommunismus in Mittel- und Osteuropa 1917–1920* (Vienna: Böhlau, 2003); Reinhard Nachtigal, *Russland und seine österreichisch-ungarischen Kriegsgefangenen 1914–1918* (Remshalden: Bernhard Albert Greiner, 2003); Wurzer, "Die Kriegsgefangenen der Mittelmächte in Rußland im Ersten Weltkrieg". In English: Rachamimov, *POWs and the Great War.*

12   An outline of Peter Pastor's "prototype thesis" can be found in Rachamimov, *POWs and the Great War*, pp. 78–82. See also Christoph Jahr and Jens Thiel (eds), *Lager vor Auschwitz: Gewalt und Integration im 20. Jahrhundert* (Berlin: Metropol, 2013).

13   Lohr, *Nationalizing the Russian Empire*, pp. 121–65.

social composition of the inmates, and the use of the inmates' labour could be staggering. If there are sources on such camps at all, they are generally contained in local archives, which further complicates research. And even in cases where this information has been studied, the analysis remains largely limited to local histories.[14] A shift of focus towards the regional practices of mass internment and an initial investigation of the camps that emerged during the revolution and the civil wars would not only shed light on these important yet understudied institutions, but would also be the next step towards understanding the later Soviet mass internment practices. Their history can elucidate, more generally, the flexibility of camps as instruments of confinement and coercion. These cases show how camps were used simultaneously as part of the arsenal of political violence and of population politics.

Western Siberia offers an apt case for a study of early mass internment for three main reasons: it was an important destination of tsarist exile and katorga; during World War I, it was the primary location of POW camps in the empire; finally, revolutionary struggles were particularly long and arduous there. Thus, three unique factors overlapped as the revolutionary camps were established: the heritage of the tsarist forced displacement, the strong presence of modern camps for war captives, and the relatively weak early influence of the Bolsheviks.

The POW camps marked a transition towards a fundamentally new regime of internment: the number of imperial convicts through the region pale in comparison to the masses of war captives. The camps for the rank-and-file POWs, which were constructed en masse in different parts of the Russian empire and especially in Western Siberia, were the embodiment of this regime. In many cases, internment went hand in hand with forced labour, and some of these cases will be analysed here. These camps were gradually installed by combatants in response to the military necessity to confine the large number of captive enemy soldiers, but this experience was used far beyond the immediate military goals. In the Russian case, a focus on the dynamic development of various camp forms as the conflict unfolded highlights the flexibility of camps and helps to pinpoint the ways in which these institutions of internment could be adapted to local conditions. The flexibility and adaptability of camps as institutions, combined with the militarization of societies and the elaboration of new forms of political control over populations, made camps, in their multiple variations, globally present.

---

14   See, for example, a recent publication of the lists of inmates of the Ryazan concentration camp: A.I. Grigorov and A.A. Grigorov, *Zakliuchennye Riazanskogo gubernskogo kontslageria RSFSR 1919–1923 gg.* (Moscow: Tipografiia OOO "MID", 2013).

Western Siberia played a key role in the penal architecture of the Russian empire. It was, on the one hand, a destination for administrative exile, with as many as 20,227 exiles and 15,937 family members (including 11,163 children) arriving in the Tobolsk and Tomsk regions between 1892 and 1896 alone.[15] On the other hand, two Western Siberian cities – first Tyumen then Tobolsk – acted as the main convict transportation hubs. Convicts from the European part of the empire were sent to the prisons in these cities, where the local exile department (*Prikaz o ssylnykh*) would distribute them throughout the regions lying further east. However, this distributed exile infrastructure, together with the increasingly centralized prison system, were only capable of accommodating convicts of the empire. World War I triggered a wave of mass internment that became a shared European experience and necessitated the creation of a parallel system of confinement. Internment thus became a prerogative of the military authorities. During the war, all fighting sides together mobilized approximately 65 million soldiers, and 9 million of them became prisoners of war.[16] According to contemporary observers, Russia captured more than 2.3 million POWs, most of whom (around 2.1 million) were from the Austro-Hungarian Empire.[17] The sheer scale of POW internment was unprecedented, and apart from being a social problem (especially when we take into account repatriation and returns), it also represented a technical challenge for governments and the military alike.

Another issue arose as the war dragged on: for many POWs captivity went from being a relatively short experience of incarceration to a semi-permanent condition. The attempts of military authorities to accommodate these captives led to a period of intensive carceral innovation. As Heather Jones has observed, initially the POW camps had a purely military function of preventing the captive enemy combatants from returning to the battlefield, but towards the end of the war the camps functioned as "a sophisticated system of state control and as a laboratory for new ways of managing mass confinement, forced labour and new forms of state-military collaboration".[18]

15   Salomon, *Ssylka v Sibir'*, Appendix I, pp. 20–23. I offered an overview of research on the condition of families of exiles and convicts in Zhanna Popova, "Exiles, Convicts, and Deportees as Migrants: Northern Eurasia, Nineteenth–Twentieth Centuries", in Marcelo J. Borges and Madeline Y. Hsu (eds), *The Cambridge History of Global Migrations* (Cambridge: Cambridge University Press, 2023), pp. 240–58.
16   Leidinger and Moritz, *Gefangenschaft, Revolution, Heimkehr*, p. 46.
17   Elsa Brändström, *Among Prisoners of War in Russia & Siberia* (London: Hutchinson, 1929), p. 35.
18   Heather Jones, "Discipline and Punish? Forms of Violent Punishment in Prisoner of War Camps in the First World War: A Comparative Analysis", in Jahr and Thiel, *Lager vor Auschwitz*,

In the Russian empire, the creation of POW camps was controlled by the central authorities. However, no single blueprint existed for how the POW camps should be replicated in various locations. Indeed, during the first two years of the war, POWs were accommodated in empty buildings next to the caserns of the Russian military.[19] During this early period, Russian authorities struggled to accommodate rank-and-file POWs and were generally unable to keep the speed of camp construction on par with the influx of captives. Captive soldiers were frequently kept in empty Russian army barracks, stalls, abandoned prisons, or simply any available large building. The captivity experiences of the Central Powers' soldiers in the Russian empire were thus much more diverse than only internment in barracks behind barbed wire.[20] Even later, as camp construction was in full swing, the camps still differed tremendously in size. At the beginning of the war, there were camps for the officers, which contained as few as several dozen prisoners. In European Russia, many mid-range camps for rank-and-file captives existed. They usually accommodated between two and ten thousand POWs.[21] Truly giant camp complexes were created in Siberia and the Far East. The one in Krasnoyarsk, for instance, contained at times as many as 35,000 POWs. In Novo-Nikolaevsk (now Novosibirsk), at least two POW camps were constructed during the first years of the war: first, a camp for 10,000 people, and then another, with the capacity to accommodate another 4,500 captives.[22] For the latter, there is archival evidence recording different stages of its construction in 1915.[23] According to the plans, it was intended to be a large complex of buildings, including a hospital, a bakery, kitchens, and barracks. Reports on its construction suggest that it was closely supervised by the military commission, which recorded considerable deviations from the original blueprints.[24] At the time, Novo-Nikolaevsk was a booming commercial town. However, even for such a growing urban centre, this camp represented a technological advance: for example, there was no central water supply system in the town, and thus the construction of the camp's water supply was one of the largest projects of

19   Wurzer, "Die Kriegsgefangenen der Mittelmächte", p. 55.
20   Rachamimov, *POWs and the Great War*, p. 92.
21   *Ibid.*
22   State Archive of the Novosibirsk Region, Novosibirsk (*Gosudarstvennyi arkhiv Novosibirskoi oblasti,* hereafter GANO), f. D-97, op. 1, d. 198, l. 3 and l. 12., and d. 204, l. 1.
23   GANO, f. D-97, op. 1, d. 204.
24   *Ibid.*, ll. 3–5.

its kind.[25] The material aspects of camps were crucial, as they demonstrate the necessities and capacities for wartime mass internment.

Some authors have suggested that an even more important premonition of the later use of camps as instruments of political violence could have manifested itself in the Russian POW camps during World War I, namely the preferential treatment of soldiers depending on their ethnicity. Peter Pastor has suggested that there existed a hierarchy of camps in the Russian Empire, with Slav POWs being sent to the camps with better living conditions, while the German, Austrian, and Hungarian POWs were sent to the most distant and run-down destinations.[26] Ivan Völgyes, in his article on Hungarian POWs in Russia in the second half of World War I, has also suggested that the Magyar POWs were sent further east and north as compared to captives of Slavic origin.[27]

As already discussed in the first chapter, a distinctive hierarchical geography of forced displacement was present during the nineteenth century, if not earlier. Both Eastern and Western Siberia served as destinations for different groups of exiles, but they were distributed depending on the gravity of their wrongdoings: those sentenced to administrative exile were settled in Western Siberia, while those serving katorga terms were exiled much further east, in Transbaikalia and on Sakhalin Island. It appears that the stark distinctions between the conditions in various sites depending on their geographical location flattened out at the beginning of the twentieth century, especially after convicts had to be evacuated from the Sakhalin Island after the Russo-Japanese war. In 1913, for example, the chief of the Main Prison Administration (GTU) remarked that the prison conditions in Western Siberia were no worse than in European Russia.[28] The newly constructed POW camps were frequently flawed, but it appears that the problems did not depend so much on the east/west distribution, but rather on the local conditions of each individual camp. Alon Rachamimov has convincingly demonstrated that "although the Russian leadership (both military and political) intended to favor Slav, Italian and Alsatian POWs, they did not make it a high priority and did not allocate sufficient personnel to implement it".[29] Pastor's view of the POW camps in Russia is crucial for

25   GANO, f. D-97, op. 1, d. 225.

26   Peter Pastor, "Introduction", in Samuel R. Williamson and Peter Pastor (eds), *Essays on World War I: Origins and Prisoners of War* (New York: Brooklyn College Press, 1983), pp. 113–17.

27   Ivan Volgyes, "Hungarian Prisoners of War in Russia, 1916–1919", *Cahiers du Monde russe et soviétique*, 14:1 (1973), pp. 54–85.

28   Gran, *Katorga v Sibiri*, p. 7.

29   Rachamimov, *POWs and the Great War*, p. 96.

his reasoning, as he suggests that there existed a direct continuity between the POW camps in Russia and the concentration camps in Nazi Germany and the Gulag camps. He was the first researcher to explicitly formulate the continuity hypothesis, and although his premises have been challenged, the issue of continuity does still need to be investigated.[30] Here, I do not intend to draw direct comparisons between the POW system and the Stalinist camps, but interpret these camps as the first occurrence of truly mass confinement in the camp environment in Western Siberia and thus an important milestone in the larger history of the spread of camps globally.

If there was a systematic differentiation in terms of the conditions of captives, it was the difference between the camps for officers and those for the rank-and-file soldiers. It was deeply rooted in long-running military practice and, as Joan Beaumont has remarked, despite the nineteenth-century development and codification of the international law regarding conditions of prisoners of war, the privileged treatment of officers has not been challenged, but quite to the contrary, "gradually formalized".[31] This preferential treatment started with superior lodging conditions: officers were far more likely to be accommodated in private houses.[32] The privilege then extended to other facilities, namely washing and dining. Disciplinary punishments were also stricter for the rank-and-file.[33] Some officers were fortunate enough to receive, at times, almost luxurious treatment. Alon Rachamimov describes the life of Roman Dyboski, who would later become the rector of Jagiellonian University in Krakow: "[he] had been interned for lengthy periods in the prisoner of war camp of Krasnaia Rechka (near the city of Khabarovsk in the Russian Far East) and in the mammoth camp in Krasnoyarsk, but had also long intervals as an archivist and teacher at the University of Kazan, an interned guest at the house of a retired Russian field marshal and for a duration of eight months a prisoner 'in the custody of Prince Nicholas Gagarin enjoying a wonderful view of the Moscow River'".[34]

Mass internment and the creation of the camp network was related to the condition of rank-and-file POWs, rather than captive officers. POW labour was another domain where the preferential treatment of officers

30   Peter Whitewood, "Failing to Create Revolutionaries: Polish POWs in Soviet Captivity, 1920–21", *Revolutionary Russia*, 35:2 (2022), pp. 185–205.

31   Joan Beaumont, "Rank, Privilege and Prisoners of War", *War & Society*, 1:1 (1983), pp. 67–94, 69.

32   Rachamimov, *POWs and the Great War*, pp. 90–91.

33   Beaumont, "Rank, Privilege and Prisoners of War", p. 71.

34   Rachamimov, *POWs and the Great War*, p. 92, quote from Roman Dyboski, *Seven Years in Russia and Siberia, 1914–1921* (Cheshire, CT: Cherry Hill Books, 1971), pp. 35–36.

was manifested. The use of POW labour, as with the conditions in captivity in general, was outlined in 1907 in the Second Hague Convention. This allowed the use of the labour of rank-and-file captives, though officers were exempted from any obligation to work.

Russia started to use POW labour on a large scale only in the fall of 1915, considerably later than other combatants. Legally, the labour of the internees could be used for state, public, and private works, but not for the war effort.[35] In practice, their labour was also used for the front, but such employment did not reach a large scale in the Russian case: only around 100,000 POWs were engaged in the summer of 1916.[36]

Similar to the variations in size and living conditions in the camps, the labour conditions of POWs demonstrated a significant lack of uniformity. The prevalent form of labour was agricultural work at private farms among the rank-and-file. Inadvertently, such small-scale, decentralized employment helped to partly alleviate the biggest crisis of the camps: epidemics.[37] During the winter of 1915–1916, approximately 400,000 prisoners died in Russian camps from typhus, malaria, cholera, and other infectious diseases.[38] Those interned in the larger camp complexes in Siberia, Turkestan, and the Far East were particularly vulnerable, but as soon as they were sent to engage in agricultural work starting in the spring of 1916, the mortality rate dropped, and "during the summer months, when the agricultural season in Russia was at its peak, the rank-and-file camps would [be] almost completely empty", as the captives were moved to work.[39]

Not all internees were equally fortunate, however. The construction of the Murmansk Railway, discussed briefly in the previous chapter in the context of the use of forced labour for infrastructural construction – represents a radically different example of the use of POW labour. The construction of this railroad was dictated by the military imperative: Russian imperial authorities were eager to connect the ice-free port of Murmansk, situated in the Russian far north, with the central part of the country, and hastily initiated

35   Wurzer, "Die Kriegsgefangenen der Mittelmächte", pp. 312–13.

36   Nachtigal, *Russland und seine österreichisch-ungarischen Kriegsgefangenen*, pp. 183–85, 201–3.

37   Interestingly, this type of employment had relatively little precedent in the history of the Russian imperial penal system: convicts were generally employed in extramural public works in the cities, such as canalization or road construction, while agricultural penal colonies remained rather experimental.

38   Reinhard Nachtigal, "Seuchen unter militärischer Aufsicht in Rußland: Das Lager Tockoe als Beispiel für die Behandlung der Kriegsgefangenen 1915/1916?", *Jahrbücher für Geschichte Osteuropas*, 48:3 (2000), pp. 363–87.

39   Rachamimov, *POWs and the Great War*, p. 89.

the railway construction in 1915, as the lack of arms and supplies became more acute. More than 70,000 POWs of the Central Powers were forced to work under dangerous conditions. The harsh climate, administrative disarray, and the extreme remoteness of the location, far from any substantial infrastructure, all contributed to high mortality among the labourers.[40] The use of POW labour in World War I marks not only the first case of the use of forced labour on such a scale, but also the pervasiveness of the use of such labour: POWs worked on large state projects, in agriculture, and on public works; later, when the Russian military administration collapsed, some of the POWs even had to assume the responsibilities of the camp administrators themselves.

As the Bolsheviks took power, they created a refugee section within the People's Commissariat of Internal Affairs.[41] In April 1918, following the Brest-Litovsk Treaty of 3 March 1918, they established a special agency that was charged with managing the population displacement. It was called *Tsentroplenbezh*, or the Central Collegium for the Affairs of Captives and Refugees (*Tsentral'naia kollegiia po delam plennykh i bezhentsev*). Charged with a large number of tasks concerning refugees and POWs, *Tsentroplenbezh* managed the POW camps and the repatriation of captives, sought to provide POWs and refugees with medical care, compiled statistics of the displaced populations, and unified the relating bureaucratic structures.[42] It was also supposed to facilitate the return of the country's own POWs and the resettlement of refugees. This was a Herculean task: after armistice was achieved in November 1918, almost one million captives returned to Russia within two months.[43] All in all, more than 3.5 million refugees and 1.4 million war captives leaving Russia were administratively processed by the *Tsentroplenbezh*.[44] Shortages of food, the animosity of locals, lack of income, and uncertainty about the future defined the condition of these refugees and released prisoners of war. Some of the refugees, forced to live in squalid transit camps on the western border, moved to work on farms in Prussia under quasi-coerced conditions.[45]

40 Reinhard Nachtigal, *Die Murmanbahn: Die Verkehrsanbindung eines kriegswichtigen Hafens und das Arbeitspotential der Kriegsgefangenen (1915 bis 1918)* (Grunbach: Bernhard Albert Greiner, 2001).
41 Commissariats were structures of executive power in the Soviet Union and its republics, and can be understood as similar to ministries.
42 Gatrell, *A Whole Empire Walking*, pp. 188–90.
43 Ivan Petrovich Shcherov, *Tsentroplenbezh v Rossii: Istoriia sozdaniia i deiatel'nost' v 1918–1922 gg.* (Smolensk: Smolenskii gosudarstvennyi pedagogicheskii universitet, 2000), p. 24.
44 *Ibid.*, p. 20.
45 Gatrell, *A Whole Empire Walking*, p. 190.

Tsentroplenbezh was also integrated within the penal system, as the camps it ran emptied due to the repatriation of the POWs during the summer of 1918. Along with the All-Russia Extraordinary Commission for Combating Counter-Revolution and Sabotage (*Vserossiiskaia chrezvychainaia kommissiia po bor'be s kontrrevoliutsiei i sabotazhem*, or the *Vecheka*, also known as the Cheka), which will be discussed in greater detail in the next chapter, the Bolshevik authorities used *Tsentroplenbezh* as part of the militarized alternative to the penal system, and the camps it managed were used for interning criminals and political enemies.[46] This agency was eventually dissolved in January 1923.

The emergence of mass internment in Western Siberia was tightly connected to the military and militarized conflicts that unravelled in the region and in the world. Local developments took place against the backdrop of the world war, the long and violent civil conflicts, continuous peasant rebellions, and the general lack of support for the Bolsheviks among the Siberian peasants.[47] As the system of the POW camps disintegrated under the pressures of revolution and civil war, new revolutionary camps emerged in the region.

Camps transform and linger, 1918–1921

Despite the collapse of the POW camp system, the institution of the camp was far from disappearing in Western Siberia. On the contrary, it became an integral part of the civil war as well as Soviet state building on the local scale. In this turmoil of war and revolution, lines between soldiers and civilians were becoming blurred. In this respect, Western Siberia also provides rich material: the revolutionary conflicts there lasted a particularly long time, and the establishment of Soviet power was extremely challenging. The camps emerged against the tumultuous background of World War I, the civil war, and the Soviet consolidation of power.[48] Historian Jonathan Smele has also urged scholars to look beyond the confrontation between the "Reds" and the "Whites" and delve instead into the multitude of overlapping armed conflicts of numerous different interest groups, including those on the

46 Dzhekobson and Smirnov, "Sistema mest zakliucheniia v RSFSR i SSSR".

47 Jonathan Crompton, "Resistance and Authority in Siberia, 1920–21: The Bolsheviks and the Siberian Peasantry with Reference to the Novosibirsk Region", *Revolutionary Russia*, 10:2 (1997), pp. 1–24.

48 Peter Holquist, *Making War, Forging Revolution: Russia's Continuum of Crisis, 1914–1921* (Cambridge, MA: Harvard University Press, 2002).

fringes of the former empire.[49] This perspective highlights the connections between the local and the global scales of these wars.

As the protracted and bitter revolutionary struggles went on, attempts to build a new normality and restore social order led to the re-establishment of some version of the penal system. In the regions, camps emerged as part of an arrangement which was only very loosely coordinated from the centre. The local authorities generally established them according to their own capacities and conceptions. This led, on the one hand, to an extreme variety of organizational forms of repression and, on the other, to the ephemeral character of these carceral institutions that often existed very briefly and left few historical sources behind. As Smith and Stucki have remarked, comparing the cases of the British concentration camps in South Africa and the Spanish camps during the Cuban War for independence, "it takes a strong, developed, adequately funded administration to organize and run a concentration camp *system*" (emphasis in the original).[50] In revolutionary Western Siberia, it took years for such administration to be built.

Exile and katorga disappeared from the punitive repertoire shortly after the February revolution, as all political prisoners were released on 7 March 1917.[51] A month and a half later, on 26 April, the Provisional Government abolished exile to Siberia, a hated symbol of the tsarist oppression. The revolutionary period was a relatively short interlude when the central government did not rely on exile and attempted to create an alternative to it, a penal system without forced displacement.

In the early Soviet period, like during late imperial times, there was no single institution of confinement that dominated the punitive landscape. Newly established concentration camps existed along with prisons that were now known under the new name of "correction houses"; agricultural colonies and youth rehabilitative colonies opened up in various regions. Conceptions of punishment and rehabilitation as they were created in the centre of the nascent Soviet state are the subject of the following chapter, while here the focus is on the local camps as they emerged in the Western Siberian cities of Tyumen, Tobolsk, and Novosibirsk. A brief remark regarding the general state of the early Soviet penal system is nevertheless in order. As Aaron Retish has

49   Jonathan Smele, *The "Russian" Civil Wars, 1916–1926: Ten Years That Shook the World* (London: Hurst, 2016).

50   Smith and Stucki, "The Colonial Development of Concentration Camps", p. 419.

51   Robert Paul Browder and Aleksandr Fyodorovich Kerensky, *The Russian Provisional Government, 1917*, 3 vols (Stanford, CA: Hoover Institution Press, 1961), vol. 1, pp. 196, 207–8.

underlined, the revolutionary penal reforms had two distinctive aspects. First, the early Soviet reformers were the first to represent the convict as their ally rather than enemy, a proletarian in need of rehabilitation and guidance. They considered labour as a rehabilitative educational force that propelled criminals toward a productive life in the new socialist society. As I show, this reformative aspiration was from early on confronted with realities of running a place of confinement in a revolutionary situation, which often meant that labour of convicts was above all a means of keeping the places of confinement afloat, and inmates alive, while the rehabilitation of criminals remained out of reach. Second, "the revolution itself and the social upheaval of the civil war undermined the very reforms that the state promoted". This revolutionary experimentation was ambitious, yet largely unsuccessful due to the lack of funding and qualified personnel, administrative disarray, and chaos in the society overall. Retish relied on sources from several locations in the European part of Russia, especially on documents from the Samara province.[52] The limited archival materials on the early Western Siberian camps that I was able to review in Tyumen support this conclusion too.

The post-revolutionary places of confinement were run by three different state agencies (Commissariat of Justice, Commissariat of Internal Affairs, and the *Vecheka*). From mid-1922, the places of confinement that were managed by the Commissariat of Justice no longer received any funding from the centre. According to the decree "On forced labour camps", such camps were to be managed by the Commissariat of Internal Affairs.[53] It is possible to suggest that differences in size and regime between the various camps, not to mention other places of confinement, were considerable, even within the Western Siberian region.[54] However, a systematic analysis of all these institutions is impossible, because often even the most basic facts cannot be established due to the lack of documents. Locations of the Moscow concentration camps, for instance, are well documented, which is

52 Aaron B. Retish, "Breaking Free from the Prison Walls: Penal Reforms and Prison Life in Revolutionary Russia", *Historical Research*, 90:247 (2017), pp. 134–50, quote p. 150.

53 Decree of the All-Russian Central Executive Committee, 17 May 1919, see I.T. Goliakov (ed.), *Sbornik dokumentov po istorii ugolovnogo zakonodatelstva SSSR i RSFSR, 1917–1952 gg.* (Moscow: Gosiurizdat, 1953), pp. 45–46.

54 On the eve of the February revolution, the following places of confinement existed in Western Siberia: an imperial katorga prison and a regional *guberniia* prison in Tobolsk; eight smaller *uezd* prisons in Tyumen, Ishim, Kurgan, Tara, Turin, Tiukalinsk, Ialutorovsk, and Berezovskii; and, finally, a corrective arrest department. In this chapter, I mainly discuss the places of confinement that were located in Tobolsk and Tyumen. This choice was defined by the availability of sources and also by the fact that these two towns were crucial for the imperial penal system.

not the case for the majority of regional camps.[55] Conditions in the regional places of confinement are also hard to reconstruct.

Statistics regarding the overall number of prisoners in the immediate aftermath of the revolution are also elusive. Some places of confinement did not communicate their numbers to the centre, or only did so intermittently. In 1919, the Central Penal Department of the Ministry of Justice published some data. As of 1 October 1919, the report states, the department had information about 23,501 men, 2,406 women, and 40 children incarcerated in various places of confinement within the Russian Soviet Federative Socialist Republic (RSFSR). However, these numbers do not provide even a remote estimate of the true total, as only 148 prisons out of 217 submitted their reports.[56] In 1921, the Central Penal Department received significantly more consistent reports: the published report states that there were 73,194 people imprisoned as of 1 November 1921.[57] The other two departments managing places of confinement did not publish their statistics and it is therefore necessary to refer to alternative sources. Mary Schaeffer Conroy has suggested the following conservative estimates of the prison and camp population for the end of 1921.[58] She refers to the "Report on Sanitary Conditions in Places of Confinement in the RSFSR", contained in the State Archive of the Russian Federation according to which the overall number of inmates incarcerated in the country was estimated to be at least 220,000 people.[59] These prisoners were held in various institutions that were run either by the Commissariat of Justice, the Commissariat of Internal Affairs, or the *Vecheka*. This report states that there were approximately 85,000 people contained in 257 correction and work houses and agricultural labour colonies (compared to the number of prisoners published in the report). In addition to that, approximately 45,440 people were interned in 111 concentration camps. A further 58,400 people were detained in jails and arrest houses. Finally, the political prisons of the *Vecheka* contained up to 53,000 people. Even though

---

55 A virtual museum of Soviet repression in Moscow has been created by the Moscow Memorial. It features information on several concentration camps that functioned in the early 1920s. Several of them were located in monasteries. Available at https://topos.memo.ru, last accessed 6 April 2022.

56 *Tiuremnoe delo v R.S.F.S.R. Otchet Tsentral'nogo Karatel'nogo Otdela N.K.Iu. VII-mu S'ezdu Sovetov* (Moscow, 1919), pp. 11–12.

57 Information from 267 prisons: *Tiuremnoe delo v 1921 godu. Otchet Narodnogo Komissariata Iustitsii, po Tsentral'nomu Ispravitel'no-Trudovomu Otdelu, IX-mu Vserossiiskomu S'ezdu Sovetov R., Kr., i K. D.* (Moscow, 1921), p. 8.

58 Mary Schaeffer Conroy, "Health Care in Prisons, Labour and Concentration Camps in Early Soviet Russia, 1918–1921", *Europe-Asia Studies*, 52:7 (2000), pp. 1257–74, 1258.

59 According to Schaeffer Conroy: GARF, f. 482, op. 12, l. 9.

these are just estimates, it is possible to suggest that concentration camps were much smaller that the POW camps and had not yet come to constitute the central element of the penal system. Michael Jakobson and M.B. Smirnov have offered differing estimates for the end of 1921 and suggested that the places of confinement under the jurisdiction of the Commissariat of Internal Affairs contained 40,913 (this number included POWs), while another 73,194 were incarcerated in the institutions of the Commissariat of Justice (this number included people under investigation), and approximately 50,000 were interned by the *Vecheka*.[60]

The use of camps as an instrument of terror during the revolution in Western Siberia is unclear. The *Vecheka*'s order from 2 September 1918 explicitly lists the concentration camps as an alternative to prisons: while the Mensheviks and the Left Socialist Revolutionaries were to be incarcerated, "representatives of bourgeoisie, the landlords (*pomeshchiki*), the factory owners, the merchants, the counterrevolutionary priests, all of the officers hostile to the Soviet power" were to be placed in the concentration camps and forced to work.[61] In Moscow, more than a dozen such camps were created. They were all closed down during the winter of 1922–1923, and the camps on the Solovki islands in the north of Russia became the main place for the repression of political dissidents and "enemies of the revolution".[62] As I will demonstrate below, sources in Western Siberia indicate that very different categories of people found themselves in the camps there.

Later sources from the Commissariat of Internal Affairs also outline a completely different set of people who should be confined in the camps. They list several very particular groups which were defined according to the type of infraction, rather than the prisoner's social background. The definitions of these infractions are very precise, and it is clear that they were not the crimes deemed most dangerous. Instructions from 1 October 1921 state that only the following groups of inmates could be confined in the camps:

1. People who were not working/loiterers;
2. Saboteurs;
3. Those guilty of small-scale speculation;
4. Counter-revolutionaries not deemed dangerous to the republic;

60 Dzhekobson and Smirnov, "Sistema mest zakliucheniia v RSFSR i SSSR".
61 For the *Vecheka* order on the Red Terror from 2 September 1918, see A.I. Kokurin and N.V. Petrov (eds), *GULAG (Glavnoe upravlenie lagerei). 1917–1960* (Moscow: MFD, 2002), p. 14.
62 "Kontslageria i ardoma 1920-kh", available at https://topos.memo.ru/category/1, last accessed 6 April 2022.

5. First-time deserters from the army who did not forge their documents;
6. Labour deserters;[63]
7. Those who committed non-lucrative crimes of workplace misconduct.[64]

Another circular from 3 January 1921 demonstrates that such distinctions were frequently disregarded and thus required constant reaffirmation. According to this circular, some of the inmates of the concentration camps were there due to an "imprecise formulation of the sentence" and actually belonged in a prison.[65] These early camps appear to have had a far more forgiving regime than either the political police camps or the labour camps that were established at the end of the 1920s.

In Siberia, the civil war was characterized by particularly long clashes between the contending sides; the Siberian Revolutionary Committee (*Sibirskii revoliutsionnyi komitet*, or *Sibrevkom*), a temporary agency of revolutionary governance installed by the Bolsheviks, existed until 1926 – considerably longer than other such committees.[66] Scattered evidence indicates that some of the POW camps were reappropriated by the fighting sides during the civil war for the incarceration of civilians. Some of the old tsarist prisons were also used by the *Sibrevkom* for extra-judicial confinement, under the name of camps or houses of compulsory work (*lageria i doma prinudrabot*).[67] These institutions appear to have been a more flexible and lower-cost alternative to prisons.

The central authorities encouraged local prison management to introduce (or re-introduce) convict labour shortly after the revolution. In a circular to the regional departments of justice from 28 December 1918, the chief of the Central Penal Department stated that some of the cells were to be transformed into workshops, and in cases where this was impossible, work tables were to be placed inside the common cells.[68] Against the backdrop of local reports decrying the staggering prison overpopulation and the undernourishment of inmates, such circulars can hardly be considered

63 This implied, most likely, people who tried to avoid universal compulsory labour. It is not clear what the distinction was between the first and the fifth categories.
64 GANO, f. R-1133, op. 1, d. 137. l. 2.
65 State Archive of the Tyumen region, Tyumen (*Gosudarstvennyi arkhiv Tiumenskoi oblasti*, hereafter GATO), f. R-126, op. 1, d. 10, l. 44.
66 Roza Shteinman, "Sibirskii revoliutsionnyi komitet" (Kandidat dissertation, University of Sverdlovsk, 1975).
67 This was, among others, the case for the Tobolsk prison in 1920: State Archive in the town of Tobolsk (*Gosudarstvennyi arkhiv v g. Tobol'ske*, hereafter GBUTO), f. R-168, op. 1, d. 22.
68 GATO, f. R-126, op. 1, d. 10, l. 770b.

as anything more than recommendations. In the case of Tobolsk, there is no evidence of any attempts to restore the pre-revolutionary workshops. During tsarist times this town hosted one of the hard labour prisons with a range of well-developed workshops, including a brick factory. During the revolution, however, most prison facilities were destroyed and the building was re-purposed as a house of compulsory work.

The organization of work was conducted on a small scale and was expedient: as the documents from Tyumen show, the heads of Soviet institutions as varied as hospitals and windmills would demand from the revolutionary committees small groups of workers for unqualified labour on a daily basis, or, rarely and generally for qualified workers, for longer term engagements.[69] These latter workers enjoyed a significant alleviation of the camp regime: in some cases, the administrative authorities of the places where these convicts were employed could petition the camp authorities to let the inmates live freely in rented houses closer to their workplace, instead of requiring them to return to the camp every evening. The Central Penal Department (*Tsentral'nyi Karatel'nyi Otdel*) decried and banned this practice in 1920, but it is highly unlikely that this ban was immediately implemented in the regions.[70]

Correspondence between the camps and the local Soviet institutions describes some of the types of forced labour employed and the conditions under which labourers had to work. Even the smallest institutions, like the camps and work houses in Tobolsk and Tyumen, sought to enforce compulsory labour, but this was largely limited to extramural work. The number of workers that such institutions could provide – often just small groups of three or four convicts, rarely up to two dozen – once again demonstrate that these revolutionary camps were much more modest in scale than both the earlier POW camps and the Gulag camps that were to come. Like the imperial prisons, they were generally urban. The dire shortage of guards, which was a problem for the early Soviet prisons, was also a problem for the provincial camps.[71] The camp administration sometimes required the assistance of the local militia, and, again, in some cases allowed inmates to work outside the camp without a convoy.[72]

69   GATO, f. R-126, op. 1, d. 24. l. 20, d. 22, l. 20b and l. 3, and d. 24, l. 109.

70   *Sbornik materialov Tsentral'nogo Karatel'nogo Otdela* (Moscow, 1920), p. 42. The Central Penal Department (*Tsentral'nyi karatel'nyi otdel*) of the People's Commissariat of Justice (*Narkomiust*) was an agency that existed between May 1918 and October 1921. See Dzhekobson and Smirnov, "Sistema mest zakliucheniia v RSFSR i SSSR".

71   *Tiuremnoe delo v R.S.F.S.R.*, p. 2.

72   GBUTO, f. R-168, op. 1. d. 22, l. 7. and d. 25. l. 18.

The concentration camps in Tyumen and Tobolsk were closed down at the beginning of December 1922, and other concentration camps in the country were closed down over the course of 1923.[73] A report covering the last two months of their existence provides a detailed account of the employment of inmates.[74] In Tyumen, the number of inmates during these two months fluctuated between seventy and seventy-eight people, of whom only five on average were hired out to local enterprises. In Tobolsk, the percentage was only slightly higher: on average, four inmates out of forty worked at local enterprises. This low number is not surprising considering the lingering effects of the destruction of industry caused by the civil war.

Unlike the enterprises, the Soviet institutions were more eager to employ inmates. In the case of Tyumen, fifteen inmates were hired as white-collar workers, while another seven performed unqualified labour. Similarly, in Tobolsk fourteen people performed white-collar work in Soviet institutions. In both camps, workshops (locksmithing, shoemaking, and carpentry) existed, but generally only served the needs of the camps without producing anything marketable. This desire to employ inmates as white-collar workers reflects the lack of qualified personnel for the institutions of the nascent Soviet state, but it was also more profitable for both the inmates and the camp authorities: until the introduction of the new economic policy, such workshops could only sell at low fixed prices.[75] This ambiguous position of revolutionary inmates offers an interesting potential line of inquiry: what was the role of inmates in the earliest Soviet state-building efforts? Where exactly were they directed and how were the conditions of labour in these institutions? Such a study would not only shed light on the functioning of the revolutionary penal system, but would also contribute to the debate on the permeability of the borders of penal sites.[76]

---

73 Dzhekobson and Smirnov, "Sistema mest zakliucheniia v RSFSR i SSSR".

74 GATO, f. R-127, op. 1, d. 14, l. 71.

75 *Tiuremnoe delo v 1921 godu*, p. 2.

76 For the Soviet case, scholars have offered highly original research on the topic of the labour of Gulag convicts outside camps that was not subject to surveillance. See especially: Alan Barenberg, "Prisoners without Borders: Zazonniki and the Transformation of Vorkuta after Stalin", *Jahrbücher für Geschichte Osteuropas*, 57:4 (2009), pp. 513–34 and Wilson T. Bell, "Was the Gulag an Archipelago? De-convoyed Prisoners and Porous Borders in the Camps of Western Siberia", *The Russian Review*, 72:1 (2013), pp. 116–41. For a more general reflection on the complex interrelationships between the Gulag and the Soviet system, see Oleg Khlevniuk, "The Gulag and the Non-Gulag as One Interrelated Whole", *Kritika: Explorations in Russian and Eurasian History*, 16:3 (2015), pp. 479–98. For articles investigating Italian, Indonesian, Australian, and Senegalese cases of permeability of penal sites' borders, with a particular focus on labour, see:

In order to tackle the persistent food supply crisis, prison authorities in Tyumen began soap production. This had a dual benefit: inmates worked during confinement, and the soap could be sold locally in order to buy food supplies.[77] Soap production was recommended by the officials of the Central Penal Department as a sustainable and profitable activity for prisoners. Eager to contribute to the war effort and to support the Bolsheviks in the civil war, officials sometimes suggested exotic measures. For instance, in 1919, during a congress of penitentiary officials, an officer voiced a proposal to create weapons repair workshops in prisons, as this would both occupy the prisoners and enable the authorities to put the vast number of broken guns back into use; this officer even argued that such a workshop was already functioning in a prison in Moscow.[78]

The camp in Novosibirsk was considerably larger than those in Tyumen and Tobolsk: perhaps a heritage of the large POW camp complex that was located there during World War I played a role in this. A report from the camp regarding compulsory work states that in May 1922 there were 986 men and 24 women listed as camp inmates, but only 278 men and 22 women were physically present in the camp.[79] As many as 681 people were absent "on work-related trips" (v komandirovkakh), as they had been sent to various Soviet institutions, including the railroad. Once again, we see the permeability of the borders of these early camps, with more than two-thirds of inmates absent from the camp. Another seventy-five people were listed as missing. This could mean that they had either tried to escape for good or that their work leave was unaccounted for. In any case, this demonstrates the issue with sources on these camps, which are inconsistent, particularly because the criteria for statistics collection were constantly changing.

The same report gives an impression of the social composition of the camp population. The data are incomplete, but none of the categories of the "enemies of the revolution" or disenfranchised groups (lishentsy) make their appearance: 363 people were "workers on the land" (in other words, peasants), 150 were unqualified workers, and 84 were soviet officials. The types of crimes listed also differed significantly from the wrongdoings that were outlined for punishment by camp internment as prescribed by the October 1921 circular quoted above. The most striking discrepancy consists

Zhanna Popova and Francesca di Pasquale (eds), Special Theme "Dissecting Sites of Punishment: Penal Colonies and Their Borders", International Review of Social History, 64:3 (2019), pp. 415–513.

77   GATO, f. R-127, op. 1, d. 14, l. 83.

78   Sbornik materialov Tsentral'nogo Karatel'nogo Otdela, p. 26.

79   GANO, R-1133, op. 1, d. 62, l. 101.

in the fact that 553 inmates were still under investigation and had not yet been convicted. This was a direct contradiction of the legislation, which stated that the camps were a destination only for those already convicted. Indeed, very few people were in the Novosibirsk camp because they had committed a relevant infraction: only two people were there because of loitering, another twenty-seven because of their participation in the "White movement", and finally another ten due to professional misconduct. Others were common criminals or "bandits". This could mean that the local courts were not observing the central guidelines, or that convicts and those under investigation could not be sent to other local places of confinement.

Another report from the Novosibirsk camp, this time regarding the use of forced labour, demonstrates that the camp management there did succeed in hiring out more prisoners to the Soviet institutions, but the organization of workshops was only marginally more efficient than in Tobolsk or Tyumen. From January to April 1922, around two-thirds of the inmates in Novosibirsk were employed by various Soviet institutions. There were also nine workshops within the camp, but production was extremely small-scale: for example, the shoemaker workshop produced only nineteen pairs of men's boots, eight pairs of ladies' boots, and ninety-seven pairs of children's shoes over the course of these four months.[80]

These regional documents suggest that during the revolution, the forced labour of prisoners was primarily used as an ad hoc substitute for the lack of a labour force in various Soviet institutions. The utter decay of places of confinement coupled with the destruction of workshops during the revolution also led to an increased use of convict labour purely for the maintenance of the camps themselves. Even though, in this situation of economic collapse, extramural labour was the most viable option, as it could have allowed the camps to garner some payments, it was not the most reliable way of implementing the central directives: direr than ever before, the lack of convoys made extramural work particularly opportune for escape.[81]

The decentralized and unplanned variation of the use of forced labour was, and could only be, a temporary solution. In these early documents, survival of the inmates and securing the most basic functioning of the camps ostensibly take priority over any orders from the central authorities. Still, this situational use of inmates' labour demonstrated that it could be integrated into the local economy without either consistent centralized oversight or a developed penal policy. This understudied revolutionary

80   GANO, R-1133, op. 1, d. 349, l. 61.
81   GATO, f. R-126, op. 1, d. 10, l. 43 (3 January 1921).

experience also brings into relief the extent to which the organization of a coordinated trans-regional system of places of confinement hinged on the strength of the central authorities.

Along with the conceptual innovations brought about by the revolution, which are the subject of the next chapter, attempts to adapt to the pressure of the economic collapse left deep marks on the penal institutions. Local administrators appear to have lacked even an approximate understanding of the progressive criminological thought promoted by the Central Penal Department, or at least struggled to implement it with any degree of coherence. As they were confronted with the daily challenges of running a prison or camp in a situation of extreme political, social, and economic disarray, they opted for short-term palliative measures rather than radical change. In the domain of forced labour, a lot of adjustments had to be made. The convicts suffered from extreme undernourishment. A report from the Tyumen region Department of Places of Confinement, for instance, states that inmates were on the brink of starvation and many died because their health was undermined by the prolonged calorie deficit.[82] The desperate tone of the report suggests that this was not in any way a deliberate policy, but a consequence of war and revolution. It is highly unlikely that there were concentration camps in other regions in 1918–1922 that consistently could provide their inmates with sufficient food.[83] The lack of coherent and reliable statistics, as mentioned before, means that we will most likely never be able to establish the overall number of inmates who died in these camps due to malnutrition and infectious disease. Unlike the Gulag statistics, which, even though they do have to be consistently criticised, do still allow us to at least estimate the number of people who died in the camps or as an immediate result of their incarceration, data from the revolutionary camps are virtually non-existent.

Camps and the new penal system, 1922–1923

The progressive policies formulated by the central administrators were hard to implement locally for a variety of reasons, including the extreme lack of resources at the local places of confinement, a lack of guards and

---

82   GATO, f. R-127, op. 1, d. 14, l. 80b (1922).

83   Peter Whitewood has underlined that these extreme material difficulties undermined the Bolshevik project of radicalizing the POWs of the 1921 Polish-Soviet War: Whitewood, "Failing to Create Revolutionaries".

qualified personnel, and difficulties in dissemination of the progressive penological ideas. In this section, I trace a particular episode characteristic of the revolutionary developments, namely the local consequences of the decision to suspend the governmental funding of places of confinement as it played out in Tobolsk and Tyumen.

In June 1922, the Commissariat of Justice changed the funding scheme for places of confinement: the financial responsibility for prisons and labour camps was transferred from central to local government.[84] As a document from February 1923 states, in the case of Tyumen this measure resulted in a rapid degradation of the living conditions of both prisoners and prison personnel. The latter, who were still receiving minimal wages, had to serve in their own clothes, as no uniforms could be produced or bought for them.[85] In Tobolsk, the management of the correctional house (*Tobol'skii Ispravdom*) sought to improve the financial situation by trying to make all prisoners work, but some had no warm clothes and therefore, considering it was February, could not work outside.[86] Others were allowed to work in the city without surveillance. Others still were authorized to go back to their families in the rural areas with an obligation to return to the corrective house with a certain amount of agricultural goods. Surprisingly enough, they returned: this measure yielded 100 poods of potatoes and 2 poods of peas, "which the corrective house would otherwise have not been able to acquire with its finances".[87] In Tyumen, the situation was comparable. Only by July 1923 had the state of the inmates improved somewhat, perhaps due to the fact that they could work outside and also grow their own food, but they still did not receive either clothes or bed linen from the prison management.[88]

After the camps were closed down in December 1922, four places of confinement in the Tyumen region remained: correctional facilities (*ispravdom*) in the towns of Tyumen, Tobolsk, and Ishim (before the revolution, tsarist prisons existed in precisely these towns), and an agricultural labour colony.[89] They were all run by the regional administration of places of confinement (*Gubernskoe upravlenie mestami zakliucheniia*, or *Gubumzak*). The number of prisoners in these places of confinement oscillated considerably between January and September 1923. In January, the overall number of inmates was around 1,050. This number reached about 1,200 in March, then dropped again

---

84   Commissariat of Justice circular from 22 June 1922, see GATO, f. R-127, op. 1, d. 1, l. 19.
85   GATO, f. R-127, op. 1, d. 14, ll. 53, 63, and 68ob.
86   *Ibid.*, l. 54.
87   One pood is 16.38 kilograms. *Ibid.*, l. 54.
88   GATO, f. R-127, op. 1, d. 65, l. 172ob.
89   GATO, f. R-127, op. 1, d. 14, ll. 71, 86.

to around 1,080 in April, rose to 1,270 in August, and then decreased again in September to around 1,150 people.[90] Despite the fluctuations, the overall trend was a growth in the number of inmates; perhaps judges started to lengthen sentences, or the number of convictions had increased. From these numbers, around two-thirds were regular convicted inmates, while others were either under investigation or in transit to a place of confinement in another region.[91] The majority were common criminals. From January to March 1923, statistics about the crimes committed by convicts were also included in the reports. The distribution can be seen in Table 1.

Table 1   **Types of crime committed by the inmates of correctional facilities in the region of Tyumen, January–March 1923. Source of data: GATO, f. R-127, op. 1, d. 14, l. 980b., l. 89, l. 120, l. 1380b., l. 1510b, l. 1550b. Blank cells are empty in the original files.**

Types of crime	January	February	March
Murder	39	28	31
Assault and battery	5	3	2
Sex-related crimes	2	6	3
Theft	208	244	247
Qualified theft and burglary	87	70	83
Other property-related crimes	31	17	37
Abuse of work position (*prestupleniia po dolzhnosti*)	34	48	50
Forging state-issued documents	-	-	-
Crimes against universal compulsory labour (*trudovaia povinnost'*)	-	-	-
Crimes against the government order (*prestupleniia protiv poriadka upravleniia*)	59	92	122
Crimes against the state	145	102	96
Military crimes	21	23	28
Other crimes	65	46	23
Total	696	679	722

This data is clearly incomplete: only 722 out of approximately 1,200 people who were inmates in March are mentioned. It is also insufficient to make any generalizations, but it does provide a curious snapshot of the local situation. Desertion from universal compulsory labour (*trudovaia povinnost'*) was previously punished by a term in a concentration camp. Considering that the camps were closed down in December 1922, these inmates should have been sent to other places of confinement, but it is unclear to which ones exactly.

90   GATO, f. R-127, op. 1, d. 14, l. 980b., l. 89, l. 120, l. 1380b., l. 1510b, l. 1550b.
91   *Ibid.*, l. 760b.

In August 1923, the Regional Administration of Places of Confinement assumed management responsibilities for the jails – the places of temporary arrest for those who had not yet been convicted. The police, who had previously been responsible for the jails, now refused to convoy the inmates. Unsurprisingly, this caused further chaos.[92]

Reports from 1922–1923 repeat time and again that places of confinement were understaffed and underfunded.[93] The resources that the camps did possess were wearing out. The horses, for example, could no longer be used for agriculture in spring, as they were exhausted by the work for the camp and prison maintenance during the winter. Due to the lack of funds, places of confinement were routinely indebted to insurance companies, electricity providers, water suppliers, and others.[94]

Despite the material hardships, local prison management did comply with the regulations of the central authorities and attempted to implement the new rehabilitative policies in places of confinement. Understandably, these efforts had limited impact. Libraries and reading clubs, as well as music clubs and public lectures, are mentioned in the reports, but it is unclear how active they actually were, considering all the issues with material supplies. For instance, school classes for inmates of the agricultural colony were very irregular due to the absence of teachers and teaching materials. Similarly, in the Tyumen correctional house, a newspaper called *Voice of the Inmate* allegedly existed, but it was "oral".[95] This meant, in all likelihood, that some articles from printed newspapers were read out to the inmates. Only shortly before April 1923 were these "educational activities" (*uchebno-vospitatelnaia deiatel'nost'*) included in the budgets of places of confinement. Prior to that, ticket sales for theatre performances by inmates were the only source of funding.[96]

In 1923, local prison administrators still reproduced some of the fundamental ideas that guided the imperial prison reform, though they would be largely abandoned by the mid-1920s. One of the cornerstones of prison reform in the nineteenth century was the officials' fixation on prison construction. Two aspects in particular led to prison buildings acquiring this particular importance within the prison reform discourse. The first was rooted in the practical aspects of confinement and improvement of inmates'

92 *Ibid.*, l. 155.
93 *Ibid.*, l. 76, l. 90, l. 155.
94 *Ibid.*, l. 79.
95 *Ibid.*, l. 77ob.
96 *Ibid.*, l. 87.

living conditions: before the start of this construction effort, dozens or even hundreds of inmates were often put into a single cell. These cells could be, for example, created out of refurbished wine cellars, where dampness, darkness, and the lack of fresh air jeopardized inmates' health and caused chronic diseases. Such cramped conditions also facilitated the spread of infections, especially tuberculosis, but also cholera and typhus. They also opened up possibilities for interpersonal violence among inmates. Transit prisons in particular were considered to be breeding grounds for disease and recidivism alike.[97] The second factor, however, was connected to the compelling ideal of the rehabilitation of convicts by placing them in the "correct" environment. Solitary confinement, or at least the night-time separation of prisoners – and, more generally, their maximum possible isolation – were considered to have a redemptive effect on the morals of the prisoners because it separated them from other criminals and the conditions in which they committed their crimes. In the early ideas, isolation per se was redemptive because it gave the convicts an opportunity to reflect on their wrongdoings. By the end of the nineteenth century, however, imperial prison administrators, relying on the international pool of penological knowledge, promoted the idea that confinement needed to be supplemented by compulsory labour in order to be truly rehabilitative.[98] The construction of dedicated prison buildings and workshops thus became one of the central directions of the nineteenth-century prison reforms. In the reports from 1923, local administrators still stated that prison construction was "the central nerve of the entire prison apparatus", though the constant need to channel all efforts towards finding new sources of funding and sustenance for themselves and the prisoners made the construction of new buildings mostly impossible.[99]

Much like in the late imperial period, concerns for physical and moral cleanliness often went hand in hand in these early documents. In the guidelines for the newly appointed commandant of the Tobolsk workhouse, the head of the regional department of justice stated:

> it is necessary to disinfect the whole building from top to bottom and clean it; to implement categorization of the cells and put those who give hope for rehabilitation in improved conditions; to combine the strictness

---

97   N. Lebedev, "Peresyl'noe otdelenie tiur'my, kak istochnik infektsii", *Tiuremnyi vestnik*, 5 (1909), pp. 578–602.

98   Dril', "Tiuremnye raboty, ikh znachenie i organizatsiia", p. 23.

99   GATO, f. R-127, op. 1, d. 14, l. 90.

of following the absolute letter of the law with the work of systematic rehabilitation; to deprive the inmate of any contact with the outside world, to isolate him from society; not to torture his soul, but to try by any means to eradicate unruly behaviour; to lead agitation and propaganda, as it is a powerful instrument of political education. We need to start the most severe attack against dim-wittedness [*temnota*] and ignorance [*nevezhestvo*].[100]

Here, the administrator refers to another pre-revolutionary practice, that of separating convicts into categories depending on their previous convictions, length of the term, and type of committed crime. Belonging to one of these categories translated, in theory, into better conditions of confinement, but it is hard to estimate if observing these categories was actually widespread. This justice department official still mobilized the "old" ideas about punishment (strict isolation and the separation of prisoners of different categories), which created a peculiar dissonance with the revolutionary ideals of educating prisoners about politics and society in accordance with Bolshevik principles. Discursively, this passage, which is quite typical of the time, refers to the old narrative of the reformative potential of incarceration: the official here still referred to notions of the soul and the letter of the law. In the next chapter, I will discuss how the officials of the Commissariats of Justice and of Internal Affairs fought these notions that they perceived as bourgeois and obsolete, and sought for alternatives to prisons.

Conclusion

War and revolution changed the penal landscape in Russia. These changes stemmed from several sources external to the penal system and related to the political change and the wartime situation. Already after the February revolution, the most notorious tsarist punishments, katorga and exile, were abolished, and political prisoners were free to return from exile. Some of them stayed and participated in the local Siberian revolutionary movements instead of returning to European Russia. For many common criminals as well, revolution meant a pre-term release: as the Provisional Government struggled to keep places of confinement functioning, amnesties emptied the prisons, and the number of inmates decreased to only 34,084 in September 1917.[101]

---

100 GATO, f. R-126, op. 1, d. 10, l. 86 (28 May 1921).
101 Dzhekobson and Smirnov, "Sistema mest zakliucheniia v RSFSR i SSSR".

After the October 1917 revolution, the chaos of the civil war, constant financial penury, and the ever-growing lack of qualified prison personnel all contributed to a rapid degradation of the inmates' living conditions. At the same time, crime was rising. In an attempt to alleviate prison overpopulation, a large number of prisoners were released again. Others were allowed to leave the prisons and camps for work, often without a convoy. At least in Siberia, but most likely in other regions as well, local officials were left to their own devices in terms of funding the confinement, a policy that became official in 1922, while the central Bolshevik government announced self-sufficiency as one of the two guiding principles of the prison and camp organization, with the full re-education (*perevospitanie*) of criminals being the second.[102] Both of these principles largely hinged upon the use of convict labour, which was the main tool for places of confinement to receive income in the absence of central funding. Compulsory labour was not only seen as a practical tool of prison management, but was also conceptualized as a compelling force to reform common criminals. Neither of these two principles could be implemented in the realities of the early Soviet state, but they did push prison and camp administrators towards increased reliance on forced labour in its most basic, low-cost, and often particularly exploitative forms.

The creation of a wide network of POW camps during World War I marked a profound change in the materialities of internment. Camps provided a militarized alternative to traditional prisons, which could hold only a fairly limited number of inmates, were increasingly expensive to maintain, or were simply destroyed. As these early camps were used for the wartime necessity of containing large numbers of captives, two crucial characteristics that made the camp as an institution so appealing for the authorities became apparent: camps were highly adaptable and scalable. They created the technical possibility of making internment, including the internment of civilians, a truly mass phenomenon. Established with the militarized regime and modern technologies of confinement, such as barbed wire, the camps could be created in a variety of settings, including former prisons, monasteries, or military barracks, but they also were considerably cheaper to construct from scratch than traditional prisons. The mix of conceptual and material characteristics that made prisons so expensive (such as the need for complex architectural arrangements, thick walls, and a focus on the maximal separation of inmates) could be abandoned in the camps. Camps had the potential for interning extremely large numbers of people that prisons did not possess. These characteristics also made places

102 *Ibid.*

of confinement mobile in an unprecedented way: unlike prisons, camps could be significantly expanded or even moved altogether in a matter of days or weeks. Although camps did not become the dominant repressive institution immediately after the revolution, this wartime experience was not discarded. In Western Siberia, the material heritage of World War I played a particularly important role, and camps were quickly and firmly integrated within the local penal system. In other parts of the country as well, concentration camps were used alongside other places of confinement as the new Soviet authorities experimented with various measures to punish wrongdoers and decrease crime. The camp, a distinctly militarized place of confinement, quickly became one of the tools the *Vecheka* used against political opponents of the regime.

Conceptions of the punishment and reformation of criminals did not change quite as profoundly as the material aspects of confinement. Despite the Bolsheviks proclaiming their definitive break from the bourgeois penal system, much of its organizational structure and theoretical premises continued to bear a lot of resemblance to the late imperial penal system. In the later years, progressive penologists came to play a greater role in the elaboration of penal policy. They were generally wary of incarceration as punishment, and tended to look for alternatives, which they considered to be not only cheaper, but also more reformative. In the first post-revolutionary years, these specialists had an unprecedented opportunity to create the penal system of the young Soviet republic anew. They sought to overcome the heritage of imperial punishment and create a progressive penal system that did not rely on forced displacement and incarcerations, but rather on other, milder, and more progressive alternatives. These early efforts and experiments, however, were largely undermined by the weaker position of these reformers in the interdepartmental struggles for power, and especially by the growing strength of the *Vecheka*, the political police charged with protecting the revolution.

Another obstacle to the building of a more progressive penal system stemmed from the wider social policies of the Bolsheviks, namely war communism and universal compulsory labour. These policies facilitated the use of coerced labour in society at large, making it more pervasive and blurring the lines between the different forms of labour coercion, and encouraging a growing reliance on force in the state's relationship with urban and rural labourers alike.

4 Revolutionary Utopias and Dystopias: Violence and the Making of the Soviet Man, 1923–1929

Abstract
This chapter focuses on the plethora of early Soviet uses of forced labour. It discusses coercion in state-building, including the policies of war communism and universal compulsory labour, and outlines the experiments with forced labour without deprivation of liberty characteristic of the penal policies of the 1920s. This chapter argues that the expanding use of coercion in state-building, however, did not instantly translate into a stronger reliance on camps as major institutions of repression. It offers a detailed analysis of the alternatives to incarceration promoted by the early Soviet penologists and stresses the role of labour coercion and violence in the social interventions planned by early Soviet leaders and the secret police in laying the foundation for the creation of the Gulag.

Keywords: universal compulsory labour, labour coercion, Cheka, political police, Soviet Union

In the years following the October revolution, idealistic revolutionary hopes that criminality would wane in a new, more just, society went hand in hand with Chekist terror. Penal policies were manifold and conflicting. In the aftermath of the revolution, the Bolsheviks were less concerned with crime as a threat to social order, and more preoccupied with eliminating and repressing political enemies. Prisons were symbols of the old regime, and scepticism towards incarceration as punishment was strong among Soviet officials. Instead, they promoted new experimental techniques to rehabilitate offenders, especially delinquent youths. New revolutionary concepts and practices in the domain of punishment emerged. Some were soon abandoned, while others continued to define the repressive system

Popova, Zhanna: *Coerced Labour, Forced Displacement, and the Soviet Gulag, 1880s-1930s*. Amsterdam: Amsterdam University Press, 2024
DOI: 10.5117/9789048560356_CH04

for decades. Early Bolshevik criminal policy was riddled with tensions between revolutionary terror and progressive criminological ideas. These developments and tensions of the 1920s could not possibly account for the explosive growth in the number of inmates that occurred during the 1930s, as the reasons for this growth were external to the penal system and were rooted in wider political change and consolidation of power in the hands of Stalin. Nevertheless, in these early policies the Bolsheviks already extensively relied on forced labour and direct violence as instruments of societal control.

Under the Bolsheviks, coerced labour became an integral part of a wide array of coercive measures that were intended to strengthen the new regime's grip on the country – a policy that came to be known as "war communism". Mobilization of the economy was one of the policy's goals, as were the repression of political opposition and the forceful moulding of new Soviet citizens – the making of the "new Soviet man". Forced labour in a camp implied all of these goals to varying extents. Other institutions that relied largely on coerced labour, such as the policy of universal compulsory labour and the agricultural colonies, also existed. In these times of crisis, labour coercion became a favoured tool for mobilizing, disciplining, and repressing large swathes of the population. In this context, "political opposition" did not necessitate participation in an organized political movement, nor indeed any explicit political act: the boundaries between the political and the non-political were blurred, and the definition of "counter-revolutionary action" was fluid and expansive. Actions were not the only reason for persecution: social origin could also be damning.[1] Reliance on the class principle in the prosecution of offences, paired with the criminalization and politicization of many actions, undermined the criminal justice system.

A reflection on the chronologies and consequences of this prolonged military conflict once again proves helpful in considering the development of repressive practices and policies in the context of war. The recent literature has demonstrated that what has been habitually called the "Civil War" was indeed a conglomerate of multiple conflicts – some of them localized, some overlapping, while others transcended national borders. It might therefore be more accurate to talk about multiple civil wars.[2] In addition to highlighting the enduring impact of war, this representation of multiple overlapping conflicts and several timelines across various regions is also helpful when approaching penal policy. It especially helps to bring together

---

1   For more on the later Stalinist politics of differentiation and discrimination, see Golfo Alexopoulos, *Stalin's Outcasts: Aliens, Citizens, and the Soviet State, 1926–1936* (Ithaca, NY: Cornell University Press, 2003).

2   Smele, *The "Russian" Civil Wars, 1916–1926.*

(and acknowledge the gap between) the struggles of local administrators discussed in the previous chapter and the innovative policies of the Marxist penologists in the capital.

Some scholars have gone a step further in revising the established chronologies. Italian historian Andrea Graziosi views the period as a "single great conflict in two acts, 1918–1922 and 1928–1933", while the New Economic Policy (NEP) provided a "breathing space" (*peredyshka*) that was bound to be terminated as soon as the Bolsheviks were confident enough of their power to abandon this retreat.[3] The NEP, however temporary, produced its own innovations in terms of penal policies. The struggles between the People's Commissariat of Internal Affairs, the People's Commissariat of Justice, and the All-Union State Political Administration (OGPU, *Ob'edinennoe Gosudarstevennoe Politicheskoe Upravlenie*) have already been discussed in the literature.[4] Here, I turn my attention to the distinctive policies of the Bolsheviks (or, to be more precise, of the various groups of Bolsheviks) regarding repression and violence, new conceptions of punishment and redemption, and the demise of the modern prison in the Soviet Union. Some of the reasons why certain institutions, practices, and policies were picked up and developed, while others were discarded, are also discussed.

The overlapping experiences of World War I, revolutions, and civil war had lingering political and societal consequences. George Mosse has investigated in detail the impact on Western European societies of mass death during the world wars.[5] His "brutalization thesis" suggests that the pervasive violence of the war experience led to the growing acceptance of violence in the post-war period, indifference towards human life, and the dehumanization of the enemy. In Mosse's view, this process was launched during World War I and later contributed to the emergence of fascism and, later, Nazism. Russian, and later Soviet, society shared the experience of the banalization of violence. As Aaron Retish has put it, "the sheer loss of life from the unprecedented military and civilian casualties from the First World War and the Civil War, as well as the state's reliance on political coercion, devalued human life and imbued everyday life with violence".[6] Although

3   Andrea Graziosi, *The Great Soviet Peasant War: Bolsheviks and Peasants, 1917–1933* (Cambridge, MA: Harvard University Press, 1996).
4   Michael Jakobson, *Origins of the Gulag: The Soviet Prison Camp System, 1917–1934* (Lexington: University Press of Kentucky, 1993).
5   George Lachmann Mosse, *Fallen Soldiers: Reshaping the Memory of the World Wars* (Oxford: Oxford University Press, 1991).
6   Aaron B. Retish, "Controlling Revolution: Understandings of Violence through the Rural Soviet Courts, 1917–1923", *Europe-Asia Studies*, 65:9 (2013), pp. 1789–806, 1790.

the brutalization thesis alone does not explain Bolshevik political violence, it does help to understand the background of this vast repressive system.

For the Bolsheviks, violence was not only a means of control, coercion, and domination, but was simultaneously a measure of transformation and education. State violence became one of the techniques used to reform society and the individual.[7] The representation of society as a malleable entity that could be reshaped through direct intervention was not unique to the Bolsheviks. Projects of population management were a pan-European trend and employed a wide repertoire of techniques that ranged from relatively innocuous social welfare policies to internment, sterilization, and forced displacement.[8] The perfectibility of humans continued to fascinate scientists and administrators alike, and as the power of the state grew, interventionist projects gained ground in various domains. The term "reformation" is an understatement in the Soviet context: the Bolshevik project envisioned the creation of a whole new socialist society and the "new Soviet man", thus attempting a definitive rupture with the capitalist order. For this making of the new man from the ruins of the old society, the Bolsheviks employed some of the coercive practices and institutions that emerged and became widespread during World War I and the civil war, but they also actively expanded their coercive repertoire.

This chapter explores three interrelated developments that defined the early Soviet penal system. Here, the focus shifts from local practices of punishment and incarceration to the production of knowledge about crime, the criminal, and the role of violence and forced labour in the new society at the core of the nascent Soviet system. The first topic to come into focus is the new socialist labour discipline and the discussions at higher levels of the Bolshevik leadership about the drivers necessary to build socialism. This section draws in broad strokes the background of the further developments by highlighting the lingering significance of universal compulsory labour. The second section looks into the role of terror and the political police as its chief agent. The All-Russia Extraordinary Commission for Combating Counter-Revolution and Sabotage, also known as the *Vecheka* or simply the Cheka, was established in Petrograd on 7 December 1917, and was the first

---

7   Holquist, *Making War, Forging Revolution* and Holquist, "Violent Russia, Deadly Marxism?".

8   For an introduction to the relevant discussions, see Amir Weiner (ed.), *Landscaping the Human Garden: Twentieth-Century Population Management in a Comparative Framework* (Stanford, CA: Stanford University Press, 2003); Leo Lucassen, "A Brave New World: The Left, Social Engineering, and Eugenics in Twentieth-Century Europe", *International Review of Social History*, 55:2 (2010), pp. 265–96; Philipp Ther, *The Dark Side of Nation-States: Ethnic Cleansing in Modern Europe* (New York: Berghahn, 2016).

organization of the revolutionary political police. It was the forerunner of the large Soviet political police apparatus, which at various times bore the names GPU, OGPU, and NKVD. I look into Chekist culture as it manifested during the early terror, and later during the period of the NEP.[9]

The political police acquired unprecedented power during collectivization, but already before that they represented a distinct group whose actions were driven by particularly ruthless notions of class war. The third section of this chapter is dedicated to alternatives to the dominance of the political police. These alternatives largely lost their importance by the end of the 1920s, but it is crucial to see why they failed, or rather, why they were incorporated into the official discourse about reform but had little influence on the practice of punishment. Peter H. Solomon Jr., following Stephen F. Cohen, has suggested that there existed a rupture, rather than a continuity, between bolshevism and Stalinism, and that we can observe an "abrupt departure" from the previous policies in the domain of punishment with Stalin's consolidation of power.[10] This departure signified a change in practice, but progressive ideas were still incorporated in the official discourse, especially in the notion of *perekovka* (the "re-forging" of hardened recidivists through labour), rather than abandoned. In other words, these early Soviet conceptions of reform were later used as justification for the Stalinist penal archipelago.

In the early Soviet Union, the political police not only filled the camps and other places of confinement with "class enemies" and "counterrevolutionaries", but were responsible for managing places of confinement for political prisoners. While Marxist thinkers were optimistic about the rehabilitation even of recidivists if they had a proletarian background, and the early

---

9   In her brilliant book on the genocide of Herero in German West Africa, Isabel Hull points to the catastrophic consequences of the German army's military culture and practices of war: Isabel V. Hull, *Absolute Destruction: Military Culture and the Practices of War in Imperial Germany* (Ithaca, NY: Cornell University Press, 2013). A similarly systematic analysis of Cheka culture and practice is still missing, but some elucidating works on the actions and ethos of the Cheka include: Sergei Petrovich Mel'gunov, *The Red Terror in Russia* (London: J.M. Dent, 1925); George Leggett, *The Cheka: Lenin's Political Police. The All-Russian Extraordinary Commission for Combating Counter-Revolution and Sabotage (December 1917 to February 1922)* (Oxford: Clarendon Press, 1981); Aleksei Litvin, *Krasnyi i belyi terror v Rossii: 1918–1922 gg.* (Moscow: Eksmo, 2004); and Ilya Rat'kovskii, *Krasnyi terror i deiatel'nost' VChK v 1918 godu* (Saint Petersburg: Izdatel'stvo Sankt-Peterburgskogo Universiteta, 2006).

10   Peter H. Solomon, "Soviet Penal Policy, 1917–1934: A Reinterpretation", *Slavic Review*, 39:2 (1980), pp. 195–217. For Cohen's argument, see Stephen F. Cohen, "Bolshevism and Stalinism", in Robert C. Tucker (ed.), *Stalinism: Essays in Historical Interpretation* (New Brunswick, NJ: Transaction Publishers, 1999), pp. 3–29.

Soviet penological policy tended to avoid incarceration as a measure too expensive and unnecessary for common criminals, political infringements were punished with extreme severity. In these yearly years, de facto two parallel systems of punishments emerged, one for the political and the other for common criminals.[11] The most infamous of the early camps for political prisoners run by the Chekists was the Solovki special camp, located on the Solovetsky archipelago in the northern part of European Russia.[12] The first camp on these islands, a camp for prisoners of war, was created in 1920. In 1923 this camp was transformed into the Cheka-run SLON (*Solovetskii lager osobogo naznacheniia*). In terms of its internal functioning, the Solovki special camp bore little resemblance to the POW camps and the smaller regional revolutionary camps. The Solovki camp served as an experimentation ground for officers of the secret police, who later reproduced similar repressive techniques in camps throughout the Soviet Union in the 1930s. This camp, which started as the first major place of confinement run by the OGPU, grew rapidly. The camp subdivisions sprawled from the islands to the mainland, and the number of prisoners increased steeply: by 1 October 1927, 12,896 people were incarcerated in the core Solovki camp. It has been identified as the source of many distinctive Gulag practices in terms of the organization of incarceration and forced labour, such as aspirations of self-sufficiency through inmate labour, and the use of "reliable" inmates, often professional criminals, as guards.[13] The attention here is more on the alternatives to the OGPU version of the concentration camps, and the reasons for their demise.

In the aftermath of the revolution, progressive Marxist criminologists experimented with places of confinement and attempted to introduce rehabilitative convict labour, but these experiments yielded limited results. The final section of this chapter looks into how the idea of the "modern prison" was abandoned in the Soviet Union. Taken together, these developments allow us to see how ideology drove practices, and to understand why the militarized forced labour camps emerged by the end of the 1920s as the dominant repressive institution. The first camps that would later become part of the Gulag already existed in the early 1920s, but the country-wide system that combined camps and other repressive institutions only emerged in the 1930s.

11   Kokurin and Petrov, *GULAG*, pp. 5–7.
12   For the history of the Solovetsky archipelago, its monastery, and the labour camps, see Roy R. Robson, *Solovki: The Story of Russia Told through Its Most Remarkable Islands* (New Haven, CT: Yale University Press, 2004). For a collection of testimonies and photographic evidence on the Solovki camp, see Iuri Brodskii, *Solovki. Dvadtsat' let osobogo naznacheniia* (Moscow: ROSSPEN, 2002).
13   Robson, *Solovki*, pp. 206–25.

New Soviet labour

What role was coercion, and especially labour coercion, to play in a society which promised to become the freest society on earth? In the new Soviet state, political crimes began to be prosecuted with unprecedented cruelty, but at the same time, the punishments for common crimes were liberalized. These changes in repressive policies took place against the backdrop of universal compulsory labour (*trudovaia povinnost'*, which can also be translated as "labour conscription"), which gained unprecedented momentum following the Council of People's Commissars decree of 29 January 1920, which was also approved by the All-Russian Central Executive Committee on 3 February 1920. Although at first glance universal compulsory labour appears to have had very little connection to contemporary criminological theories, upon closer investigation it becomes clear that proponents of universal compulsory labour followed similar assumptions as the progressive criminologists who elaborated the idea of obligatory labour as a means of rehabilitation.

Universal compulsory labour, in other words, was not devoid of reformatory meaning. This implied that coercion was not only a way of compensating for the severe depletion of the labour force or of subjecting the labour market to the attempts of centralized economic planning, but was also an instrument for instilling new socialist values. The idea of universal compulsory labour also stemmed from a utopian vision of a society on the way to socialism and the role of coercion in the building of such a society.

The blueprint for this type of compulsory labour was proposed by Lev Trotsky, who strongly argued in favour of the concept becoming the main driver of the movement towards socialism: "we are now advancing towards the socially regulated labour, on the basis of an economic plan which is compulsory for the whole country, i.e. compulsory for every worker".[14] Similarly, Nikolai Bukharin, the editor of *Pravda* and the leading party theorist, supported universal compulsory labour and stated that it was, in the Soviet case, a manifestation of "concentrated violence" that was directed inwards and therefore became "a factor in the self-organization

14   Trotsky's collected works on the subject constitute parts I and II of Lev Davydovich Trotsky, *Sochineniia. Tom 15. Na puti k sotsializmu, Khoziaistvennoe stroitel'stvo Sovetskoi respubliki* (Moscow, Leningrad: Gosizdat, 1927). Also see: *Tretii Vserossiiyskii s'ezd professional'nykh soiuzov* (Moscow, 1921), part 1, pp. 87–90. Quote from: James Bunyan, *The Origin of Forced Labor in the Soviet State, 1917–1921: Documents and Materials* (Baltimore: Johns Hopkins University Press, 2019 [1967]), p. 133.

and compulsory self-discipline of the labourers".[15] Along with Trotsky and later Lenin, Bukharin provided a theoretical justification for coercion, which by 1920 was already firmly a part of everyday local practices of labour mobilization.[16] According to Bukharin, compulsory labour would restructure society after the revolutionary destruction of the productive forces. As Bukharin's biographer, Stephen Cohen, has put it: "Force and coercion were the means by which equilibrium was to be forged out of disequilibrium".[17]

In *The Politics and Economics of the Transition Period*, Bukharin, following Marx, highlights the role of violence, or "extra-economic coercion", in the development of capitalism.[18] In the case of a post-revolutionary society on its way to socialism, Bukharin argues, violence was to be condoned, as it could also be a cohesive force, a force for organization and construction.[19] Moreover, for Bukharin, the introduction of labour conscription was also a sign that the dictatorship of the proletariat had a sufficiently strong grip on power.[20] Bukharin theorized, in very general terms, the role of coercion as a disciplining instrument not only applied to the working class, but also to the peasantry. For him, proletarian coercion was not only part of the class struggle, but also a method of "accelerated self-organization".[21]

Universal compulsory labour was first discussed at the VI Congress of the Russian Social Democratic Labour Party (Bolsheviks) in August 1917. These early discussions were already very heated, and many delegates predicted that the introduction of this measure would produce clashes between the workers and power.[22] The discussions evolved around the following questions: should compulsory labour be directed against the former propertied classes, or would it touch the workers as well, and how would the latter

15   These ideas of Bukharin were first published in Russian as Nikolai Bukharin, *Ekonomika perekhodnogo perioda, Chast' I: Obschaia teoriia transformatsionnogo protsessa* (Moscow: Gosudarstvennoe sotsial'no-ekonomicheskoe izdatel'stvo, 1920). Here I quote the English translation: Nikolai Bukharin, *The Politics and Economics of the Transition Period* (London, New York: Routledge, 2003 [1979]), p. 159.

16   Larisa Borisova, *Voennyi kommunizm: Nasilie kak element khoziaistvennogo mekhanizma* (Moscow: Moskovskii obshchestvennyi nauchnyi fond, 2001).

17   Stephen Cohen, *Bukharin and the Bolshevik Revolution: A Political Biography, 1888–1938* (Oxford: Oxford University Press, 1980), p. 92.

18   Bukharin, *The Politics and Economics*, pp. 157–59.

19   *Ibid.*, p. 160.

20   *Ibid.*, pp. 162–63.

21   *Ibid.*, p. 163. For the Bolshevik critique of Bukharin's book, see Borisova, *Voennyi kommunizm*, p. 45.

22   Borisova, *Voennyi kommunizm*, pp. 17–19.

react? Initially, "The declaration of rights of labouring and exploited people", approved by the All-Russian Central Executive Committee on 3 January 1918, stated only very generally that "universal labour conscription is introduced with the goal of eliminating the parasitic layers of society and organizing the economy".[23] It did not provide, however, any precise guidelines for the introduction of this policy. In July 1918, the declaration was integrated within the constitution.

The 1918 constitution took a far more radical stance on the matter of obligatory labour. Article 18 proclaimed that labour was the obligation of all citizens of the republic, under the motto "who does not work shall not eat".[24] The Labour Code of 1918 stated that labour was obligatory for all citizens from 16 to 50 years old, with the exception of disabled people and pregnant women.[25] During late 1918 and especially 1919, the centralized apparatus for the mobilization and coercion of workers was being built to serve the military industry, transport, and agriculture in particular. Three campaigns served as trials for the introduction of the centralized compulsory labour system: forcing people who were "not occupied by any socially useful labour" to work; the Commissariat of Internal Affairs' introduction of labour obligations for peasants, such as the obligation to clear snow; and, finally, the labour mobilization of several groups of highly skilled workers, as was the case with railroad workers at the end of 1919.[26] This last measure was proposed by Trotsky: the Soviet authorities could redirect qualified workers serving in the army to work in the rear, in case their skills were needed.[27] By the end of 1919, the Soviet government mobilized not only the former "non-labouring" groups and the peasants, but also prisoners of war and refugees.[28] The decree of 29 January 1920 formalized labour coercion: not only did it introduce universal compulsory labour, but it also laid out the penalties for failure to comply. The administrative punishments for labour

23 S.N. Valk and G.D. Obichkin (eds.), *Dekrety Sovetskoi vlasti*. Vol. 1: 25 October 1917–16 March 1918 (Moscow: Gosudarstvennoe izdatel'stvo politicheskoi literatury, 1957), p. 322.

24 Iu. Kukushkin and O. Chistiakov, *Ocherk istorii Sovetskoi Konstitutsii* (Moscow: Politizdat, 1987), p. 245.

25 "Sobranie Uzakonenii i Rasporiazhenii Rabochego i Krestianskogo Pravitel'stva RSFSR" (n.p., 1918), row 905.

26 A.M. Anikst, *Organizatsiia rabochei sily v 1920 godu* (Moscow: Izd. agit.-izdat. otdela GKT i NKT, 1921), p. 6.

27 Lev Davydovich Trotsky, *K istorii russkoi revoliutsii* (Moscow: Politizdat, 1990 [1930]), p. 151.

28 Elena Buriak, "Prinuzhdenie v organizatsii trudovykh otnoshenii v ramkakh mobilizatsionnoi ekonomiki v pervye gody sovetskoi vlasti", in G.A. Goncharov and S.A. Bakanov (eds), *Mobilizatsionnaia model' ekonomiki: Istoricheskii opyt Rossii XX veka* (Cheliabinsk: OOO "Entsiklopediia", 2009), pp. 317–32, 318.

desertion varied and included both arrest and forced labour in special labour detachments (*shtrafnye trudovye chasti*).[29]

Universal labour conscription was eventually adopted at the expense of other independent ways of organizing labour, such as trade unions. Lenin initially suggested that the trade unions should instil in workers a "different kind of discipline and unity", while compulsory labour only provoked their indignation.[30] For Trotsky, however, the trade unions were insufficient as a disciplinary instrument. He asserted, rather, that this shift towards a new socialist labour discipline could only occur through compulsion as part of the dictatorship of the proletariat. Like Bukharin, Trotsky saw coercion as the fundamental organizational force of the new society. But unlike "the favourite of the whole party", who mostly theorized about forced discipline, Trotsky, with his extensive experience of army organization, envisioned a precise mechanism of coercion. For him, labour had to be militarized: "Military power is the instrument of state coercion. Therefore, a certain element of militarization of labour is [...] unavoidable for the transitional economy that is based on universal compulsory labour".[31]

The merging of the military and industry occurred not only through the militarization of labour legislation (for instance, equating labour desertion to military desertion), but also through the mobilization of soldiers for the rear, and was largely orchestrated by Trotsky.[32] At the beginning of discussions about the role of coerced labour, Lenin supported the organizational potential of the trade unions. However, in January 1920, Lenin sided with Trotsky during the meeting of the All-Union Central Council of Trade Unions (*Vsesoiuznyi tsentral'nyi sovet professional'nykh soiuzov*, or the VTsSPS). At the beginning of February, Lenin once again supported the idea of militarizing labour organization and stated that it was time "to move towards the militarized solution of economic problems".[33]

At the organizational level, universal compulsory labour had several crucial implications. First, the 29 January 1920 decree created a department

29 *Sobranie uzakonenii i rasporiazhenii pravitel'stva za 1920 g.* (Moscow: Upravlenie delami Sovnarkoma SSSR, 1943), pp. 58–59.

30 Bunyan, *The Origin of Forced Labor*, p. 118.

31 "O mobilizatsii industrialnogo proletariata, trudovoi povinnosti, militarizatsii khoziaistva i primenenii voinskikh chastei dlia khoziaistvennykh nuzhd", in Trotsky, *K istorii russkoi revoliutsii*, p. 155.

32 Aleksandr Iliukhov, "Sovetskaia model' vseobschego truda v 1918–1922 gg.", in D.O. Churakov (ed.), *Rabochie v Rossii: Istoricheskii opyt i sovremennoe polozhenie* (Moscow: Editorial URSS, 2004), pp. 182–99.

33 V.I. Lenin, *Polnoe sobranie sochinenii. Tom 40 (Dekabr' 1919 – aprel' 1920)* (Moscow: Izdatel'stvo politicheskoi literatury, 1974), pp. 105–6.

that would organize it: the Main Committee of Universal Compulsory Labour (*Glavnyi komitet po vseobschei trudovoi povinnosti*, hereafter *Glavkomtrud*). This department was a part of the Council of Defence, and despite its short-lived existence (it was disbanded by the introduction of the NEP), it marked another step towards the centralization of labour control and the institutionalization of coercion. It was led by Felix Dzerzhinsky, who was also the head of the *Vecheka*, and included representatives from such crucial agencies as the Military Commissariat, the Commissariat of Labour, and the Commissariat of Internal Affairs. *Glavkomtrud* coordinated a network of sub-departments that implemented universal compulsory labour and devised new methods to do so. It is not possible to delve into the everyday functioning of this agency in great detail here, but briefly turning to the memoirs of an inmate who had experience with the *Glavkomtrud* in 1920 is useful to see one of the aspects of this agency's agenda. Vassily Klement'ev, the author of the memoirs in question, was a former officer of the tsarist army. He was imprisoned in Moscow in Butyrka prison, and unlike many other inmates was not sent to the forced labour camps, but was assigned to the *Glavkomtrud* instead. He was elated at not seeing any grills on the windows there, and initially could not believe that he would work without a convoy. He was appointed as a deputy of the financial department of the Commissariat of Land (*Narkomzem*), and the secretary also provided him with a bed in the *Glavkomtrud*'s dormitory for the first two weeks of his term. In the Commissariat of Land, he performed a white-collar job and was responsible, for instance, for accounting and budget drafting.[34] At least in the case of Klement'ev, the *Glavkomtrud* exercised milder coercion and directed educated inmates towards jobs within Soviet institutions in an attempt to smooth the dire shortage of qualified personnel.

Second, the militarization of labour implied not only stricter, military-style discipline in the workplace and harsher punishments for infringements of this discipline, but also the use of the army workforce within the civil economy. This movement was embodied in the creation in January 1920 of the first labour army. The creation of such armies continued in February and March: the Ukrainian labour army mainly worked at the mines of the Donetsk coal basin, while the Caucasian army worked in the oil industry. Much like convict workers at the beginning of World War I, whose situation was analysed in the previous chapter, the soldiers in these labour armies mainly performed work that did not

---

34   V.F. Klement'ev, *V bolshevitskoi Moskve* (Moscow: Russkii put', 1998), pp. 396–400.

require any special skills: agricultural work, snow and railway clearing, and timber works.[35]

Lastly, the adoption of the 14 November 1919 decree of the Council of People's Commissars on the disciplinary courts tightened the connections between labour coercion at large and the concentration camps.[36] The disciplinary courts were intended as instruments of worker control over labour discipline – for instance, as a means of fighting unauthorized absences. According to this decree, internment in concentration camps became one of the punishments for a breach of labour discipline. Creation of the disciplinary courts locally proved difficult, and the results of their work were limited.

Russian historian Larisa Borisova has suggested that the trade unions and other worker organizations, as more democratic institutions, could not compete in terms of efficacy with the more militarized agencies.[37] With the introduction of universal compulsory labour, even more people found themselves liable for internment for labour-related offences. Felix Dzerzhinsky underlined this connection between the concentration camps and the organization of labour and highlighted the camps' double goal: "the question of the concentration camps is, on the one hand, a question of new methods of fighting parasitism [*tuneiadstvo*] and the world of criminal speculation, and, on the other hand, a question of organization of the best possible use of the parasitic labour force in the interests of the republic".[38] Dzerzhinsky here conceptualizes the camps not only as instruments of class warfare (as they were used by the Cheka at the Solovki), but also as a radical tool for structuring the new society by disciplining the workers.

Initially, the first steps towards regulating the labour force were made through the Departments of Labour (*otdely truda*) and the trade unions. As professional unions of the organized working class, the trade unions were supposed to organize and "distribute" the labour force by directing the workers to certain enterprises. Coercion was envisioned only as an extreme measure to be used in case of dire need.[39] The outcome of the

35 Borisova, *Voennyi kommunizm*, p. 47.
36 *Dekrety Sovetskoi vlasti. Tom VII. 10 dekabria 1919 g. – 31 marta 1920 g.* (Moscow: Politizdat, 1975), p. 274.
37 Borisova, *Voennyi kommunizm*, p. 30.
38 "Vystuplenie F.E. Dzerzhinskogo na plenarnom zasedanii 4-i konferentsii gubernskikh transportnykh i osobykh otdelov Cheka posle nagrazhdeniia ordenom Krasnogo Znameni (6 Fevralia 1920)", in V. Vinogradov, A. Litvin, and V. Khristoforov (eds), *Arkhiv VChK. Sbornik dokumentov* (Moscow: Kuchkovo pole, 2007), pp. 141–48.
39 For instance, see "Rezoliutsiia Soveshchaniia otdelov raspredeleniia rabochei sily, 25–27 noiabria 1918", *Biulleten' Narodnogo Kommissariata Truda*, 7 (1918), p. 23.

1920 discussion about trade unions and their relegation to a secondary role in the organization of the economy would define the functioning of the Soviet economy in the years to come. The unions were supposed to improve productivity and discipline at the enterprises, but had little authority beyond that.[40] Paired with this, the introduction of universal compulsory labour had long-term consequences, despite the fact that it was abandoned at the introduction of the NEP. The NEP meant a stronger reliance on the economic motivation of the workers rather than coercion.[41] Nevertheless, universal compulsory labour created two important precedents: it demonstrated that coerced labour could serve as a fundamental organizing factor of the fledgling Soviet society, and that the militarization of the labour sphere, broadly defined, could be continued even once the war had ended.

Terror and the Chekist culture

The February 1917 revolution already marked a departure from tsarist penal practices, especially with respect to harsher punishments. In the last years of the Romanov empire, both domestically and abroad, katorga became the symbol of the cruelty of the tsarist regime, the epitome of the oppression of political militants. The old katorga system was abolished by the Provisional Government, as was the use of exile. The death penalty was abolished as well. Regular prisons were largely emptied by amnesties. Amnesties continued to be granted under the Bolsheviks as well, and tens of thousands of people were released from confinement even as violence grew.[42]

Under the Provisional Government, the Main Prison Administration (GTU) continued to exist, and the principles of the organization of the prison system remained largely unchanged. A professor at Saint Petersburg University, Aleksandr Zhizhilenko, was appointed the new head of the GTU, and during his short tenure introduced some measures that aimed to rehabilitate convicts, such as the introduction of libraries in prisons.[43] The penal policy

40 A.F. Kiselev, *Profsoiuzy i sovetskoe gosudarstvo: Diskussii 1917–1920 gg.* (Moscow: Prometei, 1991).
41 L.I. Borodkin and E.I. Safonova, "Gosudarstvennoe regulirovanie trudovykh otnoshenii v gody nepa: Formirovanie sistemy motivatsii truda v promyshlennosti", *Ekonomicheskaia istoriia. Obozrenie*, 5 (2000). http://www.hist.msu.ru/Labs/Ecohist/OB5/borsaf.htm, last accessed 16 November 2023.
42 Matthew Rendle, "Mercy amid Terror? The Role of Amnesties during Russia's Civil War", *The Slavonic and East European Review*, 92:3 (2014), pp. 449–78, 449.
43 Zhizhilenko was already an authority in criminal law prior to the revolution, but ostensibly had little or no first-hand experience with prisons. He studied criminal law in Russia and

of the Provisional Government, especially in the March–June period, was particularly marked by a desire to propose a more liberal alternative to the hated tsarist penal system. However, as it started to face more and more opposition, and especially after the attempted coup in July, the Provisional Government created even harsher punishments for challenges to the existing regime. A decree from 12 July 1917 created revolutionary court martials and re-introduced the death penalty for a wide range of military crimes.[44] Creating a consistent penal policy was neither a priority nor a realistic possibility under the Provisional Government.

Harsher punishments, and especially the death penalty, were at the centre of revolutionary discussions of penal policies. Abolition of the death penalty was one of the key popular demands during 1917, and it was also an issue for the new Bolshevik government. It was a matter of discussion within the party: for instance, Lev Kamenev considered the abolition of capital punishment to be desirable, and Anatoly Lunacharsky wrote in October 1917: "Capitulation is better than terror. I will not participate in a terrorist government". Lenin, however, opposed this point of view, considering it "soft", and encouraged the use of capital punishment in certain cases.[45] Reservations about capital punishment were reflected in the organization of the revolutionary tribunals in November and December 1917. Initially, these tribunals could sentence people to a wide range of punishments, from fines to imprisonment and exile, but not execution. According to Matthew Rendle, in establishing these new legal institutions, the Bolsheviks initially sought to create "an image of moderation".[46] Image concerns proved fleeting, as the Bolsheviks encountered much stronger opposition to their power than expected. Extrajudicial executions by the Cheka, which in February 1918 were considered a form of criminal disobedience towards Soviet orders, were, by April of the same year, considered just a negligence or abuse of power.[47]

Germany, then taught at Saint Petersburg University and the Imperial Lyceum. In 1911, he became dean of the Department of Law of Saint Petersburg University. Being head of the GTU under the Provisional Government marked the only period of his career that he spent outside of academia. After the October revolution, Zhizhilenko continued to work at the Petrograd University and to publish in the professional press, but mainly on theoretical subjects. See M.A. Arkhimandritova, V.N. Borisov, and M.A. Bocharnikova, *Institut zakonodatel'stva i sravnitel'nogo pravovedeniia pri Pravitel'stve Rossiiskoi Federatsii: Nezabyvaemye imena* (Moscow: Eksmo, 2010), pp. 69–70.

44   Iu.P. Titov, *Khrestomatiia po istorii gosudarstva i prava Rossii* (Moscow: Velbi, 2002). See also: Browder and Kerensky, *The Russian Provisional Government, 1917*, vol. 2, pp. 980–82.

45   Rat'kovskii, *Krasnyi terror*, p. 10.

46   Matthew Rendle, "Revolutionary Tribunals and the Origins of Terror in Early Soviet Russia", *Historical Research*, 84:226 (2011), pp. 693–721, 696.

47   Rat'kovskii, *Krasnyi terror*, p. 44.

Both individual and mass executions quickly became part of the repressive repertoire and were used on a scale that dwarfed anything carried out by the tsarist court martials.[48] From January 1905 to March 1909, tsarist court martials sentenced 4,797 people to death, while conservative estimates put the number of victims of the Soviet state at 28,000 per year from December 1917 to February 1922.[49]

The Red Terror officially began after the 2 September 1918 *Vecheka* order, but shootings and executions were also rampant before that, especially in the regions.[50] The establishment of terror marked the Bolsheviks' reliance on violence as a way of dealing with their political enemies and led to the growth of the power of the Cheka. However, this did not impact the state's policies regarding common criminals quite as strongly. Penal practices in the first years of Soviet power, especially in the regions, as shown in the previous chapter, were characterized by utmost penury and chaotic, localized arrangements. In the capitals, Marxist lawyers and administrators were elaborating new policies for criminals and were striving to eliminate criminality, with a view to building a socialist society without crime. The Chekists, however, also regarded themselves as fighters for the new Soviet society. Unlike the penologists, the Chekists were not preoccupied with the reformation of individuals, but rather with the "cleansing" of society through violence. They sought to affect the whole society by using indiscriminate terror: "Deterrence was the essence of terror as practised by the Chekas; the very fact that it was arbitrary, indiscriminate, and incalculable in its application heightened its pervasive, paralysing effect".[51] Describing the activity of the Cheka during the two years that passed following the revolution, Martin Latsis, a high-ranking Chekist, noted that "the necessity of an organ like the Cheka was particularly dire because the Soviet power did not have an apparatus of spiritual re-education".[52] The *Vecheka*, as an apparatus of "cleansing and coercion", could fulfil this goal. According to Latsis, the existence of the *Vecheka* was necessary for the survival of the dictatorship

48   Anna Geifman, *Death Orders: The Vanguard of Modern Terrorism in Revolutionary Russia* (Santa Barbara, CA: Praeger Security International, 2010), pp. 126–27.

49   Statistics from: James Ryan, *Lenin's Terror: The Ideological Origins of Early Soviet State Violence* (London: Routledge, 2012), p. 2. Before that, from 1826 to 1905, only 984 people were executed in the Russian Empire: that is, approximately eleven people per year, according to Litvin, *Krasnyi i belyi terror*, p. 28.

50   Kokurin and Petrov, *GULAG*, p. 14.

51   Leggett, *The Cheka*, p. 340.

52   M.Ia. Latsis (Sudrabs), *Dva goda bor'by na vnutrennem fronte* (Moscow: Gosudarstvennoe izdatel'stvo, 1920). p. 9.

of the proletariat: the church was still a powerful institution, schooling was still in need of reform, the army was in need of new leaders, and all of these old institutions nourished "the old spirit" in the "popular masses".[53]

In her memoirs, Nadezhda Mandelstam, wife of the poet Osip Mandelstam, remembered her encounter with a Chekist. This man, "the celebrated Christophorovich", whose full name was Yakov Christophorovich Peters, interrogated her and her husband in the late 1920s.[54] Along with Martin Latsis and Ivan Ksenofontov, Peters was a close collaborator of Felix Dzerzhinsky during the civil war and one of the most prominent members of the first generation of Chekists. Nadezhda Mandelstam noted that during the interrogations, Christophorovich "behaved like a person of superior race who despised physical weakness and the pathetic scruples of intellectuals". According to Mandelstam, it was not his personal trait but rather a defining characteristic of the group to which he belonged. She wrote that the Chekists who went through the revolution (and who were mostly killed later during the 1937–1938 terror) viewed themselves as "the avant-garde of the 'new people' and they had indeed basically revised, in the manner of the super man, all ordinary human values".[55] This observation brings us once again to reflections about the "new Soviet man" and his traits. What were his desired traits and how could they be instilled? In this section, I would like to delve into the connections between the Cheka and, later, the OGPU, and the making of the new Soviet man.

How was the new Soviet man supposed to come into existence, and through which means was this supposed to happen? Providing a satisfactory answer to these questions would require multifaceted and in-depth research; here, I will only focus on one aspect and outline the connections between the making of the new Soviet man and Chekist culture. Using the term "culture" to describe the Cheka, the dreaded perpetrators of the Red Terror, might seem misplaced. It does, however, allow me to analyse together the means that the Chekists envisioned to reach their goals and the ways in which they set those goals. In talking about "culture", I follow Isabel Hull to understand it as "habitual practices, default programs, hidden assumptions".[56] The culture of the first generation of the Soviet secret police operatives has not yet been systematically explored, but an extensive body of literature does analyse various aspects of the Chekists' activities. Here, I would like

53   *Ibid.*
54   Nadezhda Mandelstam, *Hope against Hope: A Memoir* (New York: Atheneum, 1983), pp. 79–85.
55   *Ibid.*, pp. 79–80.
56   Hull, *Absolute Destruction*, p. 2.

to highlight the points of Chekist culture that are especially relevant to the overarching question of this book, namely what kind of continuities and ruptures can be observed throughout Russian history regarding the ideas and practices of forced labour.

First, the emergence of the Cheka marked a break from the tsarist political police, at least on the level of personnel: if many other Soviet agencies and institutions, including the Red Army, heavily relied on "bourgeois specialists" for their functioning, the Cheka "was the only state organ which recruited all of its personnel from scratch".[57] Party membership was a pre-requisite for the leaders of the Cheka, and even more importantly, many of them were "Old Bolsheviks": for instance, in 1920, the majority of the high-ranking Chekists (fifty out of sixty-nine) had joined the party before the revolution.[58] Among the rank and file Chekists, there were also more party members than in any other Soviet agency: an August 1918 survey among employees of the *Vecheka* showed that 52.2 per cent were organized communists, and 37.3 per cent had joined the party before the revolution.[59] This produced a group that shared a mindset shaped both by the experience of the underground political struggle and the fight for power during the civil war; as a result, this was a group that shared a particularly ruthless understanding of "class war".

Second, the Chekists were not merely an isolated, rogue group of secret police operatives; rather, the *Vecheka* was among the main agencies used by the Bolshevik leadership in order to grasp and retain power, and when it came to inter-departmental arguments, the Chekists were avidly supported by Lenin.[60] Iain Lauchlan has described the interrelationship between the Bolshevik leaders and the Chekists by saying that "over time the master began to take on some of the traits of his loyal bloodhound": Lenin sought to control the Cheka by keeping it close, but his worldview was also profoundly impacted by the information about state security that the Cheka provided him.[61] According to Lauchlan, the Cheka and the Bolshevik leadership, and especially Lenin, together underwent "a symbiotic process of cumulative radicalization, whereby paranoid managers promoted

---

57   Iain Lauchlan, "Chekist Mentalité and the Origins of the Great Terror", in James Harris (ed.), *The Anatomy of Terror: Political Violence under Stalin* (Oxford: Oxford University Press, 2013), pp. 13–29, 16. In 1918, there were only two specialists from pre-revolutionary agencies, one of whom was the former head of the Special Corps of the Gendarmes, Vladimir Dzhunkovskii (1865–1938).

58   *Ibid.*, p. 16.

59   Litvin, *Krasnyi i belyi terror*, p. 72.

60   *Ibid.*, p. 65.

61   Lauchlan "Chekist Mentalité", p. 14.

a paranoid organization, and the paranoid organization made managers more paranoid: appetite for protection grew, like an addiction, by what it fed on".[62] The Chekists themselves identified the Cheka as "the combat agency of the party of the future, the communist party, that clears the path to the kingdom [in the original – *tsarstvo*, that is, tsardom] of communism through insurmountable difficulties and carries the red banner of communism in front of the worldwide proletariat".[63] Lenin, giving a speech at the 7 November 1918 meeting of *Vecheka* employees, hailed the Cheka for "directly realizing the dictatorship of the proletariat" and underlined that there was no other way of liberating the masses but through "the violent coercion of the exploiters".[64] In 1919, while attempting to challenge the overwhelming power of the Cheka, Nikolai Krylenko, then chairman of the Revolutionary Tribunal of the All-Russian Central Executive Committee, aptly summarized the essence of the Cheka issue, stating that it was not acceptable to let the Chekists become "the monopolists of the salvation of the revolution".[65]

Here is, therefore, the third crucial characteristic of Cheka culture: the *Vecheka* as a whole and its local agencies in particular were striving for a monopoly on fighting the counterrevolution, generally at the expense of other Soviet institutions. In the immediate aftermath of the October revolution, the Bolsheviks organized revolutionary tribunals. These tribunals were part of a new legal system that was intended to remove the old oppressive social relations, fight the threats to revolution, and create new revolutionary discipline.[66] This promise remained unfulfilled: as the struggle for power continued, these tribunals proved to be a less reliable revolutionary weapon than the Bolsheviks had expected. The *Vecheka*, however, was eager to provide a harsher alternative to the tribunals, and continuously sought to expand its authority.[67] On 16 June 1918, the Commissar of Justice Petr Stuchka abolished all previous decrees on the revolutionary tribunals and stated that these institutions "should not be guided in their work by any juridical norms".[68] The tribunals' decisions,

62   *Ibid.*, pp. 15–16.
63   M.Ia. Latsis (Sudrabs), *Chrezvychainye komissii po bor'be s kontrrevoliutsiei* (Moscow: Gosudarstvennoe izdatel'stvo, 1921), p. 8.
64   V.I. Lenin, *Polnoe sobranie sochinenii. Tom 37 (Iiul' 1918 – mart 1919)* (Moscow: Izdatel'stvo politicheskoi literatury, 1969), p. 174.
65   Litvin, *Krasnyi i belyi terror*, p. 66.
66   Rendle, "Revolutionary Tribunals", p. 693.
67   Rat'kovskii, *Krasnyi terror*, p. 22.
68   Litvin, *Krasnyi i belyi terror*, p. 55.

however, remained more lenient than the "solutions" of the Chekists, who were by then already paving the way for the Red Terror. In the sentences handed out at the tribunals, imprisonment paired with forced labour remained the main type of punishment for such offences as bribery, sabotage, or incitation and participation in pogroms, while the death penalty was very rare (fourteen such sentences out of 12,223 cases).[69] Even as the number of death sentences grew, the right of convicts to appeal remained. In the centre, the revolutionary tribunals and the Chekas were perceived as competitors, but in the regions, according to Russian historian Aleksei Litvin, they collaborated closely.[70] According to Matthew Rendle, little control could be executed over the tribunals, and the sentences were, in the eyes of many Bolsheviks, too lenient.[71]

Finally, the Chekists did not limit their intervention to deterrence through terror alone, but participated in experiments involving disciplinary and penal institutions. After the Red Terror was brought to a halt, the heir of the *Vecheka*, the OGPU, participated in projects involving juvenile deviants. The next section analyses in detail the growing ambivalence towards the use of confinement as punishment: while the importance of forced labour was not questioned, the traditional prison system was continuously criticized. The political police also created institutions to function as alternatives to prison. A whole range of alternatives was suggested by officials of the Commissariats of Justice and of Internal Affairs: from agricultural colonies with porous confines to non-custodial compulsory labour for those who had committed smaller infractions.[72] These experiments were part of the wider context of vigorous early Soviet attempts to transform individuals through a change in their conditions.[73]

The connection between the correction of deviants and the making of the "new Soviet man" was clear in the youth colonies. The most famous ones were organized by Anton Makarenko, who is known internationally for his pedagogical experiments. The history of another commune presents this connection in an even starker way: the Bolshevo labour commune (*Trudovaia kommuna OGPU*) was created in 1924 by Felix Dzerzhinsky

69 *Ibid.*, pp. 57–58.
70 *Ibid.*, p. 67.
71 Rendle, "Revolutionary Tribunals", p. 704.
72 Aleksandr Estrin and V. Trakhterev, "Razvitie sovetskoi ispravitel'no-trudovoi politiki kak chasti sovetskoi ugolovnoi politiki", in A.Ia. Vyshinskii (ed.), *Ot tiurem k vospitatel'nym uchrezhdeniiam* (Moscow: Sovetskoe zakonodatel'stvo, 1934), pp. 17–71.
73 Sergei Oushakine, "Pole boia na lone prirody: Ot kakogo nasledstva my otkazyvalis'". *Novoe literaturnoe obozreniie*, 71 (2005), pp. 263–98.

under the auspices of the OGPU.[74] Although it was founded as an institution of public education and not as part of the penal system, this commune shared with the penal institutions not only the theoretical assumptions of the enforced perfectibility of humans, but also, in a very practical way, the inmates: it took in young inmates of the Butyrka prison and other prisons in Moscow, as well as offenders from the labour colony of the Solovki camp.[75]

Productive labour was intended to structure the lives of the interned youngsters, but the Bolshevo colony also had other principles: trust, the voluntary nature of the stay, and "complete initiative on the part of the commune members together with the leadership and personnel of the institution".[76] These, unsurprisingly, were coupled with strict punishments for breaches of the commune's discipline, though the power of punishment belonged to the collective rather than the supervisors. The Bolshevo commune grew fast. It became a successful, profitable production and was even featured in the first Soviet sound movie, the 1931 *Road to Life (Putevka v zhizn')*. By its tenth year, more than three thousand youths were living and working there. By 1935, the commune was fully governed by its alumni.

Support from Genrikh Iagoda, however, ultimately sealed the destiny of the commune. Iagoda was a high-ranking Chekist who was de facto the head of the OGPU in the late 1920s–early 1930s. In this role, he supervised the first large-scale construction projects that relied on the forced labour of convicts, such as the White Sea-Baltic Sea Canal. This project is known for the exorbitant number of deaths among the forced workers, with even the official data confirming 12,318 deaths in 1931–1933.[77] Iagoda reached the pinnacle of his career in 1934 when he became People's Commissar of Internal Affairs, but was arrested in March 1937 during the party purges and executed one year later.

During the years of the Great Terror the Bolshevo commune was disbanded. The founder of the commune and a close collaborator of Iagoda, Matvei

---

74   For a history of the Bolshevo commune and the project of the "new Soviet man", see Josette Bouvard, "La commune de Bolchevo (1924–1938) ou la fabrique de l'Homme nouveau?" *La Revue russe*, 39 (2012), pp. 69–80, and for Makarenko's connection to this commune, see Getts Khillig [Götz Hillig], "A.S. Makarenko and the Bolshevo Commune", *Russian Education & Society*, 44:9 (1 September 2002), pp. 75–92. Michael David-Fox has also discussed in detail the role of Maxim Gorky in the construction of the laudatory narratives of the Solovki camp and the Bolshevo commune as the sites of production of the "new Soviet people": Michael David-Fox, *Showcasing the Great Experiment: Cultural Diplomacy and Western Visitors to the Soviet Union, 1921–1941* (Oxford, New York: Oxford University Press, 2011), pp. 142–74.

75   Khillig, "A.S. Makarenko and the Bolshevo Commune", p. 77.

76   *Ibid.*, p. 78.

77   A.I. Kokurin, Iu.N. Morukov (eds), *Stalinskie stroiki Gulaga 1930–1953* (Moscow: MFD, 2005), pp. 30–37.

Pogrebinskii, committed suicide on 4 April 1937. More than ninety teachers, communards, and alumni of the Bolshevo commune were shot in 1937–1938.[78]

The new techniques of violence that the first generation of Chekists had devised to hunt down "counterrevolutionaries" and manage the camps continued to define the life and death of Gulag inmates in the decades to come. Chekists' ruthless understanding of the "class war", their reliance on terror and extrajudicial measures, and the dehumanization of political dissenters were all part of the Chekist culture. This Chekist culture impacted not only the lives within the camps: from early on, it was firmly integrated into the wider project of making the "new Soviet man" and building the new Soviet society. A monopoly on the future and the readiness to achieve it by violent means laid the foundation for the Stalinist system of forced labour and forced displacement. The heir of the Cheka, the KGB (*Komitet gosudarstvennoi bezopasnosti*, Committee for State Security) continued to play a crucial role in Soviet politics after the death of Stalin.[79] Its influence endured beyond Soviet times: Julie Fedor has argued that a whole "cult" of the Cheka has emerged, whereby the Chekists had been idealized as the saviours of Russian statehood, their values and methods legitimized and endorsed by the political leaders.[80]

Offering more examples for those who liken revolution to Saturn, the lives of many Chekists of the first generation ended in the same violent way. Iagoda was executed on 15 March 1938, Martin Latsis on 20 March 1938, Iakov Peters on 25 April 1938. This generation laid the foundation for the culture of the political police – and political violence – that at Stalin's will became the instrument of their own demise.[81]

Measures of social defence

If coerced labour was identified by the leading Bolsheviks as an instrument for ordering the economy and society and disciplining individuals, then

---

78   Svetlana Iudina, "Pamiati bolshevtsev", 5 November 2013, available at: https://urokiistorii. ru/articles/pamjati-bolshevcev, last accessed 14 March 2022.

79   See, for example, in English: Christopher M. Andrew and Oleg Gordievsky, *KGB: The Inside Story of Its Foreign Operations from Lenin to Gorbachev* (New York: HarperCollins, 1990) and John J. Dziak, *Chekisty: A History of the KGB* (Lexington, MA: Lexington Books, 1988).

80   Julie Fedor, *Russia and the Cult of State Security: The Chekist Tradition, from Lenin to Putin* (Abingdon, New York: Routledge, 2011).

81   For a close-up analysis of this "purge of the purgers" based on materials from the KGB archives in Kyiv, see Lynne Viola, *Stalinist Perpetrators on Trial: Scenes from the Great Terror in Soviet Ukraine* (New York: Oxford University Press, 2017).

what was the position of convict labour within this framework? Could forced labour still be used as punishment when it had been normalized in society at large as never before? Forced labour, as we saw in the previous chapters, had long been theorized as the key to convicts' rehabilitation by liberal imperial penologists, and was implemented in a variety of ways already in the Russian empire. What were the attitudes of the early Soviet criminologists towards this experience, and how did they tackle the challenge of devising the new, socialist penal system?

During the relatively short period of three or four decades that preceded World War I, tsarist authorities were on a quest to expand and renovate the existing prisons and to build new ones. They consistently tried to improve the conditions of prisoners and started to conceptualize productive labour as a means of rehabilitation. Despite the practical difficulties of implementing it, imprisonment combined with obligatory labour was considered the "gold standard" of punishment, while the importance of exile was waning. This slow shift was thwarted by the 1905–1907 revolution, and was further undermined by the beginning of World War I. As demonstrated in the previous chapters, the pressures of war pushed the government towards the employment of convicts on large-scale infrastructural projects that implied both hard labour and forced displacement. Later, the prison network was significantly damaged during the revolutions and the civil war. Material destruction, however, was not the primary cause of the demise of the modern prison and the rise of camps: during the revolution, for instance, the old prison buildings in Tobolsk and Tyumen were still used alongside the camps.[82] What I want to underline here, however, is that imprisonment was no longer considered the dominant type of punishment, and instead incarceration in the camps became predominant.

Louise Shelley has discussed the ways in which the regional sections of the State Institute for the Study of the Criminal and Crime (*Gosudarstvennyi Institut po izucheniiu prestupnika i prestupnosti*) contributed to research on crime in the Soviet Union, and has underlined that this research had been overlooked by most outside observers. She argues that the early Soviet criminologists were "not limited by either ideological or methodological constraints".[83] It is necessary to acknowledge the professionalism, richness, and variety of early Soviet criminological thought, but the above statement

---

82   Later, the prisons did not cease to exist, but were reserved for the most dangerous offenders, as was the case of the Tobolsk prison until 1989.

83   Louise Shelley, "Soviet Criminology: Its Birth and Demise, 1917–1936", *Slavic Review*, 38:4 (1979), pp. 614–28, 617.

nevertheless appears to be far-fetched when we consider this school of criminology in a wider context.

Criminology of the first post-revolutionary years was not defined by political power in the same way as it was during the Stalinist period, but it did remain within a very specific ideological framework. This framework was defined, firstly, by the progressive ideas uttered by jurists who had started their careers long before the revolution, and who could, prior to 1917, be situated on the more radical side of contemporary criminological and penological thought. Nevertheless, they were still firmly embedded within the imperial professional juridical community, and well-connected to their international colleagues (some of them, like Sergei Poznyshev, Mikhail Isaev, and Aleksandr Estrin, continued to define the profession for many years).[84] Peter Solomon has labelled the early Soviet criminal policy as progressive, describing it as "one which met contemporary standards, that is, one which reflected the set of reform ideas and ideals that pervaded Western penology in the late nineteenth and early twentieth centuries and which was eventually adopted, in whole or in part, by many of those countries".[85] At the same time, early Soviet criminology had a strong Marxist current that placed an emphasis on the social context of crime and the possibilities of crime prevention through societal change. This double alignment meant that the coercive transformation of individuals in order to create the desired social order was justified with a whole range of arguments.[86]

Penal policies were a crucial part of the state-building process. For the Bolsheviks, building a new penal system was a practical challenge, an ideological issue, and a symbolic matter. The prisons and hard labour sites of the Russian empire were among the most powerful symbols of the tsarist oppression. In an attempt to break all ties with the tsarist regime and demonstrate their

---

84 Sergei Poznyshev (1870–1943) published, among other works, a fundamental book on penitentiary policies: Sergei Poznyshev, *Osnovy penitentsiarnoi nauki* (Moscow: Iuridicheskoe izdatel'stvo Narkomiusta, 1923). Mikhail Isaev (1880–1950) worked on the preparation of the 1924 Criminal Code, published a textbook on criminal law titled *Obshchaia chast' sovetskogo ugolovnogo prava RSFSR* (Leningrad: Gosudarstvennoe izdatel'stvo, 1925), and continued to publish until his death. Aleksandr Estrin (1889–1938) also published extensively. Before the revolution, an article of his appeared in a volume edited by Isaev: Mikhail Isaev (ed.), *Trudy Kruzhka ugolovnogo prava pri S.-Peterburgskom universitete* (Saint Petersburg: Iurid. kn. sklad "Pravo", 1913). Later, Estrin became a collaborator of Nikolai Krylenko, see Nikolai Krylenko and Aleksandr Estrin, "Reforma sovetskogo ugolovnogo protsessa: Doklad N.V. Krylenko, sodoklad A.Ia. Estrina", *Revoliutsiia prava*, 1 (1928), pp. 98–119. In 1935, he also published a university textbook on Soviet criminal law: Aleksandr Estrin, *Sovetskoe ugolovnoe pravo* (Moscow: Gosudarstvennoe izdatel'stvo "Sovetskoe zakonodatel'stvo", 1935).
85 Solomon, "Soviet Penal Policy", p. 196.
86 Daniel Beer, "Blueprints for Change: The Human Sciences and the Coercive Transformation of Deviants in Russia, 1890–1930", *Osiris*, 22:1 (2007), pp. 26–47.

own ambitions of universal liberation, the Bolsheviks initially sought to build a system of punishments that would be more humane than that of their predecessors. Criminality was seen as an illness of the old bourgeois society, and criminals were expected to change. Some, including Lenin, hoped for a reduction in criminality after the revolution that would make the penal system obsolete. The initial hope that once the proletarian dictatorship had been installed, the social conditions that encouraged crime would disappear was extremely persistent. As late as 1927, Aleksandr Estrin, professor of criminal law at Moscow State University and one of the authors of the journal *Revolution of Law*, maintained that the growth in the level of culture and political consciousness in the proletarian state would entail a wane in criminality.[87]

Early Soviet officials and criminologists were highly averse to incarceration also because of the costs associated with it. Building new prisons and incarcerating convicts for longer terms were extremely costly, especially in a country ravaged by war and revolution. From early on, officials attempted to mitigate some of these costs by forcing both convicts and detained suspects to work. A decree published in January 1918 stated that convicts should be forced to perform labour for the benefit of the state, and one-third of profit derived from this work was to be used for the functioning of prisons, while the other two-thirds had to be paid out to the inmates upon release.[88]

During most of the 1920s two parallel systems of places of confinement existed in Russia, one for criminal and one for political convicts. They were operated by two principal agencies: the Main Administration of Places of Confinement (*Glavnoe upravleniie mest zakliucheniia*, hereafter GUMZ) and the political police, the OGPU. The camps of the OGPU contained political prisoners and common criminals considered the most dangerous. Initially, the OGPU's system could hardly be considered a rival to the penal system managed by the GUMZ, as it encompassed considerably fewer camps and prisons and had a much smaller budget.[89] In 1926, in the places of confinement operated by the GUMZ in the RSFSR alone, there were 97,300 inmates, while the OGPU camps held, according to estimates, around 11,000 people.[90] What follows focuses on the discussions that surrounded the punishments for common criminals and the alternatives to incarceration.

87   Aleksandr Estrin, "K voprosu o printsipakh postroeniia sistemy ugolovnoi repressii v proletarskom gosudarstve", *Revoliutsiia prava*, 1 (1927), pp. 74–98, 94.

88   Rabochee i Krest'ianskoe Pravitel'stvo, "Article 284," *Sobranie Uzakonenii i Rasporiazhenii Rabochego i Krestianskogo Pravitel'stva RSFSR*, no. 19 (January 30, 1918).

89   Solomon, "Soviet Penal Policy", p. 202.

90   John L. Scherer and Michael Jakobson, "The Collectivisation of Agriculture and the Soviet Prison Camp System", *Europe-Asia Studies*, 45:3 (1 January 1993), pp. 533–46, 533.

In 1920, according to Aleksei Litvin, approximately one quarter of all convicts were sentenced to compulsory work without imprisonment, the majority of criminal offenders did not experience incarceration, and many were released on parole or were amnestied. In 1920, the people's courts sentenced 582,571 people, and for 199,182 of them this involved a deprivation of liberty. Of this number, 79,979 people were released on parole. Other sentences implied non-custodial punishments.[91] Following this practice, later legislation also demonstrated aversion towards imprisonment. As Peter Solomon has underlined, the 1922 Criminal Code listed punishments that were lenient compared to both the tsarist and contemporary Western legislations, and relied heavily on non-custodial sanctions such as fines or compulsory labour.[92]

The preparation of this first Soviet Criminal Code posed many problems. One of the challenges that lawyers faced was the redefinition of what constituted a criminal act. In 1922, a lawyer and statistician Viktor Iakubson published a snippet of the data from the regular (non-political) places of confinement in 1919–1920. After having reviewed 8,568 personal prisoner files that had been sent to him from across the country, he stated that these people were subject to sixty-five different punishments, varying from 2.5 days of arrest to life imprisonment and capital punishment.[93] Of the total eight and a half thousand, 240 prisoners had been sentenced to imprisonment conditionally – for instance, until the end of the civil war. This mostly applied to those accused of "active political crimes" (*aktivnye politicheskie prestupleniia*) and "crimes against the alimentary and economic state system" (*prestupleniia protiv prodovolstvennoi i khoziaistvennoi gosudarstvennoi sistemy*). In 1919, 37.2 per cent of convicts were sentenced to terms of less than six months, a number that decreased significantly in the following year to 29.9 per cent. According to Iakubson, not only the punishments, but also the crimes, were extremely diverse: after the revolution and before the introduction of the 1922 Criminal Code, there existed no pre-established classification of crimes. Among those whose files Iakubson reviewed, some were accused of "drowning a cow", "being rude to the wife and children", and "hitting a horse", and they received punishments that were specific to the crimes thus defined.[94] No matter how sceptical the leading Bolsheviks

91 Litvin, *Krasnyi i belyi terror*, p. 57.
92 Solomon, "Soviet Penal Policy", pp. 198–99.
93 Viktor Iakubson, "Ugolovnaia repressiia v pervye gody revoliutsii", *Ezhenedel'nik sovetskoi iustitsii*, 4 (1922), pp. 3–4.
94 *Ibid.*

were towards legal standardization, this situation could not last: such a criminal justice system was not only inefficient, but also hard to monitor, and even more so to control.

Along with routine smaller offences, there also existed crimes that were labelled as counter-revolutionary, which thus implied a much harsher punishment. One such crime, for instance, was "speculation" or peddling, or, in Russian, *meshochnichestvo* – that is, selling goods, especially bread, outside of the state distribution system. These pedlars were considered to be more dangerous political criminals than robbers, for instance, because their actions were considered counter-revolutionary, as they challenged the state monopoly. As Lenin put it in a speech on 30 July 1919, peddling bread was "the source of horrible oppression and the wildest, most abominable, completely unregulated profit for the speculators".[95] Peddling was one of the new crimes against the socialist order, and was deemed dangerous: it could be punished by imprisonment and, in some cases, by execution.

Marxist conceptions of law and legality, as well as the transformations of the Bolsheviks' view of the law, are well studied.[96] I will only briefly discuss here the foundational principles of the Soviet penal system – namely the class principle, the principle of analogy, and the principle of revolutionary expediency – and look at how they played out in the practice of building the Soviet penal system. The class principle was first expounded in the 1919 "Guiding principles of RSFSR criminal law",[97] and was revisited in the 1924 "General principles of the criminal legislation of the USSR and the union republics".[98] The "class principle" can be interpreted in a variety of ways. It could mean, and perhaps most often did mean, that the social background of an offender played a role in the verdict, with disenfranchised groups and "former people" (*byvshie liudi*), that is, members of the imperial aristocracy that was outlawed after the October revolution, experiencing stricter treatment. But, at least in theory, the class principle was intended to guide the judges to sentence people "according to the interests of the working class as a whole".[99]

Another legal innovation that further undermined the legal system was the principle of analogy. The introduction of this principle induced

95   V.I. Lenin, *Polnoe sobranie sochinenii. Tom 39 (Iiun' – dekabr' 1919)* (Moscow: Izdatel'stvo politicheskoi literatury, 1970), p. 121.
96   Peter H. Solomon, *Soviet Criminal Justice under Stalin* (Cambridge, New York: Cambridge University Press, 1996).
97   Goliakov, *Sbornik dokumentov*, pp. 57–60.
98   *Ibid.*, pp. 199–207.
99   Estrin, "K voprosu o printsipakh postroeniia", p. 98.

heated discussion among legal scholars and party officials. The principle of analogy meant an abandonment of the principle of *nulla poena sine lege* (no punishment without the law), and suggested that even when a crime was not listed in the Criminal Code, it could still be prosecuted according to the principle of analogy, whereby an "analogous" crime listed in the Criminal Code was applied. The introduction of these principles contributed to the possibility that some actions that were previously considered non-criminal could become criminalized. The system was becoming more and more flexible to the point of blurring the lines between criminal and non-criminal behaviour.

According to Peter Solomon, there were three types of crimes that the Bolsheviks defined extremely vaguely in their own political interest. These were counter-revolutionary and economic crimes, and misdemeanours committed by Soviet officials (*dolzhnostnye prestupleniia*).[100] The extreme elasticity of the definitions of such crimes allowed almost any crime to be politicized, and the politization of economic crimes continued after the end of the civil war: in 1925, Viktor Iakubson stated that "for us [Soviet officials] a murder, under certain conditions, can play a smaller role and represent a smaller danger for the state than some crimes that are harmful for the economy".[101] The principle of revolutionary expediency continued to define repression in the 1920s. In 1927, Aleksandr Estrin underlined that this principle, along with the notion of "measures of social defence", defined the Soviet system as fundamentally distinct. This principle suggested that the law was a manifestation of "bourgeois juridical fetishism", and in the proletarian state, revolutionary expediency had to become the guiding principle for the judges.[102] In other words, it was in the hands of the judges to decide which actions constituted a danger to the Soviet order and the revolution.

Peter Solomon has outlined three main problems that riddled the Soviet penal system in the 1920s: "inadequate budgets for prisons, overcrowding, and a tendency toward homogenised leniency in judicial and penal practice".[103] These problems were persistent, but it appears that, along with several other issues that are discussed below, they not just complicated the execution of progressive policies, but undermined them altogether.

100 Solomon, *Soviet Criminal Justice under Stalin*, p. 26.
101 Viktor Iakubson, "Klassifikatsiia zakliuchennykh i izuchenie vliianiia na nikh ispravitel'no-trudovogo vozdeistviia", *Pravo i zhizn'*, 4–5 (1925), pp. 88–95, 90.
102 Estrin, "K voprosu o printsipakh postroeniia", pp. 77–78.
103 Solomon, "Soviet Penal Policy", p. 203.

The materials of the All-Russian Congress of Workers of the Penitentiary (*Vserossiskiii s'ezd rabotnikov penitentsiarnogo dela*), which took place in October 1923, outlined some of the early responses to the challenges. Creating a Marxist theoretical framework for a penal system was a fundamental problem, and there was no example to follow. Devising the specific punishments that would become part of such a system and which also could be realized in the prevailing conditions of economic crisis and lack of funding was another challenge. According to the Commissar of Internal Affairs Aleksandr Beloborodov, forced labour during confinement could both satisfy the criminological imperative to re-educate deviants and provide a much-needed source of funding for the penal system. On the same occasion, Nikolai Krylenko, then a Deputy Commissar of Justice, stated, in contradiction to Beloborodov, that the "labour-corrective influence" on the offenders was not the primary goal of the penal system.[104] According to Krylenko, the primary goal was the protection of the collective (*kollektiv*), and not the reform and protection of the individual (*lichnost'*). In an even more contradictory fashion, he stated that the length of the terms of incarceration had to be decreased from years to months, as longer terms were far too costly.[105]

And reduce the terms they did. Once again, the statistics collected by Viktor Iakubson bear witness to this. In 1928, he published another article on the deprivation of freedom during the first years of Soviet power. There he relied on more extensive data: he worked with 34,693 personal files dating back from 1918 to 1921. According to his calculations, during this period only 40.7 per cent of convicts were sentenced to terms of below one year, while the rest – almost 60 per cent – were sentenced to longer terms, with 5.2 per cent receiving terms of more than ten years. By 1926, as the data of the People's Commissariat of Justice showed, the situation had changed profoundly: only 15.2 per cent of convicts had to serve sentences of more than one year.[106] By 1927, however, this change of course was considered a mistake, and Aleksandr Beloborodov decried this practice as sabotaging the idea of punishment. According to him, inmates who served such terms bore the stigma of incarceration but, at the same time, were no longer scared of it, and went on to commit new crimes.[107] Instead, the idea was to keep

104 "Vserossiskiii s'ezd rabotnikov penitentsiarnogo dela", *Ezhenedel'nik sovetskoi iustitsii*, 41 (1923), pp. 949–53, 949.

105 *Ibid.*

106 Viktor Iakubson, "Lishenie svobody, kak mera sotsial'noi zashchity po Ugolovnomu i Ispravitel'no-Trudovomu Kodeksam RSFSR", *Problemy prestupnosti*, 3 (1928), pp. 189–96, 195.

107 A.G. Beloborodov (ed.), *Sovremennaia prestupnost'* (*prestuplenie, pol, repressia, retsidiv*) (Moscow: NKVD RSFSR, 1927), p. 5.

the longer terms of imprisonments and substitute the shorter ones with non-custodial forced labour.

Marxist criminologists considered imprisonment, and the deprivation of liberty in general, to be the fundamental punishment of the bourgeois penal system, and sought to create alternatives to confinement as punishment and prisons as penal institutions. Even in the cases where confinement was initially implied, it could be abandoned: it was stated in the earliest Soviet legislation on labour camps, for instance, that inmates who demonstrated a particular zeal for work could be released from the camps and allowed to live in private households.[108] More importantly, non-custodial compulsory labour became not only a privilege provided the inmates, but a sentence of its own, one which did not imply any incarceration at all. Already the 1922 Criminal Code had given a full definition of this penal measure, with more than one-third of all articles dedicated to punishments mentioning it. Fairly quickly, however, the implementation of obligatory labour without confinement was undermined by growing unemployment. Even in Moscow, where such labour was considered to function fairly well, 48.3 per cent of all those sentenced to it only registered at the Bureau of Compulsory Labour, but did not perform any work, while another 17.4 per cent did not even register themselves following their sentence.[109] The judges of the people's courts and the regional (*guberniia*) courts alike started to use this sentence less and less, and by 1926 it amounted to only 14.2 per cent of all sentences, while in 1923 it had been 20.1 per cent.[110] The 1924 Corrective Labour Code listed the deprivation of liberty and non-custodial forced labour as the two main types of punishment.[111] It implied the creation of a network of various corrective institutions: instead of prisons, this new code envisioned agricultural labour colonies, artisanal and manufacturing colonies, as well as "transitional corrective labour houses", all of which were supposed to be organized mainly on the outskirts of cities.[112] Regarding non-custodial labour, however, the discrepancy between central policy and the practice of local courts persisted: although such labour was promoted by lawyers from the capital as a more humane, low-cost alternative to imprisonment, it could rarely be organized effectively in the rural areas. Because of

---

108 Goliakov, *Sbornik dokumentov*, pp. 44–45.
109 Viktor Iakubson, "Reforma ugolovnogo zakonodatel'stva i prinuditel'nye raboty bez soderzhaniia pod strazhei", *Administrativnyi Vestnik*, 1 (1929), pp. 35–39, 37.
110 *Ibid.*
111 Goliakov, *Sbornik dokumentov*, pp. 182–92.
112 *Ibid.*, p. 182.

these difficulties, local judges tended to sentence criminals to short-term imprisonment rather than non-custodial labour.[113]

However, the Bolsheviks' desire to empty the prisons lingered, and despite its failures, this measure was rehabilitated at the end of the 1920s as a tool to diminish the prison population. The 26 March 1928 decree adopted by the All-Russian Central Executive Committee and the Council of People's Commissars pushed the local courts to increase the proportion of sentences to non-custodial labour. It also limited pre-term release of those convicted to longer prison terms. The Commissariat of Justice published further circulars and directives in order to enforce this decree.[114] The grain procurement crisis of 1928 and the collectivization of peasantry that followed created an avalanche of court cases: in the first half of 1928, 466,240 people were sentenced; the number grew to 489,389 people for the second half of the year. The following year witnessed an even steeper growth: 578,277 people received various sentences in the first half of 1929, and as many as 637,826 were convicted in the following six months.[115] As local judges were strongly pressured to prefer non-custodial labour to incarceration, the proportion of such sentences grew tremendously, increasing from 15.3 per cent in the first half of 1928 to 51.7 per cent in the second half of 1929, which amounted to 344,542 convictions applying this punishment.[116] Such drive to abandon incarceration led to serious crimes being punished with non-custodial labour: in 1930, 20 per cent of all convicted murderers and 31 per cent of convicted rapists received this sentence.[117]

What part of these non-custodial labour sentences could actually be realized is unclear. In his 1929 report, Commissar of Justice Nikolai Ianson stated that the main problems in the domain of criminal justice included the growth in the number of convicts, especially those sentenced to shorter terms; the frequency of the use of release on parole instead of acquittal; and an abundance of unfounded criminal sentences.[118] Ianson still hoped that non-custodial labour could become an alternative to short-term

113 Solomon, *Soviet Criminal Justice under Stalin*, p. 56.
114 K. Gailis, "Prinuditel'nye raboty i drugie mery sotsial'noi zashchity vmesto kratkosrochnogo lisheniia svobody", *Ezhenedel'nik sovetskoi iustitsii*, 7 (1929), pp. 158–61, 159–60.
115 Evsei Shirvindt, "Obostrenie klassovoi borby i ugolovnaia repressiia", in Evsei Shirvindt (ed.) *Klassovaia bor'ba i prestupnost'* (Moscow: NKVD RSFSR, 1930), p. 5.
116 "Rech Iansona na 3-em soveshchanii sudebno-prokurorskikh rabotnikov", *Sovetskaia iustitsiia*, 24–45 (1930), pp. 1–2.
117 Scherer and Jakobson, "Collectivisation of Agriculture", p. 536.
118 Nikolai Ianson, "Doklad Narodnogo Komissara Iustitsii RSFSR tov. Iansona – Otchet NKIu RSFSR", *Ezhenedel'nik sovetskoi iustitsii*, 9–10 (1929), pp. 193–212, 195.

imprisonment.[119] However, these hopes were not to be fulfilled, as the overwhelming majority of sentences of non-custodial labour were not actually realized.[120]

Forced labour was not the only tool that the early Soviet penal policies promoted as means of re-education. Another crucial aspect of this proclaimed drive towards the reformation of criminals was "cultural-educational work" (*kul'turno-prosvetitelnaia rabota*). Once again, the Bolsheviks were not the first to attempt to reform convicts through education: for instance, as mentioned above, the head of the GTU under the Provisional Government, Aleksandr Zhizhilenko, issued a circular introducing libraries in prisons, although the degree to which this circular was ever implemented is debatable. Officials of the GUMZ directed their efforts towards the promotion of basic literacy (*likvidatstsiia bezgramotnosti*) among convicts.[121] These measures were energetically pushed by party officials from early on and were intended to distinguish the Soviet penal system from its bourgeois counterparts. These cultural-educational works included the organization of prison and camp theatre troupes, schools and libraries, and the publication of prison newspapers and the like. Hundreds of prison and camp journals and newspapers were published from at least 1921, perhaps even earlier.[122] Material conditions did not allow all places of confinement to have a printed press. In some places "mural newspapers" (*stengazety*) were produced and exhibited on the walls of common spaces where prisoners could read them. Attempts to educate and inform inmates took place even in the early Soviet distant camps and prisons in Siberia, as the example of the oral newspaper in Tyumen correctional house mentioned in the previous chapter testifies.

Nikolai Krylenko, who in 1931 became the Commissar of Justice of the RSFSR, and then from 1936 would occupy the position of the Commissar of Justice of the USSR, campaigned to abandon the term "punishment" in favour of "measures of social defence". At first glance, it appears to be little more than a symbolic change: punishments did not disappear, they were just renamed. However, this terminological revision did reflect at least two substantial changes.

First, it demonstrated that despite the proclamations of a rupture with the "bourgeois tradition", early Bolshevik attempts to reform criminal justice

119 *Ibid.*, p. 209.
120 Estrin and Trakhterev, "Razvitie sovetskoi ispravitel'no-trudovoi politiki", p. 51.
121 "Vserossiskiii s'ezd rabotnikov penitentsiarnogo dela", p. 950.
122 Andrea Gullotta, "A New Perspective for Gulag Literature Studies: The Gulag Press", *Studi Slavistici*, 8 (2011), pp. 95–111.

were firmly connected to the positivist penological tradition: re-casting punishment as a "measure of social defence" was not a Bolshevik invention, but rather was part of the theoretical avant-garde of contemporary criminology. In 1936, American legal scholar Nathaniel Cantor wrote an overview of the "measures of social defence" as they were formulated by the various national schools of criminology. "The defence of society", Cantor wrote, employing the hygienist metaphor for crime that was so common at the time, "requires the introduction of preventive and hygienic measures which will destroy the germs of crime".[123] Cantor traced the idea of "measures of social defence" to Italian criminologist Enrico Ferri. Ferri, a student of positivist Italian criminologist and phrenologist Cesare Lombroso, developed the positivist tradition and recast punishment as "measures of social defence": thus, "preventive measures against the commission of future crimes becomes the dominant interest".[124] The Soviet version of these measures, as it was conceptualized by Krylenko, bore such close resemblance to Ferri's ideas that the old Bolshevik David Riazanov accused Krylenko of plagiarizing the Italian criminologist.[125] Cantor also observed that the Soviet Union had built its legislation on the foundations created by Ferri, and that only the Soviet Union and Cuba had fully embraced these positivist principles.[126]

The second consequence of this early recasting of punishment as a "measure of social defence", especially in combination with the introduction of the class principle, was that it laid the theoretical foundation for the possibility of repression when no crime had actually been committed. The first case of this occurred in the 1920s, with potential "counter-revolutionaries", and later, in the 1930s, large groups of people were persecuted in sweeping campaigns against "socially dangerous elements".[127] As James Ryan has remarked, the basic elements of the view of criminals and deviants as socially dangerous "contingents" that had to be removed from society did not originate in the

123 Nathaniel Cantor, "Measures of Social Defense", *Cornell Law Review*, 22:1 (1936), pp. 17–38, 18.
124 *Ibid.*, p. 20.
125 Ferri, who was initially a socialist, after World War I became a supporter of Mussolini; Riazanov said, in other words, that Krylenko was plagiarizing a fascist's view on crime. Ferri's project of making a Criminal Code, which developed the idea of social defence, was actually never ratified. See Estrin, "K voprosu o printsipakh postroeniia", p. 90.
126 Cantor, "Measures of Social Defense", pp. 26, 29.
127 On the 1930s campaigns, see David R. Shearer, "Elements Near and Alien: Passportization, Policing, and Identity in the Stalinist State, 1932–1952", *The Journal of Modern History*, 76:4 (2004), pp. 835–81 and Paul Hagenloh, *Stalin's Police: Public Order and Mass Repression in the USSR, 1926–1941* (Washington, DC: Woodrow Wilson Center Press; Johns Hopkins University Press, 2009).

police system in the 1930s, but were already expressed by high-ranking officials of the Commissariat of Justice as early as in 1918.[128]

The intensive experimentation of the 1920s did not yield a single dominant penal regime. The aspiration to make places of confinement self-sufficient was a continuous effort, but the agencies managing places of confinement were unable to achieve consistent results in this respect. Some of these penal institutions were organized along principles similar to those of the pre-revolutionary era, and they failed for similar reasons: mainly financial penury, the absence of competent instructing personnel for the prison workshops, and a lack of guards. Progressive policies were abandoned not only because of external pressures, as Peter Solomon has suggested, but also, to some extent, due to the material inability to adequately implement them.[129] This demise of the modern prison in the Soviet Union contributed to the growing use of camps as alternative places of confinement. In April 1928, Commissar of Justice Nikolai Ianson, Commissar of Internal Affairs Vladimir Tolmachev, and Deputy Head of the OGPU Genrikh Iagoda suggested that they "move away from the current places of confinement towards a system of concentration camps organized following the prototype of the OGPU camps".[130]

Inter-departmental struggles added to the disarray in the penal system. Critique of the more experimental punishments gained momentum in 1928, and the final demise of the Main Administration of Places of Confinement and its policies was marked by accusations that it belonged to the Right Opposition in 1929 and early 1930. Two officials of the People's Commissariat of Justice, Naum Lagovier and Iakov Perel', published a two-part article outlining the results of inspections of places of confinement by the public prosecutors.[131] According to them, the introduction of compulsory labour without deprivation of liberty was mainly spurred by the prosecutors,[132] while officials of the GUMZ failed to administer and inspect places of confinement, and did not properly instruct local prison administrators about the new priorities in the use of compulsory labour.[133] Lagovier and

---

128 James Ryan, "The Sacralization of Violence: Bolshevik Justifications for Violence and Terror during the Civil War", *Slavic Review*, 74:4 (2015), pp. 808–31, 829.

129 Solomon, "Soviet Penal Policy", p. 196.

130 Oleg Khlevniuk, "Prinuditel'nyi trud v ekonomike SSSR. 1929–1941", *Svobodnaia mysl'*, 13 (1993), pp. 73–84, 75.

131 Iakov Perel' and Naum Lagovier, "Pravyi uklon v karatel'noi politike", *Sovetskaia iustitsiia*, 3 (1930), pp. 14–17 and 4 (1930), pp. 14–17.

132 Perel' and Lagovier, "Pravyi uklon v karatel'noi politike", *Sovetskaia iustitsiia*, 3, p. 15.

133 Perel' and Lagovier, "Pravyi uklon v karatel'noi politike", *Sovetskaia iustitsiia*, 4, p. 16.

Perel' enumerated the "perversions" of the GUMZ officials: "unfounded pre-term release of socially dangerous and alien elements; authorization of leave for people who do not deserve this privilege; mechanical count of the workdays that sometimes turn out to be fictitious; payment and use of [inmates'] labour in a way that contradicts the class principles".[134] These accusations were so all-encompassing that it was, most likely, possible to use them against most officials within the penal system. Most such actions sought to alleviate prison overpopulation, which was rampant in 1929 even though a large number of convicts were released in 1927 thanks to the amnesty marking the tenth anniversary of the October revolution. The prosecutors found the qualifications, as well as the level of political awareness of the employees of local places of confinement, to be lamentable, and they considered many of their efforts to empty the prisons reprehensible. In 1928, the public prosecutors initiated 1,183 disciplinary and 537 criminal cases against guards and other officials.[135] Perel' and Lagovier suggested several measures to improve the situation, and promoted a leading role for the People's Commissariat of Justice in this prospective endeavour.

In 1930, Evsei Shirvindt, Head of the Main Administration of Places of Confinement, penned an article entitled "The Strengthening of the Class Struggle and Criminal Repression", perhaps in an attempt to mitigate the accusations made by Perel' and Lagovier.[136] In this article, he outlined the reasons why criminality would grow, rather than disappear, during the transition to socialism. In contradiction to his earlier writings, Shirvindt condoned both harsher punishments and capital punishment. If this was an attempt to protect the GUMZ, it was unsuccessful: Shirvindt and his agency faced more attacks. In 1931, Ivan Apeter, who since January 1931 had been head of the Main Administration of Corrective Labour Institutions of the Commissariat of Justice, condemned the policies of the Commissariat of Internal Affairs as "incorrect" and "liberal".[137] Apeter reiterated the accusations of Perel' and Lagovier: according to him, too, the policies of the Commissariat of Internal Affairs during the period when it was responsible for places of confinement undermined the purpose of incarceration and punishment: too many convicts were let out on parole (*uslovno-dosrochnoe*

134 *Ibid.*, pp. 14–15.
135 *Ibid.*
136 Shirvindt, "Obostrenie klassovoi bor'by i ugolovnaia repressiia".
137 Ivan Apeter, "Osnovnye printsipy ispravitel'no-trudovoi politiki NKIu i tipy mest lisheniia svobody i organov ispravitel'no-trudovykh rabot bez soderzhaniia pod strazhei: Tezisy k dokladu tov. Apetera na V soveshchanii rukovodiashchikh rabotnikov organov iustitsii kraev i oblastei RSFSR", *Sovetskaia iustitsiia*, 18 (1931), pp. 23–26.

osvobozhdenie), and many terms were significantly reduced.[138] Representatives of the Commissariat of Justice sought to weaken the authority of the People's Commissariat of Internal Affairs by presenting the policies of the Main Administration of Places of Confinement as "soft", not protective enough, and therefore dangerous. Their efforts in the struggle over places of confinement were not in vain. On 15 December 1930, the Commissariats of Internal Affairs of the Soviet republics were disbanded, and the Commissariat of Justice became the managing agency for all places of confinement that were previously under the jurisdiction of the GUMZ.

The places of confinement operated by the GUMZ were by then a lost cause. Departure from the previous policies was clear. In May 1929, the Politburo approved the use of the mass forced labour of inmates serving terms longer than three years in the already existing labour camps of the OGPU around Ukhta and Indigo.[139] In June, the Politburo commission that was in charge of planning the labour camps system suggested that new camps would have to be created in the distant regions of the Soviet Union, especially in Ukhta, and that the inmates would have to remain in the vicinity of the camps even upon release.[140] Geographical distance and the harsh climate were intended to exacerbate the punishment, and the freedom of movement of ex-convicts was limited in order to keep them isolated, even after they had served their sentences. On 11 July of the same year, the Council of People's Commissars, the highest executive authority in the Soviet Union, issued a decree on the use of convict labour in camps controlled by the OGPU that would shape the Soviet labour camp system for decades to come. The OGPU was encouraged to build more camps in other distant regions, and all convicts serving terms of more than three years came under its jurisdiction.[141] Very little is known about the Commissariat of Justice's system of places of confinement for those serving terms shorter than three years; this system existed in 1929–1934, and to date no academic research has explored the conditions there.

Conclusion

In his 1920 treatise on *The Politics and Economics of the Transition Period*, Nikolai Bukharin wrote: "In a classless, stateless communist society where,

138 *Ibid.*, p. 24.
139 Kokurin and Petrov, *GULAG*, document nos. 12 and 13.
140 *Ibid.*, document no. 15.
141 *Ibid.*, document no. 16.

in place of external discipline, there will be the simple inclination to work on the part of the normal social being, external norms of human behaviour will become meaningless. Coercion, in any form whatsoever, will disappear once and for all".[142] Made at the height of war communism, this promise, predictably, remained unfulfilled as the war ended. The classless, stateless society remained out of reach, and coercion continued to be the state's main instrument for reordering society in accordance with the new principles. Despite all the Bolsheviks' attempts to break with the burden of the past, early Soviet criminal policy bore a significant resemblance to the tsarist penal framework, and the shape of the camp system as it was built at the end of 1920s was connected not only to ideological pressures and perceived political imperatives, but also to the failures of these experiments in the 1920s on a practical level.

Examining criminological conceptions, Chekist terror, and the policy of compulsory labour within the same analytical field might seem a peculiar choice. I hope, nevertheless, to have demonstrated that they all resonated with "the Soviet state's constant devotion to the sculpting of its raw, human material" and placed strong emphasis on the role of coercion in Soviet society.[143] In the late 1920s, political change, along with the failure to implement any sustainable rehabilitative policies and disillusionment in some of the milder measures, such as non-custodial compulsory labour, brought this early progressive experimentation to a halt. Some of the penological ideas about the rehabilitative capacity of labour were taken up by writers, journalists, and Marxist theorists and reworked into the concept of "*perekovka*", or the re-forging of recidivists through labour. This concept, widely popularized in the 1934 book *The White Sea Canal* ("*Belomoro-Baltiiskii kanal imeni Stalina*"), served as a smokescreen that obfuscated the actual conditions of forced labourers during the construction of the White Sea Canal, while promoting the socialist methods of reforming deviant individuals and society.[144] Steven Barnes, who has analysed in detail the precise ways in which this book whitewashed the camp conditions, has called this publication "something of an ideal-type presentation of early Stalinist

---

142 Bukharin, *The Politics and Economics of the Transition Period*, p. 166.
143 Peter Holquist, "State Violence as Technique: The Logic of Violence in Soviet Totalitarianism", in David L. Hoffmann (ed.), *Stalinism: The Essential Readings* (Malden, MA: Blackwell, 2003), pp. 127–58, 138.
144 Published in English as Maxim Gorky, Leopold Leonidovich Auerbach, and Semen Georgievich Firin, *The White Sea Canal: Being an Account of the Construction of the New Canal between the White Sea and the Baltic Sea* (London: John Lane, 1935).

penal ideology".[145] The concept of *perekovka* proved to be captivating and convincing for many external observers, especially intellectuals, yet it remained a concept rather than an organizational principle of the labour camps.[146] To put it simply, those who theorized *perekovka* and those who ran the camps were two distinct groups who, socially, had little in common: the former were the well-read and articulate "engineers of the human soul", excellently trained in Marxist theory, while the camps, especially early on, were run largely by uneducated people who had mainly received their experience of socialist discipline in the military, often in combat, and relied on violence as a disciplining measure.[147]

Moreover, even in theory, *perekovka* applied chiefly to members of the working class who committed non-political crimes, while the potential for the rehabilitation of "counter-revolutionaries" was rarely mentioned, if at all. Penologists were preoccupied primarily with common criminals and stressed that their corrigibility depended on their social environment. High-ranking Chekists, in the meantime, did not consider political criminals to be capable of reform.[148]

Finally, I would like to return to the issue of local violent practices and the state sanctions thereof. Even at the discursive level, the highest-ranking Bolsheviks did little to discourage violence as long as it was applied in a manner that conformed to the goals of the revolution, most broadly defined. Local violent practices were not suppressed by the state, but rather taken up and spread more widely. The leaders indeed supported local outbursts of violence as long as they were directed against alleged counter-revolutionaries, which broadened the ranks of agents of repression. In December 1917, Lenin wrote a piece entitled "How to Organize Competition?", in which he appealed to the initiative of the proletarians and poorer peasants in the fight against enemies of the revolution:

145 Steven A. Barnes, *Death and Redemption: The Gulag and the Shaping of Soviet Society* (Princeton, NJ, Oxford: Princeton University Press, 2011).

146 Studies of this concept belong to literary studies rather than to the history of the Gulag. For an analysis of the notion of the "criminal" within the concept of *perekovka*, see Anne Hartmann, "Concepts of the Criminal in the Discourse of 'Perekovka'", in Riccardo Nicolosi and Anne Hartmann (eds), *Born to Be Criminal: The Discourse on Criminality and the Practice of Punishment in Late Imperial Russia and Early Soviet Union. Interdisciplinary Approaches* (Bielefeld: transcript, 2017), pp. 167–96.

147 For instance, in 1921, only 1.03 per cent of Chekists had received higher education, while 57.3 per cent of 49,995 employees of the *Vecheka* had only received elementary education; Litvin, *Krasnyi i belyi terror*, p. 73.

148 As an example of the Chekist understanding of political crimes, see Latsis, *Dva goda borby na vnutrennem fronte*, pp. 11–16.

Thousands of practical forms and methods of accounting and controlling the rich, the rogues and the idlers must be devised and put to a practical test by the communes themselves, by small units in town and country. Variety is a guarantee of effectiveness here, a pledge of success in achieving the single common aim – to clean the land of Russia of all vermin, of fleas-the rogues, of bugs-the rich, and so on and so forth. In one place half a score of rich, a dozen rogues, half a dozen workers who shirk their work [...] will be put in prison. In another place they will be put to cleaning latrines. In a third place they will be provided with "yellow tickets" after they have served their time, so that everyone shall keep an eye on them, as harmful persons, until they reform. In a fourth place, one out of every ten idlers will be shot on the spot. In a fifth place mixed methods may be adopted, and by probational release, for example, the rich, the bourgeois intellectuals, the rogues and rowdies who are corrigible will be given an opportunity to reform quickly. The more variety there will be, the better and richer will be our general experience, the more certain and rapid will be the success of socialism, and the easier will it be for practice to devise – for only practice can devise – the best methods and means of struggle.[149]

Here, Lenin condones violence against enemies of the revolution, but also expresses rare optimism concerning their corrigibility. He mobilizes the hygienic, almost medical, metaphors that were shared by progressive penologists and Chekists alike. As James Ryan has underlined, "the discussion of crime and counterrevolution through medicalized language was a significant feature of Bolshevik discourse and its justification of violence and repression".[150] The same metaphor of vermin and purification was used in the 1930s: Gorky's image of society, for instance, was haunted by vermin – rats, mice, lice, and flees – and he indulged "freely in the fantasies of extermination".[151] But perhaps most telling is the fact that this work of Lenin was not published when he wrote it, neither in 1917 nor in the following years. It would be twelve years before it first appeared in the main Soviet newspaper, *Pravda*, on 20 January 1929, exactly as the Soviet leadership had begun the final stage of the crackdown on those labelled as wealthier peasants, the "*kulaks*". This example illustrates how Bolshevik

149 Vladimir Lenin, "How to Organize Competition?", *Pravda*, no. 17, 20 January 1929, available at: https://www.marxists.org/archive/lenin/works/1917/dec/25.htm, last accessed 2 July 2022.
150 Ryan, "The Sacralization of Violence", pp. 827–28.
151 Hartmann, "Concepts of the Criminal in the Discourse of 'Perekovka'", p. 186.

discursive measures and repressive practices shaped by the revolutionary experience could be taken up again to serve the Stalinist goals of subsuming the peasantry into the socialist order, but also how the regime sought to enrol wider groups of population to wage its repressive policies.

5 "Special Settlements" and the Making of the Gulag, 1929–1934

Abstract

This chapter argues that the building of the large-scale system of the camps of the Gulag first relied on the creation – in the course of collectivization – of a system of settlements for deported peasants. It discusses in detail the diverse and changing uses of coerced labour of deportees at various sites in Western Siberia. Building on the discussions in previous chapters, it offers a comparative analysis of the politics of forced displacement in the Russian empire and the Soviet Union; it also discusses how "special settlements" served to form a pool of highly mobile disenfranchised labourers who could be deployed in industrialization. Moreover, forced labour was also used to create an elusive perspective for the deportees to be reintegrated into Soviet society.

Keywords: special settlements, Soviet Union, Gulag, forced labour, industrialization, Western Siberia

Repressive policies related to industrialization and forced collectivization profoundly changed both the countryside and the urban areas of the Soviet Union. The shift towards intensifying repression in peasantry-related policies began in 1927 and by 1930 led to the emergence of a new type of repressive institution: the "special settlements".[1] These settlements became a crucial instrument for crushing peasant resistance and consolidating Soviet power in the countryside. The political police played the chief role in this process, as they were responsible for the mass deportations of peasants to these settlements and, later, for use of the deportees' labour. The functions of the

---

[1] I place the term "special settlements" in quotation marks to underline its nature as a Soviet euphemism intended to mask the punitive nature of these settlements. In the following pages, however, for the reader's convenience the quotation marks are omitted.

Popova, Zhanna: *Coerced Labour, Forced Displacement, and the Soviet Gulag, 1880s-1930s*. Amsterdam: Amsterdam University Press, 2024
DOI: 10.5117/9789048560356_CH05

political police expanded during these years, and the number of police staff grew. Collectivization and the installation of these settlements also marked a shift towards an unprecedented use of forced displacement and forced labour, and were directly connected with the establishment and growth of the Gulag as a whole. Pressures to fulfil the first Five-Year Plan, launched in 1928, and urges to "secure" the countryside spurred these repressive policies that the Soviet leadership deemed necessary for the regime's survival.

In a January 1933 speech addressed to the plenum of the Central Committee, Joseph Stalin announced that the goals of the first Five-Year Plan had been accomplished, and that socialism had been victorious.[2] In July 1934, policing was reorganized, and the All-Union People's Commissariat of Internal Affairs (the NKVD) was created. It was controlled by Genrikh Iagoda, who, as mentioned in the previous chapter, had already become the de facto chief of the OGPU. The OGPU was integrated within the NKVD, and Iagoda came to enjoy even vaster powers of policing and repression. All institutions of confinement in the Soviet Union were brought under the jurisdiction of the NKVD, which became the chief implementer of the repressive policies distinctive of Stalinism.[3]

This chapter discusses the developments that preceded this consolidation of power: the explosive growth of the Soviet repressive system during the years of breakneck industrialization. This is an investigation of a particular repressive institution, the special settlements. The emergence and spread of the special settlements marked both a quantitative and a qualitative rupture in the uses of forced displacement and coerced labour. These colonies for deported peasants were constructed in distant areas of the Soviet Union starting in 1930, in the process of "dekulakization" that persecuted wealthier peasants as "class enemies" and which intended to "liquidate the *kulaks* as a class". Dekulakization, a particularly violent part of the collectivization of agriculture, had the goal of transforming the processes of agricultural production, destroying the traditional peasant way of life, and crushing peasant resistance against Soviet policies. As noted by Russian historian Andrei Sokolov, the establishment of collective farms (*kolkhozes* and *sovkhozes*) expanded the use of coercion in agricultural production, effectively tying peasants to these farms.[4]

---

2   I.V. Stalin, "Itogi pervoi piatiletki: Doklad na ob'edinennom plenume TsK i TsKK VKP(b) 7 ianvaria 1933", in I.V. Stalin, *Sochineniia. Tom 13* (Moscow: Gosudarstvennoe izdatel'stvo politicheskoi literatury, 1951), pp. 161–215.

3   For more on these developments, see David R. Shearer and Vladimir Khaustov, *Stalin and the Lubianka: A Documentary History of the Political Police and Security Organs in the Soviet Union, 1922–1953* (New Haven, CT: Yale University Press, 2014), pp. 159–70.

4   Andrei Sokolov, "Prinuzhdenie k trudu v sovetskoi ekonomike, 1930-e – seredina 1950-kh", in Leonid Borodkin, Pol Gregori [Paul R. Gregory], and Oleg Khlevniuk (eds), *Gulag: Ekonomika*

The focus of the state and party leadership on forced displacement as a repressive tool that complemented the use of forced labour crystallized during this time. During the revolution and in its aftermath, the Bolsheviks, preoccupied with the consolidation of power rather than expansion and the exploitation of resources, mobilized the practice of forced displacement relatively sparingly. With the installation of the "special settlements", however, Soviet authorities launched a campaign of deportations that dwarfed the tsarist exile. The regime in these settlements was distinct from that of the "corrective labour camps" that constituted the other, better known, part of the Gulag. The settlements generally had no armed guards and no barbed wire, and the settlers' labour was coerced but not forced with the threat of direct violence.[5] These settlements embodied the Soviet agenda of forced colonization and demonstrated the ever-growing reliance on coerced labour.

Compared to camps, the emblematic punitive institutions of the Gulag, special settlements have remained a relatively under-studied part of the Stalinist architecture of repression. Numerous collections of documents were published in Russian in the 1990s and early 2000s, but the interest of researchers, with several notable exceptions, has been rather limited.[6] In

---

prinuditel'nogo truda (Moscow: ROSSPEN, 2005), pp. 17–66, 28–29.

5   Later, especially during the war, the use of physical coercion in the settlements intensified, and life there came increasingly to resemble the camp regime. This concerned especially those mobilized as part of the *Trudarmiia*, or "labour army". In some cases, the conditions of the settlers were worse than those of camp inmates. See Viktor Berdinskikh, *Spetsposelentsy: Politicheskaia ssylka narodov Sovetskoi Rossii* (Moscow: Novoe literaturnoe obozrenie, 2005 [Kirov, 2003]), pp. 389–444.

6   The present analysis relies primarily on these rich published sources. Archival documents on collectivization were published in Russian as Viktor Petrovich Danilov, Roberta Manning, and Lynne Viola (eds), *Tragediia sovetskoi derevni: Kollektivizatsiia i raskulachivanie. Dokumenty i materialy, 1927–1939*, 5 vols (Moscow: ROSSPEN, 1999) and N.N. Pokrovskii, V.P. Danilov, S.A. Krasil'nikov, and Lynne Viola (eds), *Politbiuro i krestianstvo: Vysylka, spetsposelenie. 1930–1940*, 2 vols (Moscow: ROSSPEN, 2005, 2006). Documentation on the conditions of the special settlements was also published in volume 5 of the seven-volume *Istoriia stalinskogo Gulaga* (T.V. Tsarevskaia-Diakina (ed.), *Istoriia stalinskogo Gulaga. Konets 1920-kh – pervaia polovina 1950-kh godov*, vol 5. *Spetspereselentsy v SSSR* (Moscow: ROSSPEN, 2004). English-language resources are more limited, but nevertheless extensive, and I refer to the document collections throughout the text: when the possibility presented itself, I used the published English-language translations of the document extracts. The Western Siberian case of special settlements is perhaps the best studied, especially thanks to the efforts of collections and research entertained over the years by Sergei Krasil'nikov and his collaborators; in addition to the outstanding academic research by these Siberian scholars to whose work I continually refer, a scholar like myself can also profit from multi-volume annotated publications of sources from the local archives, especially the four-volume collection S.A. Krasil'nikov *et al.* (eds), *Spetspereselentsy v Zapadnoi Sibiri*, 4 vols (Novosibirsk: EKOR, 1992, 1993, 1994, 1996).

Russian, major research into this topic was done mostly in the early 2000s, with several fundamental volumes published within a short timeframe.[7] In English, the seminal work of Lynne Viola continues to be the fundamental reference on the topic.[8]

Still today interrelations between the settlements and the camps remain to be systematically researched. Attempts to evaluate the connections between forced collectivization and the growth of the camp system have already been made, and this chapter develops further this line of inquiry.[9] As such scope is extremely wide, I focus here on the case of Western Siberia to demonstrate the local dynamics of this process. Working with the Western Siberian material, I discuss the use of settlers' forced labour, some similarities and differences between the conditions in the camps and in the settlements, as well as continuities and ruptures between the tsarist exile and the Stalinist peasant deportations.

The first half of the 1930s was the formative period of the Gulag system. A focus on the special settlements during this time helps to highlight how political repression attained an unprecedentedly mass scale and an extreme level of violence, and how inextricably the use of forced displacement and coerced labour were intertwined within the Soviet project of colonization and industrialization. As noted by the chief Russian expert on the history of the Gulag, Oleg Khlevniuk, the decision to create a network of self-supporting camps "could have remained just another attempt to reorganize the penitentiary system had it not coincided with events that changed the course of Soviet history" – namely, forced collectivization and dekulakization.[10] During this time, various repressive institutions sprawled throughout the Soviet Union in both urban and rural areas, and acquired unprecedented importance as tools of governance, population control, and extraction of resources.

In the early projects of the penal settlements, the agenda to forcefully colonize the distant, uninhabited parts of the Soviet Union was coupled with

7   Berdinskikh, *Spetsposelentsy*; N.F. Bugai, *L. Beria – I. Stalinu: "Soglasno Vashemu ukazaniiu…"* (Moscow: AIRO-XX, 1995); P.M. Polian, *Ne po svoei vole… Istoriia i geografiia prinuditel'nykh migratsii v SSSR* (Moscow: OGI – Memorial, 2001), V.N. Zemskov, *Spetsposelentsy v SSSR, 1930–1960* (Moscow: Nauka, 2003), and S.A. Krasil'nikov, *Serp i molokh: Krestianskaia ssylka v Zapadnoi Sibiri v 1930-e gody* (Moscow: ROSSPEN, 2009). For an English-language review of some of these volumes, see Oxana Klimkova, "Special Settlements in Soviet Russia in the 1930s–50s", *Kritika: Explorations in Russian and Eurasian History*, 8:1 (2007), pp. 105–39.
8   Lynne Viola, *The Unknown Gulag: The Lost World of Stalin's Special Settlements* (Oxford: Oxford University Press, 2007).
9   For an early analysis that relied on the newly available archival sources, see Scherer and Jakobson, "The Collectivisation of Agriculture".
10   Oleg Khlevniuk, *The History of the Gulag: From Collectivization to the Great Terror* (New Haven, CT: Yale University Press, 2004), p. 9.

some of the progressive ideas of the 1920s. An aversion to confinement, the blurring of borders between penal institutions and society at large, as well as proposals for "freer" rehabilitation through labour were present in the early documents. In a 12 April 1930 message to some of the highest-ranking Soviet officials, Genrikh Iagoda proposed his vision of the development of the Soviet penal system:

> The question of the camps must be resolved from a different perspective. Today the camp is a mere gathering of inmates, whose labour we use without any prospects for either the inmates or ourselves. It is essential to make labour more voluntary by giving the inmates more freedom after work. We have to convert the camps into colonization settlements without waiting for the conclusion of prison terms. Reducing a sentence for good behavior, out of philanthropic impulse, is unacceptable and often quite harmful. This also gives the wrong impression that the inmate has been rehabilitated and a hypocritical notion of good behavior, which may be suitable for bourgeois states, but not for us. The whole purpose of transferring the inmates to us is to liquidate prisons. It is clear that, under the existing system, their liquidation will take many years, because a camp per se is worse than prison. We have to colonize the North in the shortest possible time.[11]

In Iagoda's proposal, both the work that the settlers would have to perform during their work days and their allegedly "freer" labour after the end of the shift were intended to work for the overarching goal of colonization. It was supposed to be achieved through the combination of forced displacement, forced labour on a large scale, centrally coordinated projects, and the continuous presence of convicts and deportees in these distant regions, assured by a developed policing infrastructure. This project was not realized: instead of merging the camps with the penal settlements, the Bolshevik leadership opted for the creation of two distinct, yet interconnected networks of repressive institutions: labour camps and special settlements.

Installation of the special settlements

The relationship of the Bolshevik authorities with the peasantry in the aftermath of the revolution was, to put it mildly, strained: the ruthless grain

11   *Ibid.*, p. 23.

requisitions of the civil war and the attempts of the Bolsheviks to enlist the poorer peasants as their main allies in the villages were met with resistance from large parts of the peasantry.[12] State policies became outright hostile by the end of the 1920s. After the years of the New Economic Policy, which allowed small-scale entrepreneurship and commerce, starting in 1928 it was repression that came to define the relationship between the Soviet authorities and the peasantry.[13] A campaign of collectivization of agriculture, aimed at the aggregation of cultivated land in the hands of the state and peasant collectives, rather than private peasant households, was launched in 1928 to support the accelerated industrial production of the first Five-Year Plan. Collectivization was aimed at the profound reorganization of Soviet agriculture, as the collective farms were expected to be more efficient than smaller private producers, thereby freeing up workers from agriculture to work in industry. The Communists used it to secured the countryside to establish a tighter control over grain extraction.

Stalin's desire to control the grain supply meant that the political leadership started to use increasingly violent measures to "squeeze" grain from the peasantry. The grain procurement crisis of the autumn and winter of 1927–1928 was mainly interpreted by the party leadership in political terms, and used as a pretext for launching a repressive campaign against the grain traders.[14] Not only was violation of the trade regulations criminalized, but also the withholding of goods from the market.[15] This violent advance against the peasantry, however, was not rolled out without opposition within the party.

After the critique of this campaign by Nikolai Bukharin and other members of the Right opposition during the July 1928 Central Committee plenum, some compromises were made, and the dominant group promised a return to the regular, non-extraordinary grain requisition system. However, these compromises were only temporary. The problems with the grain supply persisted throughout the second half of 1928, and the Right opposition was losing political power. In the spring of 1929, another tool was added

12   Alessandro Stanziani, "La gestion des approvisionnements et la restauration de la gosudarstvennost'. Le Narkomprod, l'arm'ee et les paysans (1918–1921)", *Cahiers du monde russe*, 38:1–2 (1997), pp. 83–116.

13   Sheila Fitzpatrick, *Stalin's Peasants: Resistance and Survival in the Russian Village after Collectivization* (Oxford: Oxford University Press, 1996), pp. 24–28.

14   Lynne Viola, V.P. Danilov, N.A. Ivnitskii, and Denis Kozlov (eds), *The War against the Peasantry, 1927–1930: The Tragedy of the Soviet Countryside* (New Haven, CT: Yale University Press, 2005), p. 18.

15   These were Articles 105 and 107 of the Criminal Code, see *ibid.*, p. 58.

to the array of extraordinary measures: Article 61 of the Criminal Code was now used against the peasants. The 1929 edition of this article implied that the refusal to fulfil one's obligatory services to the state in terms of the compulsory labour policy or tax payments (*povinnosti, obshchegosu-darstvennye zadaniia ili proizvodstvo rabot*) entailed a fine of up to five times the monetary equivalent of the service for first-time offenders, and the deprivation of freedom and "corrective labour works" for a term of up to one year for second-time offenders.[16] These fines came to be known as *piatikratka*, which can be roughly translated as "five-fold [payment]". In order to realize this new punitive measure, Soviet authorities exploited power relations and conflicts in the countryside for their own profit and enrolled poorer peasants to conduct surveillance of and control over other inhabitants of the villages. The view of collectivization and dekulakization held by Stalin and his closest circle was radical: they envisioned it to be, as Molotov called it in a telegram to Stalin, "a tumultuous, mass movement" that did not necessitate much planning or administrative oversight.[17]

These extraordinary repressive measures sowed discontent among the peasants and elicited strong resistance, but they also antagonized the most disadvantaged groups of villagers against their better-off neighbours, turning social conflicts into political ones, and giving local party activists carte blanche against those they labelled as *kulaks*.[18]

In 1929, the regime started to identify *kulaks* as the chief class enemies. The goal of dekulakization, which was rolled out simultaneously with collectivization, was the confiscation of land and other property from wealthier peasants, as well as the repression of political opponents. Some of the *kulaks* actively protected their property, either with weapons or by hiding it, or, on the contrary, they sabotaged the grain requisitions by wasting their grain stock (a resistance practice known as *razbazarivanie*).[19]

In December 1929, Stalin and Iagoda vehemently argued that *kulak* resistance was intensifying, and thus posed a threat to collectivization, and stated that the "liquidation of kulaks as a class" was the only response

16   S.A. Papkov, *Obyknovennyi terror: Politika stalinizma v Sibiri* (Moscow: ROSSPEN, 2012), p. 45.

17   Viola *et al.*, *The War against the Peasantry*, p. 171.

18   The definition of a *kulak* was extremely vague and could be used to persecute an ever-widening group of people. The borders between the definitions of poor, middle, and well-off peasants were largely arbitrarily constructed by the central authorities, without much attention to the local contexts, and shifted depending on the political situation.

19   For more on peasant resistance, see Lynne Viola, *Peasant Rebels under Stalin: Collectivization and the Culture of Peasant Resistance* (Oxford: Oxford University Press, 1999).

to this threat.[20] Combined with their previous agitation among the poorer peasants, these statements prompted the start of the "elemental" (*stikhiinaia*), hectic phase of dekulakization. Finally, on 30 January 1930, the Politburo issued a decree "On Measures for the Liquidation of Kulak Farms in the Areas of Wholesale Collectivization" that prescribed the dekulakization procedure. It differentiated the repression of *kulaks* by dividing them into three categories:

A. Category 1 – immediately liquidate the counterrevolutionary *kulak aktiv* [core militant group] elements by incarcerating them in concentration camps, not stopping at the death penalty for organizers of terrorist acts, counterrevolutionary disturbances, and insurrectionist organizations;
B. Category 2 should comprise the remaining elements of the *kulak aktiv*, especially the richest *kulaks* and quasi-landowners, who are to be exiled to remote localities of the USSR and, within the borders of a given region, to remote areas of the region;
C. Category 3 consists of *kulaks* who are left within the borders of the district [*raion*]; they are to be resettled on new land plots allotted to them outside collective farms.[21]

By the time this decree was issued, dekulakization in the regions had already acquired its own logic. Reports from the regions decried a plethora of abuses: dekulakization of Red Army soldiers' families and the families of poor and middle peasants; confiscation of goods that were then never handed over to the authorities, but appropriated by party activists and local officials; deportations that were unauthorized by the OGPU; direct violence and other atrocities.[22] "Elemental" dekulakization meant that in many places, women, children, and the elderly were thrown out of their homes during the night, and stripped of all their possessions, including bedding and the most basic household items.

Those labelled as *kulaks* were deported to the special settlements. Some deportees were settled among the locals in already existing villages, but many of them were locations in the distant areas of the Soviet Union that did not have any infrastructure or even lodgings.[23] These settlements were

20 Viola *et al.*, *The War against the Peasantry*, pp. 176–78.
21 *Ibid.*, pp. 228–29.
22 *Ibid.*, p. 212.
23 V.P. Danilov and S.A. Krasil'nikov (eds), *Spetspereselentsy v Zapadnoi Sibiri: 1930–vesna 1931 g.* (Novosibirsk: EKOR, 1992), p. 176.

overseen by the commandants (*komendant*), who controlled the deportees' movements. On paper, the shape of the special settlements was described by the central authorities in great detail, and it was reflected in the multiple circulars of the OGPU and the Council of People's Commissars. The settlements were supposed to be small, with thirty to fifty households, but in practice they could include more than one hundred households, and in some cases more than five hundred. The main representative of power in the special settlements was a commandant. The deportees were stripped of their political rights. They were obliged to confirm their presence in the settlement at the commandant's office (*komendatura*) every week, and were not allowed to leave the settlements without special permission, even for short trips. The regime in the settlements was not as strict as in the camps, but it was nevertheless a coercive, limiting regime that was intended to prevent a restoration of the traditional peasant way of life.

Peasant deportations began in January 1930, and by 1932 as many as 1,317,022 people found themselves in settlements. In 1939, before the start of a new wave of deportations, the number of special settlers had decreased to 938,552.[24] In the case of Western Siberia, at the beginning of March 1930, the local authorities "identified" around fifty thousand *kulak* households that were supposed to be displaced within the region.[25] In the typical fashion of Stalinist repression, central authorities set the "quota" for the deportations, aiming for the forced displacement of twenty-five thousand households. Eager to show their vigilance against the *kulaks*, regional authorities increased this quota to thirty thousand households.[26]

During these operations, whole families were deported by the political police – the OGPU. Escorted by soldiers with fixed bayonets, these families had to leave most of their belongings behind, board the trains in cattle cars, and hope to survive the unknown. Their homes and land, as well as any savings exceeding 500 rubles, were confiscated.[27] These peasant families were sometimes displaced within the same region (this was especially typical in Western Siberia), but more often had to endure much longer transits. Transportation was one of the most gruesome parts of the deportation experience. Two main destinations of these peasant deportations were the Northern European part of Russia and Siberia. Colonization of these regions

24 Viktor Zemskov, "Spetsposelentsy (po dokumentatsii NKVD–MVD SSSR)", *Sotsiologicheskie issledovaniia*, 11 (1990), pp. 3–17, 6.
25 Danilov and Krasil'nikov, *Spetspereselentsy v Zapadnoi Sibiri: 1930–vesna 1931 g.*, pp. 50–51.
26 *Ibid.*, p. 89.
27 Viola *et al.*, *The War against the Peasantry*, p. 209.

was the proclaimed goal, but there was no coordinated plan for such an endeavour. Local authorities, who were charged with providing food, work, and lodging for the settlers, were often criminally unprepared. The fact that the deportees often found themselves in extremely remote areas that lacked any infrastructural connections suggests that the logic of preventing escapes might have played a bigger role than the colonization agenda when the choice of destinations had been made. Indeed, many settlements were abandoned as soon as the deportees were allowed to leave.

In the administrative chaos of the displacements, the peasants could find themselves in unfamiliar regions, often in freezing temperatures, without food or adequate housing.[28] In their reports, official inspectors found the degree of neglect exhibited by the local authorities towards the settlers shocking. Labour played an ambivalent role in this early period: both the lack of an occupation and forced labour could have catastrophic results. Forced labour was physically exhausting and generally performed with the most primitive instruments, if any. Not everywhere were settlers forced to work; in some settlements, they ended up unemployed and impoverished, because the local administrators did not find any work for them. In others, like in the settlements of Chainskoe (*Chainskaia komendatura*) in the Tomsk region of Western Siberia, adult male settlers were forced to work in the timber industry throughout the summer of 1930, and therefore could not build any houses for their families; as the winter advanced, people found themselves without any shelter, and mortality rates among settlers in Chainskoe soared.[29] Settlers were supposed to provide two months' worth of food for themselves, but many households that had previously had to pay the five-fold fines for the refusal to provide grain (*piatikratka*) were already too impoverished to provide such supplies.[30]

Neglect, administrative disarray, harsh climatic conditions, and abuses by the political police and local activists resulted in extremely high levels of mortality among the deportees. The most vulnerable, children and the

---

28   These cases of criminal neglect and administrative dysfunction that led to catastrophes were not limited to the first year of mass deportations. In 1933, thousands of "alien elements" were rounded up in Moscow and Leningrad following the passportization campaign, and then deported to the remote island of Nazino in Western Siberia. Once again, these deportees included children, pregnant women, and the elderly. More than six thousand people found themselves without food, shelter, or medication. Within a month, more than one quarter had died. See a collection of published documents: S.A. Krasil'nikov (ed.), *Iz istorii zemli Tomskoi. 1933 g. Nazinskaia tragediia* (Tomsk: Volodei, 2002). For an English-language account, see Nicolas Werth, *Cannibal Island: Death in a Siberian Gulag* (Princeton, NJ: Princeton University Press, 2007).

29   Krasil'nikov, *Serp i molokh*, p. 247.

30   Danilov and Krasil'nikov, *Spetspereselentsy v Zapadnoi Sibiri:1930–vesna 1931 g.*, p. 91.

elderly, suffered especially, and many succumbed to illness and exhaustion already during transit. Among those who survived deportation, many tried to flee the settlements. The rates of escape were high, especially during the first months and even years. From May to September 1930, more than four thousand families out of fourteen thousand deported to Western Siberia abandoned the settlements.[31]

At the onset of the deportations, the political police were responsible only for the arrest and transportation of the deported families, while responsibility for the organization of the special settlements and for overseeing the settlers' forced labour was placed on the local authorities. However, as the latter continually failed to provide for the settlers, and the settlements descended further into chaos, the central government allocated more responsibility over the special settlements to the OGPU. In early March 1930, the head of the Tomsk region decried the situation in a letter to the secretary of the Siberian party commission Robert Eikhe. He stated that there were five thousand deportees in the district, while the central authorities had only provided three hundred rations. He was also concerned about security issues: in the camp subdivisions of the district, seven thousand people were forced to work, but the camps lacked guards and this role was performed by the inmates themselves. Several thousand suspected *kulak* families had relocated themselves within the district in order to avoid deportation.[32] In May 1930, a special regional committee was organized in Siberia to oversee and manage the special settlements and direct the use of the deportees' labour.[33] By June, it was clear that the administration of the settlements was catastrophic.[34] Starting from August 1931, the OGPU became fully charged with the colonization of the northern part of Western Siberia, the Narym region, instead of the local economic agencies.[35] This also led to a steep growth in OGPU staff numbers. For instance, the party cell of the OGPU of Tomsk district grew from fifty-nine people in May 1929 to eighty-nine people in May 1930.[36]

By the end of 1931, the Council of People's Commissars had developed a more detailed plan for the colonization of the northern region Narym, which stated that the region had to become agriculturally self-sufficient and

31 Krasil'nikov, *Serp i molokh*, p. 247.
32 Danilov and Krasil'nikov, *Spetspereselentsy v Zapadnoi Sibiri: 1930–vesna 1931 g.*, p. 56.
33 *Ibid.*, p. 172.
34 *Ibid.*, p. 173.
35 Krasil'nikov, *Serp i molokh*, p. 250.
36 A.G. Tepliakov, *Mashina terrora: OGPU-NKVD Sibiri v 1929–1941 gg.* (Moscow: AIRO-XXI, 2008), p. 32.

should end all import of grain, fodder, and vegetables by the end of 1933.[37] This document prescribed that at least twenty-five thousand former *kulaks* had to perform agricultural labour, while another sixty thousand were to be employed in the timber industry. Overall, according to the decree, there were more than 215,000 special settlers in the region. Local economic agencies remained in charge of the day-to-day administration of the coerced deported labourers, but the secret police had obtained an unprecedented degree of control over the distribution of adult settlers to various employers. The 15 April 1932 report regarding the fulfilment of this plan by the Narym commission, however, once again decried a host of administrative failures and abuses. The network of *komendaturas* that were supposed to conduct surveillance the settlers was seriously understaffed, more than half of the supplies necessary for the settlers to start the agricultural season, mainly seeds and horses, was not delivered, and only one third of the lodgings planned were actually constructed.[38]

The deportation campaign was disastrous from the very beginning, even from the point of view of the authorities who ordered and orchestrated it. The deportees' labour could rarely be used for productive agricultural work in the hostile northern lands, escape was extremely common, and violence was ubiquitous. The 25 April 1930 report of the OGPU plenipotentiary in Siberia stated that many local activists viewed the deportations as the first step towards the physical destruction of the *kulaks*. This OGPU plenipotentiary, following Stalin's speech that interpreted the atrocities committed against the peasantry in the early 1930 as local activists being "dizzy with success", labelled such actions as "excesses and perversions" (*peregiby i izvrashcheniia*), and denied the systemic violence of dekulakization.[39]

The modus operandi of the secret police itself was, however, overwhelmingly violent, as *kulak* families were treated as enemies of the regime. The extreme violence of the dekulakization campaign, paired with the fact that the authorities were neither willing nor able to prevent the abuses committed by the activists, destroyed many peasant families even before they were deported. If the deportees managed to arrive at the settlements, they were often exhausted, undernourished, and unprepared for everyday

37 The Council of People's Commissars' decree from 28 December 1931 "O khoziaistvennom ustroistve spetsposeletstev v Narymskom krae", published in Pokrovskii *et al.*, *Politbiuro i krestianstvo*, vol. 1, pp. 456–60.

38 Danilov and Krasil'nikov, *Spetspereselentsy v Zapadnoi Sibiri: 1930–vesna 1931 g.*, pp. 141–45.

39 *Ibid.*, p. 86. Stalin's article "Dizzy with Success" (*Golovokruzhenie to uspekhov*) was first published in *Pravda*, no. 60 (2 March 1930).

life and for the grand proclaimed goal of colonization alike. There was no single plan for the creation of the special settlements system; rather, it was "an amorphous conglomeration of orders, directives, decrees, and special commissions, beset by a multitude of contradictions".[40] These contradictions and the bureaucratic chaos they produced became a source of additional pain for the deportees even as they arrived at their destination.

Administrative disarray did not remain the definitive feature of the system of special settlements beyond the initial several years. As the settlements sprawled throughout Siberia and the Russian North, and new groups of "enemies of the state" arrived, the OGPU tightened its grip over this system, and its management became more coordinated.

Initially, adult deportees were obliged to stay in the settlements for five years, but in 1935, following a suggestion by Genrikh Iagoda, this term was prolonged indefinitely. This decision reflected the political leaders' anxieties concerning the ability of special settlers to reform and the capacity of the former *kulaks* to be fully integrated into the Soviet way of life. But it also was dictated by practical considerations: as the term of release of those deported in 1930 approached in 1935, Iagoda and his subordinates realized that the settlers would leave en masse, if given an opportunity. This would have undermined the agenda of forced colonization, but also confronted the wider Soviet population with the former *kulaks*, whose return was "politically undesirable".[41] The desire to keep this large pool of forced workers readily available must have also played a role.

The special settlements were an important element in the Soviet architecture of repression and their initial installation and development were inextricably connected to the development of the camp system. While camps were used as instruments of more individualized political repression for years before the start of peasant deportations, it was dekulakization that gave a particularly forceful impetus to the use of forced labour of both convicts and the deportees on a mass scale. Apart from the deportations, dekulakization was accompanied by numerous executions as well as mass arrests that filled the camps. For instance, starting already in February 1930, each week in Siberia alone up to two thousand peasants were arrested as "*kulak* activists" (*kulatskii aktiv*), and by the end of March, around nine thousand people had been placed under arrest.[42]

40 Lynne Viola, "The Aesthetic of Stalinist Planning and the World of the Special Villages", *Kritika: Explorations in Russian and Eurasian History*, 4:1 (2003), pp. 101–28, 111.
41 Tsarevskaia-Diakina, *Istoriia stalinskogo Gulaga*, vol. 5, pp. 209–10.
42 Papkov, *Obyknovennyi terror*, p. 57.

Ruptures and continuities in the deportations to Western Siberia

Over the course of modern Russian history, state authorities repeatedly turned to forced displacement in order to control both population and territories. As centralized power crumbled in the course of the revolution, forced displacement disappeared from the repressive repertoire. The authorities could no longer forcefully and systematically direct masses of exiles towards certain regions: the only practised form of forced displacement was banishment, or *vysylka*, which was used to expel undesirable individuals, generally political militants, from the cities important for the regime. It was, most notably, one of the measures of the Petrograd *Vecheka* in its early days, before the start of the Red Terror.[43] The most notorious example of early Soviet banishment was the case of the "Philosophers' steamboats": two German ships which transported more than 160 intellectuals and their families from Petrograd to Stettin during the autumn of 1922.[44] These actions were intended to wipe out altogether the influence of the Bolsheviks' political opponents, but they resembled more the tsarist exile of political dissenters than the mass, and often deadly, deportations that were to follow.

The Soviets' first truly mass deportations occurred in 1919, when more than 45,000 people were deported from the south of Russia as part of "decossackization". This campaign bore a resemblance to the sweeping wartime campaigns of the imperial government, especially the deportations of "enemy minorities".[45] As Peter Holquist has underlined, "while decossackization deserves comparison with the later Soviet policy of dekulakization, it merits equal comparison with the tsarist regime's policies of ethnic population management, practiced in the western territories of the Empire during the course of the First World War".[46] Decossackization was an early Bolshevik experiment of mass deportation, which was still significantly connected to the tsarist deportation campaigns.

While these mass deportations took place in European Russia, in Siberia, according to Siberian historian Sergei Krasil'nikov, exile did not exist from 1917 to 1922, and only in 1922 did the Bolsheviks begin, not unlike the tsarist authorities before them, to banish political dissenters. By mid-1922, around five hundred people had been extrajudicially exiled in the region, and by

43 Rat'kovskii, *Krasnyi terror*, p. 13.

44 See Lesley Chamberlain, *Lenin's Private War: The Voyage of the Philosophy Steamer and the Exile of the Intelligentsia* (New York: St. Martin's Press, 2007).

45 Lohr, *Nationalizing the Russian Empire*.

46 Peter Holquist, "'Conduct Merciless Mass Terror': Decossackization on the Don, 1919", *Cahiers du monde russe*, 38:1/2 (1997), pp. 127–62, 128.

1924 this number had not yet reached one thousand.[47] As the Bolshevik state slowly consolidated its grip over the territories and the populations, and especially as the power of the secret police grew, forced displacement became more and more widely used. It was not, however, until the first peasant deportations of 1930 that forced displacement truly became a large-scale instrument of Soviet social engineering. Over the course of the dekulakization campaign, the special police revived the same method of mass persecution that was first employed during the civil war: namely, the organization of special committees known as *troikas* as the main organs with extrajudicial repressive power over the *kulaks*.[48]

At first glance, it is quite inviting to make some comparisons between the tsarist practice of exile and the Soviet peasant deportations. Perhaps the starkest apparent similarity between exile and deportation to special settlements is the fact that apart from being punitive practices, both were inscribed within a wider state agenda of colonization, which largely justified most abuses in the eyes of the authorities. As discussed in the first chapter, exile to Siberia had a limited impact on the colonization of the region in the way that the central authorities imagined it, but it was nevertheless preserved due to its other proclaimed function, namely the expulsion of "undesirables" from European Russia. Another goal, one that was never explicitly stated in the documents produced by the central authorities but that becomes clear as we delve into the long-running discussions that surrounded the abolition of exile, was the maintenance of the peripheral, subaltern position of this region within the country. Exile demanded the compliance of local authorities, and it was maintained despite these authorities' complaints of its destructive effects on the society and economy of the local regions.

Despite certain similarities with tsarist exile, the special settlements do mark a rupture with the previous repressive uses of forced displacement, both qualitatively and quantitatively. Outlining these differences helps us to characterize the Soviet repressive repertoire, to identify the defining traits of the Stalinization of the penal system, but also to elucidate the role of technological and bureaucratic advances in the establishment of the Gulag. During Soviet times, all of those deported to the special settlements were deported extrajudicially. Deportations also occurred on a completely different scale: while in tsarist Russia they only targeted individuals, the families of whom could, at least on paper, choose whether or not to follow them into exile, in the Soviet case the peasant family, rather than the individual, was

---

47 Krasil'nikov, *Serp i molokh*, pp. 239–40.
48 Papkov, *Obyknovennyi terror*, p. 56.

the "basic unit" of these deportations. These deportations and the special settlements clearly aimed at the destruction of the traditional peasant way of life and production. Direct violence and crushing any resistance were part of it, but the Soviet state sought to employ more subtle goals to achieve this goal as well. For instance, a range of policies existed that aimed at breaking up the connections between different generations of deportees and incorporating the children of the settlers into the Soviet system. In this coercive system, children enjoyed some minimal privileges compared to adults: they could freely leave the settlements once they reached the age of sixteen, and faced fewer limitations than released adult deportees in terms of choice of education, occupation, and place or residence. These privileges aimed at separating the younger generation from the older peasants. Another subtler policy included schooling, as the children from deported peasant families were, at least until the age of twelve, fully integrated into the Soviet school system and followed the same curriculum. This policy, however, was hard to implement. Finding reliable Soviet teachers in the Siberian wilderness, and amidst the chaos of creating the settlements, was challenging. In the spring of 1932, for instance, three quarters of all teachers in the special settlements of the Narym region in the north of Western Siberian were settlers themselves, and seventy school headmasters were also settlers.[49]

The goal of removing and isolating "undesirables" appears to be comparable, but it hardly is: the ways of identifying undesirables and the means of their removal were fundamentally different. The Soviet peasant deportations were guided by the definition of *kulaks* as the state's main political enemies, and they envisioned "the liquidation of the *kulaks* as a class". This targeting of vast masses of people as political enemies marked a clear rupture with previous policies. The deportations also started to target whole groups (this was first social groups loosely defined by state agents, and later ethnic groups) rather than individuals. The Soviet forced displacements did not follow the vague agenda of social control that targeted the subaltern groups, as was the case with tsarist exile, but implied a profound social "cleansing" of the strategically important bigger cities, the more productive agricultural regions, and the borderlands. Creating "quotas" for the deportations, and encouraging the over-fulfilment of these quotas, was also typical of Soviet repression, an indiscriminate and ruthless tactic that secured the participation of the local authorities and led to indiscriminate repression. Unlike tsarist exile, which implied the routine transportation of smaller groups of

49   V.P. Danilov and S.A. Krasil'nikov (eds), *Spetspereselentsy v Zapadnoi Sibiri: Vesna 1931–nachalo 1933 g.* (Novosibirsk: EKOR, 1993), p. 142.

convicts and administrative exiles to Siberia, the Soviet peasant deportations were "operations", large-scale logistical efforts orchestrated by the
secret police. In both cases, however, an important factor of administrative
disarray, especially when it came to transit and transportation, played a
significant role and compounded the hardships of the exiles and deportees.[50]
The Cheka and its heir, the OGPU, were charged with the persecution of
political enemies, and while the tsarist secret police were notorious for
their persecution of political militants, the Soviet secret police operated
on a completely different scale, and acquired an incomparable level of
control over society.[51]

   The Soviet special settlements were presented as instruments of colonization, but Soviet officials understood colonization in the narrow and
exploitative way, and the settlements became tools of resource extraction,
both in terms of natural resources, above all timber, and the labour of
the deportees. But this agenda of forced labour use was not what guided
the dekulakization campaign from the start. During the initial stage of
deportations, political repression and the confiscation of property were
the two main goals. This becomes clear when we take into account how
the deportations unfolded: while arrest and removal from places of origin
were clearly a logistical priority for the authorities, the administration of
deportees in the settlements was neglected, especially in 1930.[52] There was
no coherent centralized plan of how the deportees were to be settled and put
to work. Instead, the local authorities failed tragically in administrating the
early peasant deportees. Settlement of the deportees, and even more so the
use of their labour, was not among the priorities of the central authorities
in the first months of the *kulak* deportations. The committee charged with
the oversight of accommodation and employment of the deportees, led
by V.V. Schmidt, was created only in April 1930.[53] The idea that deportees
could provide a stable coerced labour force for forestry in the distant and
underpopulated areas of the Russian North and Siberia crystallized only
by the autumn of 1930.[54]

50   Beer, "Penal Deportation to Siberia".
51   N.V. Petrov, "Vvedenie", in N.V. Petrov and N.I. Vladimirtsev (eds), *Istoriia Stalinskogo Gulaga: Tom 2: Karatel'naia sistema: struktura i kadry* (Moscow: ROSSPEN, 2004), p. 17. In Russian, see A.I. Kokurin and N.V. Petrov (eds), *Lubianka. VChK-OGPU-KVD-NKGB-MGB-MVD-KGB. 1917–1960* (Moscow: MFD, 1997). In English, see Shearer and Khaustov, *Stalin and the Lubianka.*
52   For detailed accounts of the condition of the settlers, see Viola, *The Unknown Gulag* and Krasil'nikov, *Serp i molokh.*
53   Danilov *et al., Tragediia sovetskoi derevni*, vol. 2, p. 354.
54   Viola, *The Unknown Gulag*, p. 60.

A clear agenda of the utilization of deportees' coerced labour for industrial goals emerged even later, as the secret police's influence in the whole enterprise grew further. There was a notable contradiction between the agenda of forced colonization, which implied stable settlement of the deportees and their work in agriculture in distant areas of Siberia, and the use of forced labour for industrialization, overseen by the OGPU and later the NKVD, which hinged upon distribution of the deportees in the already populated areas and their frequent relocation depending on labour needs in various construction and extraction projects. Keeping the deportees in the settlements was a priority for the officials, which made it extremely difficult for the settlers to leave even if they were able to prove that their deportation was unlawful. While reviewing settlers' appeals in 1930, a committee found that at least 10 per cent of them were deported unlawfully. These included families of Red Army soldiers, civil war veterans, the elderly and children under sixteen deported without any other family members, families of poor and middle peasants, and rural intelligentsia. The chair of the committee insisted, however, that only 2–3 per cent could be allowed to return to their places of origin, while others had to be resettled in other villages in the North as "free citizens with privileged conditions". Although this suggestion elicited objections from other members of the committee, it was ultimately supported by Genrikh Iagoda, and the Politburo allowed only 6 per cent of the incorrectly deported to return.[55]

Central authorities proclaimed that the deportees retained the potential to be "reformed" into loyal Soviet citizens. As the decree of the People's Commissariat of Agriculture from 1 April 1930 stated, the "settlements must be located outside of the areas of wholesale (*sploshnaia*) collectivization and, when possible, between such areas, so that they [the inhabitants] would exercise an ideological influence on the population of the settlements".[56] Despite these announcements, however, the only consistently employed measure to integrate adult settlers into Soviet society was forcing them to work.

At the beginning of the 1930s, the Soviet authorities characterized Western Siberia as suffering from underdeveloped infrastructure, overwhelming criminality, and a lack of policing, and still considered it to be a frontier zone. Throughout the 1930s, they conceptualized their policies in Western Siberia in terms of "colonization" and "taming".[57] Special settlements can be

55   *Ibid.*, pp. 62–65.
56   Danilov and Krasil'nikov, *Spetspereselentsy v Zapadnoi Sibiri: 1930–vesna 1931 g.*, p. 27.
57   David R. Shearer, "Modernity and Backwardness on the Soviet Frontier: Western Siberia in the 1930s", in Donald Raleigh (ed.), *Provincial Landscapes: Local Dimensions of Soviet Power, 1917–1953* (Pittsburgh, PA: University of Pittsburgh Press, 2001), pp. 194–217.

viewed as the chief instrument of such "taming", both because they allowed the authorities to bring controllable, coerced, and repeatedly "replenish-able" populations to these regions to be used both for agricultural and industrial labour, and because the use of these settlers' labour on large-scale projects allowed them to construct infrastructure that further facilitated the deployment of coercive policies – for example, the development of the railroad network was used to strengthen control over grain extraction.

Administratively, the system of special settlements was a part of the GULAG from 1931 to 1944, and only then was a separate department for the special settlements organized.[58] Unlike the "corrective labour" camps, which were not confined to a particular type of landscape and could be both urban and rural, and where the inmates were forced to perform a large array of works, the special settlements remained largely confined to the rural territories of the most distant and climatically hostile regions. The agenda of industrialization did instigate the further displacement of former *kulaks* towards the industrial centres, but the surrounding landscapes generally remained hostile and threatening. Western Siberian industrial sites were often built and developed on barren land, and the use of deportees as a source of forced labour was crucial for this construction.

The deportations were intended as punitive campaigns against the peasantry as a whole, rather than a narrow group of wealthier peasants. Social uprooting, as well as political and economic deprivation, were constitutive elements of these campaigns. To a certain extent, material hardships, hunger, and the harsh climate were also weaponized against deported families. As Lynne Viola has made clear, both the extensive, rigid, and abstract planning and the failure of local authorities to fulfil these plans contributed to the suffering of deported peasants.[59] And, as Andy Bruno has underlined, the environment could also undermine the intentions of the Soviet authorities and their control over the desired industrial development.[60] The environment, and especially the distance, also made the special settlements very hard to flee. The settlements, despite the absence of barbed wire and armed convoys, offered few possibilities for escape: it was unlikely that a teenager or an elderly person could successfully overcome such challenges. Furthermore, escape by an adult could signify the loss of

---

58 Petrov, "Vvedenie", p. 29.
59 Viola, "The Aesthetic of Stalinist Planning and the World of the Special Villages".
60 Andy Bruno, "Industrial Life in a Limiting Landscape: An Environmental Interpretation of Stalinist Social Conditions in the Far North", *International Review of Social History*, 55:S18 (2010), pp. 153–74, 157.

the sole breadwinner of a household, resulting in extreme deprivation for the family members left behind.

Labour coercion across the rural-urban divide

Labour conditions in the Stalinist Soviet Union can be represented as a continuum of coercion. On one pole of the continuum would be the convicts, who were forced to work in the camps of the Gulag, often under the threat of direct violence from the guards and in extremely harsh conditions. In some of the camps, the hardship and violence were such that inmates were indeed annihilated through labour, although the camp system as a whole was not designed as an instrument of mass extermination.[61] At the other extreme would be the privileged officials who enjoyed the full benefits of the distributive system. The labour of the special settlers, then, could be placed closer to the "extreme coercion" pole of the continuum, but differences between the labour conditions of settlers and inmates were still crucial. The settlers did not face physical violence as punishment for not working enough, and could, especially later on, choose their occupation. At the beginning of the deportations, employed settlers were supposed to receive 75–80 per cent of the wages of free labourers, and did not enjoy social insurance.[62] Later, according to a temporary decree from 1 July 1931, deported settlers were to receive payment for their work that was equal to the salary of free workers, with a deduction of 15 per cent taken for maintenance of the settlements: the salaries of the commandants and the wider administrative control system.[63] They also had the possibility of obtaining state loans on favourable conditions for the development of the cooperatives (*neustavnye arteli*), and were exempted from taxes for the first three years.

Despite these concessions, the settlements remained territories under a special disciplinary regime. The threat of being sent to the camps was

---

61   For a discussion of violence and death in the Gulag, see Barnes, *Death and Redemption* and especially the works of Golfo Alexopoulos: Golfo Alexopoulos, "A Torture Memo: Reading Violence in the Gulag", in Golfo Alexopoulos, Julie Hessler, Kirill Tomoff, and Joshua A. Sanborn (eds), *Writing the Stalin Era: Sheila Fitzpatrick and Soviet Historiography* (New York: Palgrave Macmillan, 2011), pp. 157–76; Golfo Alexopoulos, "Destructive-Labor Camps: Rethinking Solzhenitsyn's Play on Words", *Kritika: Explorations in Russian and Eurasian History*, 16:3 (2015), pp. 499–526, and Golfo Alexopoulos, *Illness and Inhumanity in Stalin's Gulag* (New Haven, CT: Yale University Press, 2017).

62   Danilov and Krasil'nikov, *Spetspereselentsy v Zapadnoi Sibiri: 1930–vesna 1931 g.*, p. 32.

63   Tsarevskaia-Diakina, *Istoriia stalinskogo Gulaga*, vol. 5, p. 148.

constant. The distribution of food and industrial goods there remained under the control of the OGPU.[64] Moreover, in an attempt to prevent escapes, the OGPU introduced collective responsibility (*krugovaia poruka*) among the deportees, and for every ten settlers, one was made an "elder" who was responsible for conducting surveillance of the others.[65] Here, Soviet officials used a well-known, albeit dated, term for a coercive system of collective responsibility: though differently organized, the original peasant *krugovaia poruka* was the measure that the tsarist authorities had employed to secure tax payments from peasant communes until the beginning of the twentieth century.

Both the camp and the special settlement systems expanded fast across the Soviet Union. Oleg Khlevniuk has distinguished two patterns in terms of the expansion of the labour camp system: first, forced labour was used for the colonization of distant regions of the country; second, it was used in densely populated areas where additional labour was needed.[66] The spread of the Siberian division of the GULAG, the Siblag, followed the second pattern rather than the first. The Siblag was organized in the autumn of 1929. By 1 January 1930, it had 4,592 inmates, a number that increased more than five-fold over the course of that year, with the camp population reaching 21,149 by 1 January 1931.[67] The special settlers remained far more numerous than the inmates throughout the first half of the 1930s. They were also spread out across a wider territory than the inmates. Labour camps and camp subdivisions in Western Siberia were generally situated in the southern part of the region, in close proximity to the cities, often within city limits.[68]

The geography of the special settlements in Western Siberia was far more diversified. They were generally rural, and were scattered throughout the region. The types of labour that the settlers had to perform were defined by the local economy and differed between the northern and the southern settlements: in the north, in the Narym region, settlers predominantly laboured in agriculture, fishing, and the timber industry. These settlements were intended as a tool of colonization of the particularly hostile, and long considered uninhabitable, parts of Western Siberia. This expansion to the north was driven by the extraction of timber resources, and forestry was

64 *Ibid.*, p. 39.
65 Danilov *et al.*, *Tragediia sovetskoi derevni*, p. 527.
66 Oleg Khlevniuk, "No Total Totality: Forced Labor, Stalinism, and De-Stalinization", *Kritika: Explorations in Russian and Eurasian History*, 16:4 (2015), pp. 961–73, 963.
67 Wilson T. Bell, "The Gulag and Soviet Society in Western Siberia, 1929–1953" (Ph.D. dissertation, University of Toronto, 2011), p. 66.
68 *Ibid.*, p. 51.

one of the chief areas of employment for forced labourers. Already in 1926, Commissar of Internal Affairs Aleksandr Beloborodov suggested to the Head of the Main Administration of Places of Confinement Evsei Shirvindt that prisoners should be transported to the Ural region as it lacked labourers in forestry.[69] One of the earliest suggestions of the coordinated use of mass forced labour in the USSR was also made in relation to forestry: in the spring of 1928, the Commissar of Justice N.M. Ianson presented his project for the mass use of convict labour for timber extraction.[70] Forestry demanded workers in Western Siberia as well: the OGPU plenipotentiary in Siberia stated in his April 1930 report that "the biggest economic disadvantage of the Siberian forestry industry and the main setback for its development is the absence of the workforce in the region".[71] As Wilson Bell has suggested, it might be possible that only one forestry camp was installed in Western Siberia, despite its vast forests, specifically because the numerous deported *kulak* workers, as the labour force necessary for the extraction of this resource, were already being exploited.[72] This policy became official when the 18 August 1930 decree of the Council of People's Commissars stated that the deportees had to be employed primarily in forestry, fishing, and other crafts, and only allowed employment in agriculture when no other occupations were available.[73] This decree concerned not only Western Siberia, but all other deportation destinations, including the Urals and the Russian North.

In the south, in the coal rich region of the Kuznetsk Basin, or the Kuzbass, settlers were employed in the coal mining industry, metallurgy, and construction. The gigantic industrial conglomerate of the Kuznetsk metallurgical plant and the Kuznetsk coal mining plant shaped the landscape of Southwestern Siberia. The importance of this region for industrialization meant that "huge numbers of workers were recruited, mobilized, and deported to provide the workforce needed to construct one of the biggest Soviet centres of [...] heavy industry".[74] The building of the Kuznetsk metallurgical plant (*Kuznetskstroi*) became the biggest construction site in Western Siberia. Construction started in 1929 and attracted around fifty thousand workers

69 GARF, f. 4042, op. 1, d. 40, l. 11.

70 Krasil'nikov, *Serp i molokh*, p. 241.

71 Danilov and Krasil'nikov, *Spetspereselentsy v Zapadnoi Sibiri: 1930–vesna 1931 g.*, p. 112.

72 Bell, "The Gulag and Soviet Society in Western Siberia, 1929–1953", p. 52.

73 Danilov and Krasil'nikov, *Spetspereselentsy v Zapadnoi Sibiri: 1930–vesna 1931 g.*, p. 33.

74 Julia Landau, "Specialists, Spies, 'Special Settlers', and Prisoners of War: Social Frictions in the Kuzbass (USSR), 1920–1950", *International Review of Social History*, 60:S1 (2015), pp. 185–205, 186.

overall. By September 1930, 2,335 special settlers were working at *Kuznet-skstroi*.[75] Central authorities had a more ambitious plan of using deportees' labour which was, however, thwarted by administrative failures. According to a OGPU report from August 1931, ten thousand settler families were supposed to work at *Kuznetskstroi* and *Vostokougol'*, but these enterprises refused to build lodgings for these families. Only after intervention by the OGPU was the construction of lodgings initiated.[76]

Kuzbass had some of the richest coal deposits in the Soviet Union. During the first Five-Year Plan, Kuzbass coal mining became a key industrial project: the plan anticipated that annual coal production there would quadruple between 1928 and 1932. Similarly, the Kuzbass metallurgical plant was constantly in need of new workers. Despite the egalitarian propaganda of the Soviet authorities, "the Kuzbass before World War II was a strictly hierarchic society", with multiple groups of workers competing for the distribution of scarce resources, such as higher quality housing and food supplies.[77] Special settlers were the first cohort of coerced workers to labour in the mines and at the plant of the Kuzbass. The plant also employed free labourers, including a number of highly skilled "specialists", and later employed other forced labourers, namely prisoners of war. As the authorities continued to consider the *kulaks* to be class enemies, they were extremely anxious about this close interaction between deportees and free labourers, and suspected that the former could "demoralize" the latter and undermine their productivity.[78]

Such socialist anxieties notwithstanding, deportees' coerced labour was consistently employed in Kuzbass. The management of the plant faced not only a workforce shortage, but also a high rate of labour turnover: many workers had just short-term contracts, often of no more than three months, and left production immediately afterwards. Some, faced with the harsh living conditions, left even before the end of their term. Overall, up to 40 per cent of workers stayed for fewer than six months. This problem was not specific to the Kuzbass plant, but plagued many large enterprises as industrialization gained momentum. Even the emblem of Stalinist industrialization suffered from high workforce turnover: as noted by Stephen

---

75 Krasil'nikov, *Serp i molokh*, p. 245.

76 Tsarevskaia-Diakina, *Istoriia stalinskogo Gulaga*, vol. 5, p. 152. Vostokougol was organized in 1930 and was responsible for coal mining in the Urals, in Siberia, and in the Far East.

77 Landau, "Specialists, Spies, 'Special Settlers', and Prisoners of War", p. 204.

78 For boss of *kraiadmupravlenie*'s report to the Commissar of Internal Affairs Tolmachev from July 1930, see Danilov and Krasil'nikov, *Spetspereselentsy v Zapadnoi Sibiri: 1930–vesna 1931 g*, p. 194.

Kotkin, even "Magnitostroi, the biggest shock construction site in a country that worshiped bigness, did not have enough 'labor power', even of the 'unskilled' variety".[79]

The terms of employment for former *kulaks* in the agricultural and industrial sectors changed throughout the 1930s. Even though the deportees were initially peasants by occupation, local authorities sought to use their labour in the non-agricultural sphere right from the beginning, and to break the deportees' connection with agriculture. Industry and infrastructural construction were among the most significant beneficiaries of forced labourers in Western Siberia: already in the autumn of 1930, several major employers of former *kulaks* included *Soiuzzoloto* – the gold mining trust – which employed 3,225 people, the forestry trust *Siblestrest*, which hired 4,056 people, and the agricultural machinery production plant *Sibkombain*, which employed another 1,788 settlers.[80]

By September 1931, more settlers were directed towards non-agricultural labour: forty-one thousand households out of a total of sixty-five thousand were ascribed to agricultural settlements, while the rest – that is, almost one third of the total number – were involved in non-agricultural labour: coal and ore mining, the timber industry, and construction. Starting in 1932, the special settlers who were first deported to Narym were then resettled to the Kuzbass area.[81] In 1941, as the USSR entered World War II, only one third of adult special settlers were employed in agriculture.[82]

Soviet authorities continued to be suspicious of the deportees, and these special settlers did not have many ways to get rid of their limiting, stigmatizing status. While it was easier for the children to leave the settlements once they reached the age of sixteen, for the adult settlers, legal possibilities of return were limited until the 1950s. Even those who were allowed to leave the settlements struggled with stigma, and not just of a social kind: they had a special mark in their passports that limited their occupational and residential possibilities. The adult settlers could file complaints at the special commission of the Council of People's Commissars and appeal their deportation, but these petitions were rarely satisfied. Suspected of animosity towards the Soviet regime, the deportees had to prove their loyalty. Intensive industrial labour could rehabilitate them in the eyes of

79   Stephen Kotkin, *Magnetic Mountain: Stalinism as a Civilization* (Berkeley: University of California Press, 1997), p. 94.
80   Krasil'nikov, *Serp i molokh*, p. 245.
81   *Ibid.*, p. 265.
82   *Ibid.*, p. 19.

the Soviet state. Shock work, known as *udarnichestvo*, was a route to release, but also allowed deportees to get rid of the discriminating status of special settler upon liberation. Continuous over-fulfilment of the work norms allowed these deported workers to be reinstated within two or three years after deportation instead of five, and the reinstatement of the head of the family also implied the reinstatement of all the other family members. This measure was used sparingly: by December 1936, seven full years after the start of deportations in February 1930, just 57,088 people, or around twelve thousand households, had their rights reinstated in Western Siberia.[83] Later, starting in 1935–1937, deportees could also leave the settlements by marrying a non-settler or asking for a derogation to study elsewhere. These releases remained, however, comparatively small in number. The first mass releases of deportees took place only after Stalin's death. Even then, the regime kept the limitations in place for many years, and, as the French historians Alain Blum and Emilia Koustova have underlined, the process of releasing deportees, including deportees from the Western borderlands, was uncoordinated with the policy of release and rehabilitation of camp inmates. Dismantlement of the special settlements system was a slow and uneasy process, riddled by distrust or, at best, the ambiguous attitude of the authorities. The discriminating status of the "special settler" was definitively abolished only twelve years after Stalin's death, in 1965. The system's deconstruction in 1954–1965 was guided by a number of collective release decrees and other regulations that prescribed the deportees' release, return, and restitution of property.[84] Return and restitution of property did not take place automatically upon release, but required the former deportees to appeal to the authorities and go through what Blum and Koustova call "a procedural labyrinth".[85]

Conclusion

Creation of the special settlements was the definitive measure deployed by the Bolsheviks in their war against the peasantry. Throughout the 1930s, the regime's desires to subdue the peasantry, colonize the hinterlands, and

---

83   *Ibid.*, p. 278. According to the data of Viktor Zemskov quoted above, on 1 January 1936, in the whole Soviet Union, there were 1,017,133 deportees in the special settlements.
84   Alain Blum and Emilia Koustova, "Negotiating Lives, Redefining Repressive Policies: Managing the Legacies of Stalinist Deportations", *Kritika: Explorations in Russian and Eurasian History*, 19:3 (2018), pp. 537–71, 538–39.
85   *Ibid.*, p. 567.

mobilize labour and resources for breakneck industrialization, all affected the ways in which the special settlements were organized and developed. Settlements were envisioned by the Soviet leadership in a concrete and rigid way, without any regard for local contexts, and the implementation of this vision was riddled with administrative chaos and unbridled violence. The settlers' future, and even their survival, seem to have occupied only a minor place in the planning of the central Soviet authorities at the beginning of the deportations.

Gradually, central authorities managed to organize life in the settlements and mobilize the labour of the deportees. They did so by relying on the political police as the central agent of this mobilization aimed at uprooting the peasants and using their labour for industrialization, either directly as coerced industrial workers or as agricultural workers forced to comply with the state-imposed goals of grain requisition. Stalinist policies against the peasantry had devastating results, entailed the brutal destruction of the social order in the countryside, and led to the immeasurable suffering of millions of people and the deaths of hundreds of thousands as victims of deportations, direct violence, internment in camps, and manmade hunger. Russian historian Sergei Papkov conceptualized dekulakization as the first occurrence of what he calls "ordinary terror": the unprecedented mass campaigns of repression that followed one another in the 1930s and culminated in the 1937–1938 Great Terror, only to continue with varying force until Stalin's demise.[86]

The installation of the special settlements in the course of dekulakization marked a major rupture in Soviet repressive policies. With this shift, mass displacement and the large-scale use of forced labour became routine tools of governance rather than exceptional measures. The camp system of the Gulag was built on the same dyad, and it was tightly interconnected with the settlements. In the 1930s, criminologists' progressive practices were abandoned, while the political police acquired unprecedented power over the fate of millions of deportees and inmates and control over the economic development of whole regions. The logic of creating and guarding social order, typical for other contemporaneous penal systems, and aspirations to deter and reform common criminals with a host of measures of differing degrees of coercion, which characterized the developments of the Soviet penal system in the 1920s, were subsumed within a wider and much more ambitious project of using forced displacement and coerced labour for the extraction of resources, including labour, for the accelerated modernization of the

86 Papkov, *Obyknovennyi terror.*

Soviet Union. Lynne Viola has underlined that it is crucial to understand the Soviet Union as a *modernizing* state in order to grasp these dynamics of violence in the 1930s.[87] Decimation of the peasantry, persecution of perceived political opponents, and intensified criminalization of lesser wrongdoings created a pool of coerced workers who could be used in the most distant areas of the country for hard, unmechanized labour, and could also be promptly redirected from one location to another as the goals of production changed.[88] The accelerated Soviet industrialization was above all a political project, and the Gulag acquired its prime importance as a tool of such "developmental violence" directed towards the Soviet citizens.[89]

Political and economic considerations intertwined, making the Gulag a site of extreme exploitation which still left a glimpse of a hope of rehabilitation – for those who survived. In 1934, Andrei Vyshinskii, Stalin's infamous chief prosecutor, proclaimed that "the coupling of violence with persuasion and education is the distinctive trait of the dictatorship of the proletariat".[90] In the view of the Soviet authorities, the combination of brutality and the promise of reform did not represent a contradiction. Both were acceptable instruments with which the new Soviet men and women could be created.[91] Despite suspicions and outright violence towards the deportees and inmates considered politically unreliable, the Gulag, as Steven Barnes has underlined, was not devoid of reformatory aspirations. At the same time, he has acknowledged that "the death of prisoners was always accepted as

---

87   Lynne Viola, "The Question of the Perpetrator in Soviet History", *Slavic Review*, 72:1 (2013), pp. 1–23.

88   The trend towards intensifying the prosecution of petty crime, and crimes "against socialist property", rose in the 1930s. This included both harsher punishments and the extension of the criminal sanction. The 7 August 1932 decree "On protection of the property of state enterprises, kolkhozes and cooperatives, and strengthening of the public (socialist) property", known also as "the law of three spikelets", is particularly infamous, as it increased the harshness of the punishment (up to death penalty) for petty theft, including the collection of grain left in the *kolkhoz* fields after harvest, at the height of the 1932–1933 hunger. In the post-war period, it continued with more severe penalties for labour discipline infractions and other similar infractions, see Chapter 12 "The War and Postwar Trends", in David R. Shearer, *Policing Stalin's Socialism: Repression and Social Order in the Soviet Union, 1924–1953* (New Haven, CT, Stanford, CA: Yale University Press, Hoover Institution Press, 2009).

89   For more on the concept of developmental violence in the Soviet context, see Christian Gerlach and Nicolas Werth, "State Violence – Violent Societies", in Michael Geyer and Sheila Fitzpatrick (eds), *Beyond Totalitarianism: Stalinism and Nazism Compared* (Cambridge: Cambridge University Press, 2008), pp. 133–79.

90   "Vvedenie" in Andrei Vyshinskii (ed.), *Ot tiurem k vospitatel'nym uchrezhdeniiam* (Moscow: Sovetskoe zakonodatel'stvo, 1934), p. 8.

91   Barnes, *Death and Redemption*, p. 27.

part and parcel of the work of the camp system".[92] For deportees, full return to society remained elusive. As for camp prisoners, estimates suggest that between 20 and 40 per cent of inmates were released per annum between 1934 and 1953.[93] For prisons, penal colonies, and special camps such data is unavailable. For many released inmates, new arrests would follow. Even release did not mean that Gulag inmates escaped death, as incarceration took an extreme toll on inmates' health. Recent research has convincingly shown that medical discharge, introduced in 1923 as a progressive measure, was, by the 1940s, systematically used across the camp system to manipulate mortality statistics and to "release" handicapped and ill inmates who would often die shortly thereafter.[94]

Tracing the early development of the special settlements system highlights the extensive reliance on coerced labour, the strong interconnectedness of the free and unfree spheres of labour, and the political leadership's extensive use of coercion and direct violence for the fulfilment of the state's goals of resource mobilization, colonization, and industrialization alike, as well as its attempts to achieve large-scale social engineering. The immediate goals of the special settlements included the isolation of suspected enemies of the regime, the exploitation of their labour, and the forceful integration of select former "kulaks", and especially their children, into Soviet society. They were simultaneously inscribed within the wider logic of expansion and control over the distant territories. Coupled with bureaucratic inconsistencies and the unpreparedness of local authorities, they produced a hectic, arbitrary, dangerous, and often deadly system, where the condition of settlers was characterized not only by everyday material hardships and forced labour, but also by a total lack of knowledge about any prospects of return: even formal release did not always allow them to leave the "special settlements".

Despite their catastrophic consequences, the mass *kulak* deportations served as a blueprint for later campaigns. The model of special settlements as it emerged in the early 1930s was replicated with minimal changes as the regime labelled ever widening groups as its enemies. The same elements, such as the dominant role of the secret police, the extrajudicial procedure of deportation, its mass character, deportation to particularly distant regions, the shape of the settlements, and the deportation of whole families, remained

92   *Ibid.*, p. 12.
93   J. Arch Getty, Gábor T. Rittersporn, and Viktor N. Zemskov, "Victims of the Soviet Penal System in the Pre-War Years: A First Approach on the Basis of Archival Evidence", *The American Historical Review*, 98:4 (1993), pp. 1017–49, 1041.
94   Mikhail Nakonechnyi, "'Factory of Invalids': Mortality, Disability, and Early Release on Medical Grounds in GULAG, 1930–1955" (Ph.D. dissertation, University of Oxford, 2020).

characteristic of the Soviet model of forced displacement until the death of Stalin. Similar deportations were used starting in 1933 against "alien elements" from the main Soviet cities during the passportization campaign.[95] Whole ethnicities were deported in the 1930s and 1940s, including Russian Germans, Crimean Tartars, Chechens, Ingush, and others. In the wake of the Molotov-Ribbentrop pact, mass deportations were widely used against the intelligentsia and alleged *kulaks* in the Baltic countries, as well as other perceived "enemy groups" from the western borderlands of the Soviet Union.[96] Forced displacement in the form of administrative mass deportations firmly entered the Soviet repertoire of political repression and was used over several decades against various social and ethnic groups, guided by the political goals of ethnic and political cleansing and sovietization.[97]

95   Shearer, "Elements Near and Alien".

96   For accounts of deportees from the Western borderlands, see Alain Blum, Marta Craveri, and Valérie Nivelon (eds), *Deportés en URSS: Récits d'européens au goulag* (Paris: Éditions Autrement, 2012). Research in English has also explored the conditions of these deportees, their experiences during and after the exile, and attempts to leave the settlements: Emilia Koustova, "(Un) Returned from the Gulag: Life Trajectories and Integration of Postwar Special Settlers", *Kritika: Explorations in Russian and Eurasian History*, 16:3 (2015), pp. 589–620; Violeta Davoliūtė and Tomas Balkelis (eds), *Narratives of Exile and Identity: Soviet Deportation Memoirs from the Baltic States* (Budapest, New York: Central European University Press, 2017); Jehanne M. Gheith and Katherine R. Jolluck, *Gulag Voices: Oral Histories of Soviet Incarceration and Exile* (Basingstoke: Palgrave Macmillan, 2011); Katherine R. Jolluck, *Exile and Identity: Polish Women in the Soviet Union during World War II* (Pittsburgh, PA: University of Pittsburgh Press, 2002).

97   For an overview of Soviet deportations in the twentieth century, see Polian, *Ne po svoei vole* and Terry Martin, "The Origins of Soviet Ethnic Cleansing", *The Journal of Modern History*, 70:4 (1998), pp. 813–61. For the wider context of forced migrations in modern European history, see Ther, *The Dark Side of Nation-States*. For a study of the "re-sovietization" of Latvia, see Juliette Denis, "Identifier les 'éléments ennemis' en Lettonie: Une priorité dans le processus de resoviétisation (1942–1945)", *Cahiers du monde russe*, 49:2–3 (2008), pp. 297–318.

Epilogue: Paroxysms of Violence, 1937–1953

Between the 1870s and the 1930s, the penal-repressive system, like the whole country, went through turbulent changes. A protracted period of crisis followed slower-paced developments of the last third of the nineteenth century. Prior to the installation of the network of Stalinist punitive institutions, World War I marked the most significant rupture, heralding the advance of mass confinement and, in line with wider European developments, greater reliance on coercion in governance, and firmly bringing mass forced displacement and the infrastructural labour of convicts into the repressive repertoire of the tsarist authorities.

Stalin's rise to power and his ruthless drive to consolidate control over both the countryside and urban centres spurred major punitive innovations, above all the creation of the special settlements, and brought about the most significant rupture in penal-repressive policies in the observed period. Along with peasant deportations, the scaling up and expansion of the camp system – based largely on punitive practices elaborated at the OGPU Solovki camp – was another building element of the Gulag. While the Stalin-era transformations of the system as a whole marked a clear break with earlier policies, continuities with the imperial legacy remained discernible on the level of particular practices and institutions of repression.

Both failures and successes of the imperial and early Soviet penal systems informed the decisions of the Soviet leaders as they worked towards expanding the use of coerced labour and separating the Soviet Union into a multitude of "zones" of varying degrees of coercion. They also shaped this repressive system within a wider context of modern practices and concepts regarding the malleability of the "human material" and the body politic. At the most basic level, the readiness to deploy extensive state intervention to refashion society according to state goals was typical for many twentieth-century European polities, as forced sterilization, ethnic cleansing, mass deportations, and other coercive methods were used against the unwanted factions of their populations. Already the imperial officials

Popova, Zhanna: *Coerced Labour, Forced Displacement, and the Soviet Gulag, 1880s-1930s*. Amsterdam: Amsterdam University Press, 2024
DOI: 10.5117/9789048560356_EPI

and professionals had envisioned the penal system as a terrain for such interventions.[1] As David Hoffmann has argued, this interventionist ethos "provided a necessary though not sufficient condition for Stalinist terror".[2] Brought to life and shaped by the Stalinist regime, the Gulag marked a shift towards using a wide array of interventionist techniques based on violence that functioned not only as an element of penalty and an extraordinary measure of repression, but as an instrument of social engineering and governance. In the eyes of Soviet officials, coercion acquired the decisive power of transforming individuals and society. Internment, transportation, and forced labour became tools of redefining who belonged to Soviet society and who had to be expelled from it.[3] They also created a large pool of forcibly mobile disenfranchised, and typically socially stigmatized, workers. Within this system, labour retained its gruesome ambivalence: depending on its conditions, it could save an inmate's or exile's life and even eventually make possible their return to society, but for those forced to perform backbreaking outdoor labour, it often became a death sentence.

The tradition of exile in the Russian empire was extremely persistent, and traces of this imperial heritage also shaped the Gulag. With the exception of a relatively short interlude of war and revolution, Russian and, later, Soviet authorities continuously used forced displacement to solve the problems they perceived as inherent to the governance of the country's vast territories and the need to exploit natural resources, populate the borderlands with ethnically Slavic settlers, and direct coerced workforces into areas where labour supply was otherwise short. Late nineteenth-century attempts to establish a modern penal system, ultimately undermined by social and political instability and autocracy's drive to instrumentalize the penal system as a tool of suppressing political dissent, failed to provide a viable alternative to exile as punishment. Prisons never became the dominant penal institution in the Russian empire, but the drive towards centralization of the penal system administration prompted by penal reform, as well as the turn to mass confinement and the use of convict labour on large-scale construction projects during World War I mark the emergence of long-running trends in the development of the repressive system.

The point of departure for writing this book was the question "What made the Gulag possible?" Although the literature about Soviet camps and other carceral institutions produced in recent years is abundant and rich,

1   Beer, "Blueprints for Change".
2   Hoffmann, *Stalinism*, p. 130.
3   Barnes, *Death and Redemption*.

I have found that this particular question was largely sidestepped, as most authors relied – unsurprisingly, considering the lingering heritage of Cold War views on Soviet history – on short-term explanations tightly connected to the Bolsheviks taking power. Although this was unarguably a crucial pivoting point, camp-related decisions made by the Bolsheviks, as I have demonstrated in this book, were made within the context of long-term developments in imperial penal and repressive practices and policies, uses of convict labour and displacement internationally, and strong reliance on a multitude of forms of labour coercion in society at large. Fully historicizing the Gulag and situating it within the global landscape is a task that cannot be tackled within one book, but I hope to have identified some crucial connections both in temporal and spatial terms.

In these concluding pages, I would like to briefly trace Gulag developments from the late 1930s to the death of Stalin, and stress once again the long-term dimension of this history and its heritage. I focus, in particular, on the recursive history of katorga as it was reinvented during the Great Patriotic War as an instrument to persecute internal enemies deemed most dangerous. Although Stalinist carceral and repressive policies and practices marked a significant break with the past due to the scope and scale of coercion and violence, Soviet officials also could, as this example suggests, mobilize and appropriate the most notorious aspects of the tsarist punitive system. Even a brief overview of the Gulag's explosive growth alerts the reader to the fact that this vast and multifaceted system, even once formally disbanded, left profound traces on Russian society and politics.[4]

Neither in the colonial contexts nor in autocratic states did a system of scale and longevity comparable to the Gulag emerge. Between 1930 and 1952, according to the most reliable calculations, around 25 million people went through the Soviet camp system. In addition to that, up to 1 million people were tortured to death during investigation or executed before ever reaching the camps.[5] Between collectivization and the start of the Great Terror in 1937, campaigns against "alien elements" lead to a constant increase in the

---

4   This topic is so vast that it cannot be dealt with in a satisfying manner in these concluding remarks, but some long-term continuities have manifested themselves prominently during the ongoing full-scale Russian invasion of Ukraine that started on 24 February 2022. In particular, the mass conscription of prison inmates as mercenaries can be seen as another iteration of two long-term trends: first, the tendency in times of crisis to temporarily delegate deployment of violence and repression to agents only loosely (if at all) associated with the state (as was the case during the revolution and the early stage of the dekulakization) and second, reliance on convicts as a pool of mobile and expendable labourers.

5   Khlevniuk, "The Gulag and the Non-Gulag", pp. 480–81.

number of special settlers and camp inmates.[6] The further expansion of
the camp system on the eve of World War II was closely connected to the
Great Terror of 1937–1939 and led to an explosive growth in the number of
inmates. The Soviet leadership's frantic hunt for internal enemies, which
had already led to the internment, incarceration, or death of millions during
the 1930s, in 1937 turned into a full-fledged frenzy of violence. The series of
repressive operations that became known as the Great Terror was launched
when the Politburo approved the NKVD Order no. 00447 that prescribed
quotas for executions and confinement in the labour camps by region.
According to this order, 270,000 people were to be prosecuted, of which
more than 72,000 were to be executed.[7] Prior to the partial opening of
classified archives, this wave of terror was understood primarily as a party
purge, but access to documents has broadened this view.[8] This party purge
was interconnected with mass terror, most notably the operation against
"former kulaks", while separate operations also targeted Germans, Poles,
Koreans, and other nationalities living in the USSR. Ultimately, the quotas
prescribed by Order no. 00447 were over-fulfilled by far: from 1 October 1936
to 1 November 1938, 1,336,863 people were convicted, 668,305 were executed,
and 602,593 were sentenced to terms from 5 to 25 years in the camps.[9]
In order to cope with the influx of detainees, the Main Administration of
Camps was instructed to create seven new camps for 103,000 inmates.[10]
By January 1940, there were at least 1,344,408 inmates in the camps, plus at

6   Shearer, "Elements Near and Alien"; Shearer, *Policing Stalin's Socialism*; Hagenloh, *Stalin's Police*.

7   J. Arch Getty and Oleg V. Naumov, *The Road to Terror: Stalin and the Self-Destruction of the Bolsheviks, 1932–1939* (New Haven, CT: Yale University Press, 1999), p. 471.

8   On mechanisms, motivations, and the scope of the Great Terror, see: *ibid.*; Barry McLoughlin and Kevin McDermott (eds), *Stalin's Terror: High Politics and Mass Repression in the Soviet Union* (London: Palgrave Macmillan, 2003); Paul Hagenloh, "'Socially Harmful Elements' and the Great Terror", in Sheila Fitzpatrick (ed.), *Stalinism: New Directions* (London: Routledge, 2000), pp. 286–308; Mark Iunge [Marc Junge], Gennadii Bordiugov, and Rolf Binner, *Vertikal' bolshogo terrora. Istoriia operatsii po prikazu NKVD no. 00447* (Moscow: Novyi Khronograf, 2008); Karl Schl"ogel, *Terror und Traum: Moskau 1937* (Munich: Hanser Verlag, 2008); Paul R. Gregory, *Terror by Quota: State Security from Lenin to Stalin (an Archival Study)* (New Haven, CT: Yale University Press, 2009); and James Harris (ed.), *The Anatomy of Terror: Political Violence under Stalin* (Oxford: Oxford University Press, 2013). On the unfolding of the Great Terror in Siberia: S.A. Papkov, *Stalinskii terror v Sibiri: 1928–1941* (Novosibirsk: Sibirskoe otdelenie RAN, 1997) and Tepliakov, *Mashina terrora*.

9   Danilov *et al.*, *Tragediia sovetskoi derevni*, vol. 5, p. 304.

10   R.W. Davies, Mark Harrison, Oleg Khlevniuk, and Stephen G. Wheatcroft, *The Industrialisation of Soviet Russia*, vol. 7: The Soviet Economy and the Approach of War, 1937–1939 (London: Palgrave Macmillan, 2018), p. 84.

least 997,513 "special settlers", not to count the inmates of penal colonies.[11] As camp authorities were faced with a constant inflow of new convicts and became less and less concerned with inmates' health and even survival, the camps turned more brutal. This worsening of inmates' conditions hinged not only upon decisions of individual camp bosses, but was further prompted by the central officials. In 1939, the Main Camp Administration stopped counting workday credits, which meant that inmates could not shorten their sentences through the consistent fulfilment of the production norms, as had previously been the case.[12]

State security police played a pivotal role in shaping and maintaining the Soviet penal system. During the first peasant deportations and the subsequent mass operations, the OGPU and its successor the NKVD amassed tremendous power, and began to play the decisive role in the organization of the Gulag and use of the inmates' forced labour. During the Great Terror, the influence of the political police was such that it managed to temporarily shift the balance of power in its favour, undermining the supremacy of the party. As Oleg Khlevniuk has argued, Stalin manipulated this continuous power struggle between the secret police and the party, first using the NKVD to purge the party organs, and then vesting the party officials with authority to purge the political police.[13]

Until Stalin's death, the repressive network expanded and became increasingly complex: the Gulag came to include a plethora of institutions such as special settlements, penal colonies, corrective labour camps, prisons, as well as special camp sections called *sharashkas*, where scientists and engineers were held, creating a continuum of carceral labour. The Gulag population grew more heterogeneous. Adolescents who stole a few potatoes from the lands of collective farms, political activists, murderers, wives and children of political leaders and Red Army officers, professional criminals, shirkers, prostitutes, members of religious sects, embezzlers, and former priests – people of virtually any background could be sent to the camps,

11   V.N. Zemskov, "GULAG (Istoriko-sotsiologicheskii aspekt)", *Sotsiologicheskie issledovaniia*, 6 (1991), pp. 10–27, 11, and Zemskov, "Spetsposelentsy (po dokumentatsii NKVD–MVD SSSR)", p. 6.
12   Khlevniuk, "No Total Totality", p. 964. This system was only re-introduced to selected camps after the war. For an analysis of the workday credit system, see: Simon Ertz, "Trading Effort for Freedom: Workday Credits in the Stalinist Camp System", *Comparative Economic Studies*, 47:2 (2005), pp. 476–91.
13   Oleg Khlevniuk, "Party and NKVD: Power Relationships in the Years of the Great Terror", in McLoughlin and McDermott (eds), *Stalin's Terror*, pp. 21–33.

while in the special settlements, women, children, and the elderly were interned en masse.

Practices of forced displacement also transformed as the Gulag expanded. Moving prisoners from one location to another was not simply a mundane practice related to the rationale of managing separate camps and preventing overpopulation, but had strategic implications. Hard to grasp from the official documents, this dimension of the camp experience is most visible in the available memoirs, as accounts of former inmates generally bring together within one narrative elements of repression that in the archival documents are either discrete or simply absent altogether. Memoirs help to trace trajectories that spanned over thousands of kilometres, and commonly involved more than one arrest and a multitude of destinations.[14] Along with mass peasant deportations, the intense relocation of individual prisoners and groups of inmates became one of the defining characteristics of the Soviet penal system. Unlike the imperial exile, which was generally guided by the self-contradictory logic of expulsion of wrongdoers to the peripheries and the colonization of these regions, Stalin-era forced displacement was guided by a multitude of interconnected goals – punitive, economic, and security-related. The relative importance of these goals was continuously shifting. From the economic perspective, constantly changing goals of construction and production dictated the swift transportation of forced workers towards new, ever more geographically distant, sites. As a security measure, they could be seen as a way to break up prison solidarity and prevent resistance. These relocations inadvertently also contributed to the emergence of a pan-USSR network of organized crime known as the "thieves in law".[15] For political and common inmates alike, unpredictable long-haul relocations compounded the pains of imprisonment, disorienting them and exposing them to extreme hardship.[16] Relocation per se was an intense

---

14   I discuss this in detail in the final chapter of my dissertation: Z. Popova, "A Threatening Geography: Forced Displacement and Convict Labour in Western Siberia, 1879–1953" (Ph.D. dissertation, University of Amsterdam, 2019), pp. 210–25.

15   These professional criminals elaborated a strict code of conduct that they observed in the Gulag, which, along with ruthless violence against other inmates, allowed them to oppose the camp authorities and maintain criminal activities throughout the whole camp system. See: Federico Varese, "The Society of the Vory-v-zakone, 1930s–1950s", *Cahiers du monde russe*, 39:4 (1998), pp. 515–38.

16   On the concept of pains of imprisonment, see a classic ethnographic study of the New Jersey State Prison: Gresham M. Sykes, *The Society of Captives: A Study of a Maximum Security Prison* (Princeton, NJ: Princeton University Press, 1958). Based on his material, Sykes distinguished the following pains of imprisonment: deprivation of liberty, deprivation of autonomy, deprivation of goods and services, deprivation of heterosexual relations, and deprivation of security.

experience of uprooting, but the conditions of transit could make it deadly. In an attempt to bolster the secrecy of the camp system, convicts were often only moved during the night and transported in unmarked cattle cars.[17] Even against the backdrop of the camp experience, authors of the memoirs often described the transit as particularly gruesome as inmates rarely had an adequate supply of food and water, season-appropriate clothing, or places to sleep and rest inside the train car. And in the cases when fellow convicts died, sometimes they had to continue travelling alongside the dead bodies.

Consistent data on prisoner mortality during these relocations is not available, but memoirs bear witness to the extreme exhaustion of inmates during transit. Testimonies of those who survived the relocations, incarceration, and forced labour also allow us to grasp this dynamic dimension of the camp system: the camp experience was not limited to forced immobility (incarceration), but also involved extreme coerced relocation. The forced labour system served not only as a tool of compulsory colonization, by attaching groups of people to specific territories, but also as an instrument of the impetuous and ruthless extraction and exploitation of resources, both natural and human, across the entire Soviet Union, through this relentless forced movement.

Attempts to keep camps secret accompanied the growth of the system. Towards the end of the 1930s, the triumphant narratives of "re-forging through labour" that surrounded the first big projects based on convict labour disappeared from the public space. Instead, the Gulag system became more and more secretive: the "shock camp labourers" (*lagerniki-udarniki*) were no longer glorified in the press, documents related to the functioning of the camps were classified, and wage workers employed on sites controlled by the Main Administration of Camps had to sign non-disclosure agreements.[18] Along with the fear and social stigma placed on inmates and special settlers, secrecy helped to cover up the abuses systemic to the camp system. In many areas, such as Vorkuta, secrecy was hard to enforce, as the daily life of forced labourers was inextricably intertwined with the life of whole towns.[19]

The Gulag's role in the Soviet economy was its other distinctive characteristic. Recent scholarship on the camp system has offered in-depth studies of regional camps and their connections to the local and union-wide

---

17   Khlevniuk, "No Total Totality", p. 969.
18   G.M. Ivanova, *Istoriia GULAGa, 1918–1958: Sotsial'no-ekonomicheskii i politiko-pravovoi aspekty* (Moscow: Nauka, 2006), pp. 241–42.
19   Alan Barenberg, *Gulag Town, Company Town: Forced Labor and Its Legacy in Vorkuta* (New Haven, CT: Yale University Press, 2014).

economy and society.[20] We know today relatively well not only how various camp complexes functioned and impacted the economy, but also how the administration of the system as a whole developed over time.[21] The cases of camp complexes on the fringes of the Soviet Union, such as Kolyma or Karaganda, initially attracted more attention than some more centrally located camps, but new studies on the camps in the more densely populated regions are also appearing.[22] Crucial information contained in the classified archives of the Federal Security Service (Federal'naia sluzhba bezopasnosti Rossiiskoi Federatsii, FSB) is still lacking and, considering the current political climate, is unlikely to become available in the near future, but, as Oleg Khlevniuk has noted, historiography of the Gulag is already "approaching the point at which we merely begin to reproduce or touch-up a well-illustrated picture".[23] Towards the end of the 1930s the NKVD came to control such significant parts of the Soviet economy that the Gulag turned into what Galina Ivanova, seeking to highlight the penetration of convict labour into the economy, has called the "camp-industrial complex" (lagerno-promyshlennyi kompleks).[24] By 1937, the NKVD already controlled 6 per cent of the Soviet Union's capital investment.[25] The NKVD (after 1946, the MVD, the Ministry of Internal Affairs) continued to play an ever-growing role in the economy of the country, participating in some industries (for instance,

20   On Magadan and Dal'stroi, see A.I. Shirokov, Dal'stroi v sotsial'no-ekonomicheskom razvitii Severo-Vostoka SSSR (1930–1950-e gg.) (Moscow: ROSSPEN, 2014); David J. Nordlander, "Origins of a Gulag Capital: Magadan and Stalinist Control in the Early 1930s", Slavic Review, 57:4 (1998), pp. 791–812; David J. Nordlander, "Capital of the Gulag: Magadan in the Early Stalin Era, 1929–1941" (Ph.D. dissertation, University of North Carolina at Chapel Hill, 1997); and David J. Nordlander, "Magadan and the Evolution of the Dal'stroi Bosses in the 1930s", Cahiers du monde russe, 42:2–4 (2001), pp. 649–66. On Karlag in Kazakhstan, see Barnes, Death and Redemption. On the Karelian Gulag, Nick Baron, Soviet Karelia: Politics, Planning and Terror in Stalin's Russia, 1920–1939 (Abingdon: Routledge, 2007). On Norilsk, Simon Ertz, Zwangsarbeit im stalinistischen Lagersystem: Eine Untersuchung der Methoden, Strategien und Ziele ihrer Ausnutzung am Beispiel Norilsk, 1935–1953 (Berlin: Duncker & Humboldt, 2006). On the Gulag in the Urals region, see James Harris, "The Growth of the Gulag: Forced Labor in the Urals Region, 1929–31", The Russian Review 56:2 (1997), pp. 265–80 and Judith Pallot, "Forced Labour for Forestry: The Twentieth Century History of Colonization and Settlement in the North of Perm' Oblast'", Europe-Asia Studies 54:7 (2002), pp. 1055–83. On Viatlag, Viktor Berdinskikh, Istoriia odnogo lageria (Viatlag) (Moscow: Agraf, 2001). On Vorkuta, Barenberg, Gulag Town, Company Town.
21   Khlevniuk, The History of the Gulag; Paul R. Gregory and Valery Lazarev (eds), The Economics of Forced Labor: The Soviet Gulag (Stanford, CA: Hoover Institution Press, 2003); Borodkin et al., Gulag.
22   Bell, "The Gulag and Soviet Society in Western Siberia, 1929–1953.
23   Khlevniuk, "The Gulag and the Non-Gulag", p. 479.
24   Ivanova, Istoriia GULAGa, pp. 222–64.
25   Davies et al., The Industrialization of Soviet Russia, vol. 7, p. 83.

the timber industry and construction) and almost exclusively controlling others (such as gold and diamond mining). On the eve of Stalin's death, the MVD was the largest construction agency in the Soviet Union and received no less than 10 per cent of all capital investment.[26] By the beginning of the war, the economic functions of the Gulag were diverse. According to Russian economic historian Leonid Borodkin, they included the following: the Gulag was used to force the economic development of the most distant areas of the country; it created a pool of extremely mobile labourers who could be easily displaced according to the plans and needs of the political leadership; it gave the authorities the possibility of overexploiting the interned labourers; it enabled the disciplining of other labourers through the constant threat of incarceration in the camps; it reduced pressure on the weak market for consumer goods (for instance, by controlling inmates' rations); and it partially alleviated social problems in the wider society, such as the lack of housing, through the isolation and displacement of millions of inmates, deportees, and "special settlers".[27]

When the Soviet Union entered World War II on 22 June 1941, the pressure on labourers both inside and outside the Gulag increased tremendously. Already in the first weeks of the war, new regulations steeply reduced the inmates' time off work, limiting days off to three per month, and the period of daily rest to eight hours.[28] Total mobilization for the war effort led to the tightening of labour legislation in the whole country: in December 1941, in an attempt to fight high labour turnover and labour shortage, the Soviet government prohibited employees from switching between enterprises.[29] Abandonment of the workplace was now punishable with five to eight years of confinement, making incarceration a measure to discipline the workforce. Convict labour was not the only way that the Gulag was mobilized for war: over one million young healthy male convicts were released from the camps to fight in the Red Army. This concerned, above all, common criminals, especially those convicted for petty crime, while "counterrevolutionaries" were not included in these releases.

26 Oleg Khlevniuk, "Zony sovetskoi ekonomiki. Razdelenie i vzaimodeistvie", in L.I. Borod-kin, S.A. Krasil'nikov, and O.V. Khlevniuk (eds), *Istoriia stalinizma: Prinuditel'nyi trud v SSSR. Ekonomika, politika, pamiat'* (Moscow: ROSSPEN, 2013), pp. 38–54, 38.

27 L.I. Borodkin, "GULAG v gody voiny: Mobilizatsionnaia ekonomika v ekstremal'nom rezhime", *Ural'skii istoricheskii vestnik*, 61:4 (2018), pp. 46–54, 48.

28 Steven A. Barnes, "All for the Front, All for Victory! The Mobilization of Forced Labor in the Soviet Union during World War Two", *International Labor and Working-Class History*, 58 (October 2000), pp. 239–60, 244.

29 *Ibid.*

Combined with the lack of food and shortages of other essential supplies, the wartime labour rules led to a spike in inmate mortality. Already between 1940 and 1941, mortality in the Gulag more than doubled, but it became truly horrific as the war dragged on. In 1942, the average mortality rate across the Gulag reached 24.9 per cent, with an average of more than thirty thousand people dying per month in the camps, penal colonies, and prisons. In 1943 it remained exceptionally high, with 22.4 per cent of inmates dying throughout the year.[30] Annihilation through labour was not the goal of the Gulag administration as a whole, but the health of inmates was not a priority either, as the number of inmates soared on the eve of the USSR entering the war.[31] State-defined production goals had to be fulfilled, often regardless of the human cost, and both the overexploitation of inmates and intensive forced relocations served this goal with an extremely high loss of life. Reliance on forced labour also meant that the level of mechanization of labour was extremely low. As memoirs of former inmates attest, the avoidance of hard physical labour in construction, mining, or the timber industry was the crucial condition of survival. Working in the camp's medical section, at the lower levels of camp administration (for instance, as an accountant), or at an animal farm could all bring salvation from death by exhaustion, exposure, and illness.

Under wartime conditions, Soviet officials looked for an unprecedentedly severe punishment for those whom they saw as threatening to the survival of the regime. In devising this punishment, they explicitly tapped into the tsarist heritage and combined the Soviet camps with the most severe tsarist penal regime. Thus, twenty-six years after its abolition, katorga was re-introduced.

Reinventing katorga

When katorga was abolished by the Provisional Government in February 1917, its demise seemed definitive; militants across the political spectrum demonstrated a deep aversion to this particular penal regime, as it had become the symbol of the harshness and despotism of tsarist political

---

30   Kokurin and Petrov, *GULAG*, pp. 441–42, and Ivanova, *Istoriia GULAGa*, pp. 52 and 256.

31   Between 1 January 1939 and 1 January 1941, the combined population of the camps, penal colonies, and prisons grew by nearly 1 million, from almost 2 million to 2.9 million people. See: Barnes, *Death and Redemption*, p. 113. On annihilation through labour in the Nazi camps, see Nikolaus Wachsmann, "'Annihilation through Labor': The Killing of State Prisoners in the Third Reich", *The Journal of Modern History*, 71:3 (1999), pp. 624–59.

persecution. After the October revolution, the Bolsheviks experimented with a variety of new punishments, but bringing back katorga was not evoked in these early discussions. This was perhaps related to the role that former political prisoners still played in the politics of the early Soviet state. With the creation in 1921 of the All-Union Association of Former Political Prisoners and Exiled Settlers also began the institutionalization of the memory of the victims of the tsarist katorga. This association united revolutionaries, helped former inmates, and collected and disseminated knowledge about political repression in imperial Russia by publishing brochures and periodicals. The association largely shaped the vibrantly plurivocal heritage of the revolutionary struggle by telling the stories of anarchists, social revolutionaries, Mensheviks, and members of other revolutionary movements. It managed to attain relative independence, but was forcibly dissolved in 1935, as its activists were persecuted and sent to the camps.[32]

Soviet katorga was created by a decree of 17 April 1943 and punished those convicted as "Germano-fascist villains, spies, traitors of the Motherland and their cronies".[33] The choice of these offences once again highlighted the close interconnection between mass forced displacement and the camp system: wartime deportees, such as Chechens, Germans, Ingush, Crimean Tatars, and others, started to face terms of twenty years of katorga for attempting to escape the settlements into which they were forced.[34]

Like the imperial katorga, its Soviet iteration was intended as the second harshest punishment after the death penalty. It implied hard labour in the most dangerous locations, long-haul forced displacement, and a much stricter regime of isolation compared to the corrective labour camps. Special katorga sections were organized within some of the most remote camp complexes: Vorkuta, Kolyma, and Norilsk, as well as in Karaganda, where a subdivision for infirm convicts was located.[35] Although the exact locations were different to those of the imperial period, when the primary katorga sites were located in Eastern Siberia and on Sakhalin, the logic of expulsion of these convicts to the most distant and desolate areas, where geography itself became part of the punishment, persisted.

The Soviet katorga was an exceptionally harsh regime even by the brutal standards of the Gulag. Most famously, Aleksandr Solzhenitsyn called these

32   Marc Junge, *Die Allunionsgesellschaft ehemaliger politischer Zwangsarbeiter und Verbannter (1921–1935)* (Habilitation, Ruhr Universität Bochum, 2007).
33   GARF, f. 9414, op. 1, ch. 1, d. 76, l. 4.
34   Ivanova, *Istoriia GULAGa*, p. 86.
35   Barnes, *Death and Redemption*, p. 143.

204 COERCED LABOUR, FORCED DISPLACEMENT, AND THE SOVIET GULAG, 1880S-1930S

subdivisions "murder camps", where people were essentially starved and annihilated through labour.[36] A wartime punitive innovation, katorga became the most violent and deadly regime in a system where survival was already challenging. Documents show that connections between the Soviet and the tsarist katorga systems did not limit themselves to the use of the same term. Unfortunately, I could not find any documents concerning the preparation of the initial 17 April 1943 law that re-introduced this punitive regime, but dossiers on the discussions of the reform of katorga from 1945 and 1948 are available. They show that the Soviet camp administrators were more than just vaguely aware of the functioning of the tsarist system; they prepared extensive research notes on the pre-revolutionary legislation, and straightforwardly adapted some defining aspects of the punishment for their own needs.[37]

Initially, the application of katorga was relatively limited, but it expanded rapidly as the Soviet army advanced through the former Nazi occupied territories. On 1 January 1944, there were 981 katorga convicts in the camps, most of them in the region of Vorkuta, but already by mid-1944, their number had grown to 5,200.[38] The use of this new punitive regime gained momentum by the end of the war and especially in its aftermath. In the final months of World War II, large groups of people from the western territories of the USSR were sent to the camps, notably those suspected of being guerrilla fighters from Lithuania, Latvia, Estonia, and Ukraine, and their alleged supporters among the peasant population.[39] While by May 1945 around twenty-nine thousand people were serving katorga terms in the camps, already by 1 September 1945 this number had increased to 38,568.[40] Extremely high mortality rates among these inmates, however, do not allow us to determine how many people in all were sentenced to this ordeal. Convicts in Vorkuta were given numbers that consisted of a letter of the Cyrillic alphabet and a number of up to one thousand. Elena Markova (1923–2023), a katorga survivor who arrived in Vorkuta in July 1944 and eventually served a ten-year term, noted that during the first two years of her confinement in the camp, the inmates were dying so fast that the camp administration went through two

36 Aleksandr Solzhenitsyn, *The Gulag Archipelago, 1918–1956: An Experiment in Literary Investigation*. Vol. 3 (New York: Harper Perennial Modern Classics, 2007 [1974]), p. 8.
37 GARF, f. 9414, op. 1, ch. 1, d. 76 and d. 359, respectively.
38 E.V. Markova, *Vorkutinskie zametki katorzhanki "E-105"* (Syktyvkar: Komi respublikanskii martirolog zhertv massovykh politicheskikh repressii "Pokaianie", 2005), p. 5, and GARF, f. 9414, op. 1, ch. 1, d. 68, l. 8.
39 GARF, f. 9414, op. 1 ch. 1, d. 68, ll. 36–39.
40 Kokurin and Petrov, *GULAG*, pp. 132–33, and GARF, f. 9414, op. 1, ch. 1, d. 76, l. 11.

"alphabets", meaning that at least fifty-six thousand people had arrived at this camp.[41] According to Solzhenitsyn, the inmates of the first "alphabet" in Vorkuta "all passed under the earth within a year".[42] Mortality statistics are elusive, but other sources help us to see that the health and survival of these convicts were under constant threat. In 1945, a discussion of katorga and the death penalty was initiated by Nikita Khrushchev, then Secretary of the Central Committee. He suggested that all those sentenced to capital punishment should be sent to katorga instead. In response, the deputy of the People's Commissar of Internal Affairs, Vasilii Chernyshev, prepared a memo on the functioning of katorga and recommended against Khrushchev's suggestion. This memo highlights the destructive power of Soviet katorga: while Khrushchev intended to "keep the physically healthy people for use on works in the distant and hostile territories of the Soviet Union", Chernyshev argued against this by stating that out of the twenty-nine thousand katorga convicts in the Soviet Union in May 1945, more than ten thousand were physically unable to work at all, not to mention perform hard labour.[43]

Soviet legislators' reliance on the pre-revolutionary heritage manifested in three main similarities between the tsarist and the Stalinist katorga. First, the regime relied once again on the punitive use of transportation combined with hard labour. The desire to isolate the convicts deemed most dangerous was coupled with the intent to make their terms particularly punitive, as the places where these convicts were banished were the most distant parts of the realm.

The second similarity lay in the organization of punishment. The most brutal aspect was borrowed directly: convicts had to wear shackles at all times, not only while working, but also in the barracks, which were locked at all times, preventing the inmates from moving even within the camp zone. Both men and women had their heads shaved, which was not the case for inmates of the corrective labour camps. Head shaving could have been argued as a precaution against lice, but it was also another traumatizing intervention into the inmates' bodies: Elena Markova remarked that she was shocked and fascinated when she saw the female inmates working in the medical section of the camp for the first time, as they all had long shiny hair. For her, the loss of her hair was an infringement of her womanhood.

41 The Russian alphabet contains thirty-three letters, but five of them (io, i kratkoe, y, the "soft" and the "hard" signs) cannot be used in such cases. E.V. Markova, "Doroga, kotoruiu ia ne vybirala", Radost', 3 (1995), pp. 126–33, p. 130.
42 Solzhenitsyn, The Gulag Archipelago, 1918–1956, p. 10.
43 Kokurin and Petrov, GULAG, p. 132.

And, in any case, it did not help against the lice.[44] The Soviet katorga, like its tsarist predecessor, implied extremely long terms, during which the convicts could belong to one of three categories of inmate depending on their degree of compliance with the camp administration. This arrangement and even the names of the categories were directly borrowed from the tsarist legislation. Transition to a more "privileged" category could grant inmates some improvement in their condition, such as the possibility to switch from physical labour to work for which they had qualifications, the possibility of correspondence with their relatives, or even remuneration for their work.[45]

The third similarity consisted in the consequences of this hard labour regime. Even though consistent statistics on the death rates in these subdivisions are not available, it is clear that the Soviet katorga was extremely deadly, and even those who survived it bore its stigma not only after their legal rehabilitation, but indeed until the fall of the Soviet Union. The tsarist katorga left convicts no possibility of making a return to society: even after they had served their terms, they had to remain in the surroundings of the penal sites as exiled settlers, and many of them could never return to a productive life due to physical disabilities sustained during their incarceration. In the Soviet case, former convicts could leave the surrounding areas of the camp only due to political change following the death of Stalin, but the initial legislation prescribed that they remain in exile next to the camps where they had served their terms.

Building on the imperial heritage, Soviet officials and camp administrators avidly used modern technical means like barbed wire, thus enhancing control over the inmates to an unprecedented degree. Policing was also significantly more pervasive than in the tsarist period: elaborate statistics and intricate social categorizations defined the potential inmates, while the passport system had made the society more transparent.[46] The last traces of inmates' individuality were erased through the use of numbers, rather than names, during roll calls and in everyday life.

Due to this intensification of control, labour in the Soviet katorga was also organized in a manner that brought this regime close to annihilation through labour. In their choice for the main katorga location, Vorkuta, central authorities were driven by the imperatives of wartime economic mobilization: as the German army was advancing in the western territories of the Soviet Union, the coal supply from the Donbass was cut off, thus making

44   Markova, *Vorkutinskie zametki*, pp. 36–39.
45   GARF, f. 9414, op. 1, ch. 1, d. 359, ll. 3–4.
46   Shearer, "Elements Near and Alien".

alternative sources of coal crucial. The Pechora coal basin was one of the main alternative mining locations within the USSR, and a particularly crucial one due to its proximity to Leningrad.[47] Inmates had to work twelve-hour shifts under hostile weather conditions, follow an extremely strict regime both during working hours and afterwards, and had vanishing prospects of actually surviving their terms. Elena Markova described her katorga experience like this: "Reality was so terrifying that it seemed impossible to survive even one day. And I had a fifteen-year term".[48] Markova's dread echoes a dry remark made by Vasilii Chernyshev, who stated that katorga convicts in Vorkuta were "morally depressed and completely lacked stimulus for labour", as they had lost "the perspective" of completing their terms of 15 to 20 years.[49]

At the beginning of 1948, the political leadership initiated another change in the penal system.[50] Through the creation of the "special camps" (*osobye lageria*) in February 1948, a stricter, katorga-like regime began to affect a much larger group of inmates.[51] In terms of regime severity, the "special camps" were intended to fall between corrective labour camps and katorga. Initial plans envisaged the creation of "special camps" in the regions of Norilsk, Komi, Kolyma, Karaganda, and Mordovia for a total of 100,000 prisoners.[52] These camps were intended for twelve categories of inmates deemed particularly dangerous; prisoners of such categories were to be transferred to the new camps within eight months.[53] According to the MVD order that prescribed the regime in these camps, convicts were to work in ten-hour shifts (one hour more than in the regular camps), preferably performing hard labour.[54] The leadership of the Main Administration of Camps required that the local camp administrators ensure full employment of the inmates, but this generally remained an unattainable goal. As Aleksandr Mironov has observed, most

---

47 Barenberg, *Gulag Town, Company Town*, pp. 43–45.

48 Markova, *Vorkutinskie zametki*, p. 51.

49 Kokurin and Petrov, *GULAG*, p. 133.

50 Ivanova, *Istoriia GULAGa*, p. 296.

51 Barenberg, *Gulag Town, Company Town*, p. 97.

52 Nikita Petrov (ed.), *Istoriia stalinskogo gulaga. Konets 1920-kh – pervaia polovina 1950-kh godov. Tom 2. Karatelnaia sistema: Struktury i kadry* (Moscow: ROSSPEN, 2004), p. 326 and Kokurin and Petrov, *GULAG*, pp. 135–37.

53 These categories were: (1) spies; (2) wreckers (*diversanty*); (3) terrorists; (4) Trotskyists; (5) members of the Right opposition; (6) Mensheviks; (7) social revolutionaries; (8) anarchists; (9) nationalists; (10) White emigrants; (11) "members of other anti-Soviet organizations and groups"; and (12) "persons presenting danger due to their anti-Soviet relations and enemy activity". For more on these categories, see Ivanova, *Istoriia GULAGa*, pp. 300–301.

54 GARF, f. 9401, op. 2, d. 8, l. 99.

of the "special camps" were installed in regions where the use of regular camp inmates' labour was already developed, and camp administrations could rarely provide more employment for the forced labourers. This would have required either the installation of new industrial or construction sites or a reduction of the number of regular camp inmates, but the local camp bosses were not ready for either of these two options.[55] The exhaustion of inmates and the lack of guards and potential employment all meant that the central authorities' plans were rarely met. In 1949, only one special camp, the Berlag, transferred to the state budget more money than it had received.[56] Although hard physical labour was stated as one of the fundamental elements both of katorga and the special camps, implementation of the central authorities' orders continued to be a challenge for local camp bosses. For convicts, however, this provided little relief: due to the long sentences, forced collectivism, meagre rations, poor living conditions, harsh climate, and illness, these camps were among the most dangerous institutions in the Gulag.

Stalin died on 5 March 1953, and already on 27 March a decree "On amnesty" was published in the central press which prompted the release of 1.5 million inmates from the camps, colonies, and prisons, amounting to almost 60 per cent of all Gulag detainees.[57]

Stalin's death served as an impetus for the virtual dismantlement of the system of mass forced labour, but the system was already in crisis prior to that. The first post-war amnesty had already served as a shock to the Gulag and produced some lingering changes in the camp system. Almost half of the inmate labourers were released in 1945, and despite initial hopes that the amnesty would serve as a source of motivation and would help to increase inmate productivity, its overall effect on labour output in the camps was negative. Many younger and more skilled workers were released, while the number of invalids released under Stalin's amnesty was much lower. As Golfo Alexopoulos has put it, the amnesty instead simply further weakened an already crippled institution.[58]

The 1953 amnesty relied on projects that had been elaborated before the death of Stalin. Plans were made within the MVD for a deep reorganization

---

55   Aleksandr Mironov, "Trudovoe ispolzovanie zakliuchennykh osobykh lagerei MVD SSSR", in Borodkin *et al.*, *Istoriia stalinizma*, pp. 200–210, 201.

56   GARF, f. 9414, op. 1, d. 1846, l. 287.

57   Aleksei Tikhonov, "The End of the Gulag", in Gregory and Lazarev, *The Economics of Forced Labor*, pp. 67–73, 67. On the eve of Stalin's death, there were around 2.5 million people in all of these institutions, with circa 1.7 million in the corrective labour camps.

58   Golfo Alexopoulos, "Amnesty 1945: The Revolving Door of Stalin's Gulag", *Slavic Review*, 64:2 (2005), pp. 274–306.

of the Gulag, including proposals to change the status of all camp inmates to that of exiled labourers in 1951 and 1953. During the brief period when Beriia was in power following Stalin's death, these plans served as a road map for the March 1953 amnesty.[59] The rapid reduction in the number of inmates and the closure of penal institutions were just two of the aspects of the comprehensive post-Stalin reform of the penal system. These reforms also aimed for the "return to socialist legality", lifting the veil of secrecy from the Gulag, and providing some external control over the functioning of the camps. Moreover, another goal of the reforms was to reduce the economic importance of the camp system "in favour of a multifaceted correctional programme".[60]

The situation inside the camps also changed. While in the 1930s most of the inmates in the camps were peasants, workers, party members, and cadres, after the war new groups of people with experience of armed resistance were incarcerated. These included the inhabitants of the Nazi occupied territories, who had often participated in the partisan struggle, Soviet soldiers released from German POW camps, as well as members of the Russian liberation movement and the Organization of Ukrainian Nationalists, among others. Many of these inmates shared a hatred of the Soviet regime, were ready to fight it from within the camp system, and had experience with self-organization and armed resistance.[61] Despite the fact that the number of camp inmates grew consistently following the end of World War II, reaching its peak of around 1.7 million in 1953, the productivity of labour in the industries controlled by the Gulag was falling. An ever-growing number of inmates refused to work, and the strikes, armed escape attempts, and uprisings in the camps became more and more frequent.[62] Three of the largest post-Stalin Gulag uprisings, in Vorkuta (Rechlag), Norilsk (Gorlag), and Kengir (Steplag), all occurred in the "special camps".

Post-1953 transformations in Soviet politics led to the dismantlement of the gargantuan repressive system of mass forced labour and displacement within several years of Stalin's death, but even after the Gulag formally ceased to exist, its legacy continued to loom large. In the 1960s, despite the use of parole and other tactics to reduce the number of inmates, rates of

59   Tikhonov, "The End of the Gulag", pp. 69–72.
60   Marc Elie and Jeffrey Hardy, "'Letting the Beasts Out of the Cage': Parole in the Post-Stalin Gulag, 1953–1973", *Europe-Asia Studies*, 67:4 (2015), pp. 579–605, 579. The reintroduction in 1954 of parole, which was abolished in 1939, was a significant part of this reform.
61   Marta Craveri, "Krizis GULaga: Kengirskoe vosstanie 1954 goda v dokumentakh MVD". *Cahiers du monde russe*, 36:3 (1995), pp. 319–43, 320.
62   *Ibid.*, pp. 321–23.

incarceration remained high, demonstrating that the use of mass repression persisted.[63] Today, the Gulag legacy continues to manifest itself not only in the domain of memory politics, but also in the carceral experiences of prisoners. An excessive reliance on the forced displacement of inmates and the placement of the strictest places of confinement in particularly distant regions shaped the location of the post-Soviet prisons and colonies as well.[64]

63   Elie and Hardy, "'Letting the Beasts Out of the Cage'", p. 602.
64   Judith Pallot, "The Topography of Incarceration: The Spatial Continuity of Penality and the Legacy of the Gulag in Twentieth- and Twenty-First-Century Russia", *Laboratorium: Russian Review of Social Research*, 7:1 (2015), pp. 26–50 and Laura Piacentini and Judith Pallot, "'In Exile Imprisonment' in Russia", *British Journal of Criminology*, 54:1 (2014), pp. 20–37.

Bibliography

Archival collections cited

RGIA (*Rossiiskii gosudarstvennyi istoricheskii arkhiv*) – Russian State Historical
Archive, Saint Petersburg:
  f. 20 – Department of Trade and Manufactories (*Departament torgovli i manufaktur*)
  f. 1149 – Department of Laws of the State Council (*Departament Zakonov
  Gosudarstvennogo Soveta*)
  f. 1151 – Department of Civil and Religious Affairs of the State Council (*Departament grazhdanskikh i dukhovnykh del Gosudarstvennogo Soveta*)

GARF (*Gosudarstvennyi arkhiv Rossiiskoi Federatsii*) – State Archive of the Russian
Federation, Moscow:
  f. 122 – Main Prison Administration of the Ministry of Justice (*Glavnoe Tiuremnoe
  Upravlenie pri Ministerstve Iustitsii*)
  f. 4042 – Main Administration of Places of Confinement, NKVD (*Glavnoe
  Upravlenie mestami zakliucheniia (GUMZ) Narkomata vnutrennikh del RSFSR*)
  f. 9401 – Ministry of Interior, USSR (*Ministerstvo vnutrennikh del SSSR*)
  f. 9414 – Main Administration of Places of Confinement, NKVD – MVD USSR
  (*Glavnoe Upravlenie mest zakliucheniia NKVD – MVD SSSR*)

GANO (*Gosudarstvennyi arkhiv Novosibirskoi oblasti*) – State Archive of the
Novosibirsk Region, Novosibirsk:
  f. D-97 – Novonikolaevsk City Government, Novonikolaevsk, September 1909–
  December 1919 (*Novonikolaevskaia gorodskaia uprava, g. Novonikolaevsk,
  sentiabr' 1909 – dekabr' 1919 gg.*)
  f. R-1133 – Executive Committee of the Novonikolaevsk Soviet of Workers', Peasants', and Soldiers' Deputies, Novonikolaevsk, 26.07.1921–1925 (*Ispolnitel'nyi
  komitet Novonikolaevskogo gubernskogo Soveta rabochikh, krest'ianskikh i
  krasnoarmeiskikh deputatov, g. Novonikolaevsk, 26.07.1921–1925 g.*)

GATO (*Gosudarstvennyi arkhiv Tiumenskoi oblasti*) – State Archive of the Tyumen
Region, Tyumen:
  f. R-126 – Tyumen House of Correction (*Tiumenskii ispravitel'nyi dom*)
  f. R-127 – Inspection of the Places of Confinement of the Executive Section of the
  Executive Committee of the Tyumen Soviet of Workers', Peasants', and Soldiers'
  Deputies (*Inspektsiia mest zakliucheniia Otdela upravleniia Ispolkoma Tiumen-
  skogo gubernskogo Soveta rabochikh, krest'ianskikh i krasnoarmeiskikh deputatov*)

GBUTO (*Gosudarstvennyi arkhiv v g. Tobol'ske*) – State Archive in the town of Tobolsk:

f. R-168 – Tobolsk House of Correction and Tobolsk Camp of Compulsory Labour of the Department of Compulsory Labour of the NKVD USSR (*Tobol'skii ispravitel'nyi rabochii dom i Tobol'skii lager' prinuditel'nykh rabot otdela prinuditel'nykh rabot NKVD SSSR*)

Printed primary sources

Anikst, A.M. *Organizatsiia rabochei sily v 1920 godu*. Moscow: Izd. agit.-uzdat. otdela GKT i NKT, 1921.

Apeter, Ivan. 'Osnovnye printsipy ispravitel'no-trudovoi politiki NKIu i tipy mest lisheniia svobody i organov ispravitel'no-trudovykh rabot bez soderzhaniia pod strazhei: Tezisy k dokladu tov. Apetera na V soveshchanii rukovodiashchikh rabotnikov organov iustitsii kraev i oblastei RSFSR'. *Sovetskaia iustitsiia*, no. 18 (1931): 23–26.

'Arestantskii trud na nuzhdy armii'. *Tiuremnyi vestnik*, no. 5 (1916): 519–23.

Beloborodov, A.G., ed. *Sovremennaia prestupnost' (prestuplenie, pol, repressia, retsidiv)*. Moscow: NKVD RSFSR, 1927.

Bezsonov, Iu. *Mes vingt-six prisons et mon évasion de Solovki*. Paris: Payot, 1928.

Brändström, Elsa. *Among Prisoners of War in Russia & Siberia*. London: Hutchinson, 1929.

Browder, Robert Paul, and Aleksandr Fyodorovich Kerensky. *The Russian Provisional Government, 1917*. 3 vols. Stanford, CA: Hoover Institution Press, 1961.

Cantor, Nathaniel. 'Measures of Social Defense'. *Cornell Law Review* 22, no. 1 (1936): 17–38.

Dekrety Sovetskoi vlasti. Tom VII. 10 dekabria 1919 g.–31 marta 1920 g. Moscow: Politizdat, 1975.

Dril', Dmitrii. *Ssylka i katorga v Rossii*. Saint Petersburg: Tipografiia Pravitel'stvuiushchego Senata, 1898.

Dril', Dmitrii. *Ssylka vo Frantsii i v Rossii: Iz lichnykh nabliudenii vo vremia poezdki v Novuiu Kaledoniiu, na o. Sakhalin, v Priamurskii krai i Sibir'*. Saint Petersburg: Izdanie L.F. Panteleeva, 1899.

Dril', Dmitrii. 'Tiuremnyia raboty, ikh znachenie i organizatsiia'. *Tiuremnyi vestnik*, no. 1 (1902): 23–47.

Dyboski, Roman. *Seven Years in Russia and Siberia, 1914–1921*. Cheshire, CT: Cherry Hill Books, 1971.

Eikhgol'ts. 'Fizicheskii trud, kak sredstvo dlia ulutscheniia sanitarnogo sostoianiia tiur'my'. *Tiuremnyi vestnik*, no. 6–7 (1910): 923–38.

Estrin, Aleksandr. 'K voprosu o printsipakh postroeniia sistemy ugolovnoi repressii v proletarskom gosudarstve'. *Revoliutsiia prava*, no. 1 (1927): 74–98.

Estrin, Aleksandr. *Sovetskoe ugolovnoe pravo*. Moscow: Gosudarstvennoe izdatel'stvo 'Sovetskoe zakonodatel'stvo', 1935.

Estrin, Aleksandr, and V. Trakhterev. 'Razvitie sovetskoi ispravitel'no-trudovoi politiki kak chasti sovetskoi ugolovnoi politiki'. In *Ot tiurem k vospitatel'nym uchrezhdeniiam*, edited by A.Ia. Vyshinskii, 17–71. Moscow: Sovetskoe zakonodatel'stvo, 1934.

Gailis, K. 'Prinuditel'nye raboty i drugie mery sotsial'noi zashchity vmesto kratkosrochnogo lisheniia svobody'. *Ezhenedel'nik sovetskoi iustitsii*, no. 7 (1929): 158–61.

Galkin, Mikhail. *Materialy k izucheniiu tiuremnogo voprosa*. Saint Petersburg: Tipografiia Vtorogo otdeleniia sobstvennoi E.I.V. kantseliarii, 1868.

Gessen, V.M. *Iskliuchitel'noe polozhenie*. Saint Petersburg: Pravo, 1908.

Goliakov, I.T., ed. *Sbornik dokumentov po istorii ugolovnogo zakonodatelstva SSSR i RSFSR, 1917–1952 gg.* Moscow: Gosiurizdat, 1953.

Gorky, Maxim, Leopold Leonidovich Auerbach, and Semen Georgievich Firin, *The White Sea Canal: Being an Account of the Construction of the New Canal between the White Sea and the Baltic Sea*. London: John Lane, 1935.

Gradusov, Vladimir. 'Zheleznodorozhnye raboty arestantov'. *Tiuremnyi vestnik*, no. 6–7 (1916): 657–58.

Gran, P.K. *Katorga v Sibiri. Izvlecheniia iz otcheta o sluzhebnoi poezdke Nachal'nika Glavnogo Upravleniia P. K. Grana v Sibir' v 1913 godu*. Saint Petersburg: Tipolitografiia S.-Peterburgskoi Odinochnoi Tiur'my, 1913.

Gur'ev, N. 'Sanitarnoe sostoianie nashikh tiurem'. *Tiuremnyi vestnik*, no. 1 (1910): 65–85.

Iadrintsev, Nikolai. *Sibir' kak koloniia*. Saint Petersburg: Tipografiia M.M. Stasiulevicha, 1882.

Iakubson, Viktor. 'Klassifikatsiia zakliuchennykh i izuchenie vliianiia na nikh ispravitel'no-trudovogo vozdeistviia'. *Pravo i zhizn'*, no. 4–5 (1925): 88–95.

Iakubson, Viktor. 'Lishenie svobody, kak mera sotsial'noi zashchity po Ugolovnomu i Ispravitel'no-Trudovomu Kodeksam RSFSR'. *Problemy prestupnosti*, no. 3 (1928): 189–96.

Iakubson, Viktor. 'Reforma ugolovnogo zakonodatel'stva i prinuditel'nye raboty bez soderzhaniia pod strazhei'. *Administrativnyi Vestnik*, no. 1 (1929): 35–39.

Iakubson, Viktor. 'Ugolovnaia repressiia v pervye gody revoliutsii'. *Ezhenedel'nik sovetskoi iustitsii*, no. 4 (1922): 3–4.

Ianson, Nikolai. 'Doklad Narodnogo Komissara Iustitsii RSFSR tov. Iansona – Otchet NKIu RSFSR'. *Ezhenedel'nik sovetskoi iustitsii*, no. 9–10 (1929): 193–212.

Ignat'ev, V. 'Chto nuzhno dlia razvitiia arestantskikh rabot?' *Tiuremnyi vestnik*, no. 5 (1908): 432–34.

Isaev, Mikhail. *Obshchaia chast' sovetskogo ugolovnogo prava RSFSR*. Leningrad: Gosudarstvennoe izdatel'stvo, 1925.

Isaev, Mikhail. *Osnovy penitentsiarnoi politiki*. Moscow: Gosizdat, 1926.

Isaev, Mikhail. 'Predstoiashchee preobrazovanie katorgi'. *Pravo*, 6 (13 February 1911): 321–32.

Isaev, Mikhail. 'Predstoiashchee preobrazovanie katorgi (prodolzhenie)'. *Pravo*, 7 (20 February 1911): 393–404.

Isaev, Mikhail, ed. *Trudy Kruzhka ugolovnogo prava pri S.-Peterburgskom univer- sitete*. Saint Petersburg: Iurid. kn. sklad "Pravo", 1913.

Khrulev, S.S. *Katorga v Sibiri: Otchet nachal'nika Glavnogo tiuremnogo upravleniia S.S. Khruleva o sluzhebnoi poezdke v 1909 v Irkutskuiu guberniiu i Zabaikalskuiu oblast'*. Supplement to *Tiuremnyi vestnik*, no. 8-9 (1910).

Klement'ev, V.F. *V bolshevitskoi Moskve*. Moscow: Russkii put', 1998.

'Kratkaia ob'iasnitel'naia zapiska po proektu Ministra Iustitsii o preobrazovanii katorgi'. *Tiuremnyi vestnik*, no. 12 (1915): 1952–2018.

Kratkii ocherk meropriiatii v oblasti tiremnago dela v Rossii za period s 1900 po 1905 god, sostavlennyi dlia VII Mezhdunarodnogo tiuremnogo kongressa v Budapeshte Nachal'nikom Glavnogo Tiuremnogo Upravleniia A.M. Stremoukhovym. Saint Petersburg: Tipografiia S.-Peterburgskoi tiur'my, 1905.

Krylenko, Nikolai, and Aleksandr Estrin. 'Reforma sovetskogo ugolovnogo protsessa: Doklad N.V. Krylenko, Sodoklad A.Ia. Estrina'. *Revoliutssia Prava*, no. 1 (1928): 98–119.

Krzhivetskii, B. 'Vnutrenniia arestantskie raboty i kustarnyi trud'. *Tiuremnyi vestnik*, no. 5 (1913): 839–71.

K.V.N. 'Ssylka po prigovoram krestianskikh i meshchanskikh obshchestv'. *Russkaia rech'*, no. 3 (1881): 49–78.

Latsis (Sudrabs), M.Ia. *Chrezvychainye komissii po bor'be s kontrrevoliutsiei*. Moscow: Gosudarstvennoe izdatel'stvo, 1921.

Latsis (Sudrabs), M.Ia. *Dva goda bor'by na vnutrennem fronte*. Moscow: Gosudarst- vennoe izdatel'stvo, 1920.

Lebedev, N. 'Peresyl'noe otdelenie tiur'my, kak istochnik infektsii'. *Tiuremnyi vestnik*, no. 5 (1909): 578–602.

Lenin, Vladimir. 'How to Organize Competition?'. *Pravda*, no. 17, 20 January 1929. Available at: https://www.marxists.org/archive/lenin/works/1917/dec/25.htm, last accessed 2 July 2022.

Lenin, V.I. *Polnoe sobranie sochinenii. Tom 37 (Iiul' 1918–mart 1919)*. Moscow: Izdatel'stvo politicheskoi literatury, 1969.

Lenin, V.I. *Polnoe sobranie sochinenii. Tom 39 (Iiun'–dekabr' 1919)*. Moscow: Izdatel'stvo politicheskoi literatury, 1970.

Lenin, V.I. *Polnoe sobranie sochinenii. Tom 40 (Dekabr' 1919–aprel' 1920)*. Moscow: Izdatel'stvo politicheskoi literatury, 1974.

Luchinskii, Nikolai. 'Arestantskie raboty vo Frantsii i v Rossii'. *Tiuremnyi vestnik*, no. 1 (1906): 39–56.

Luchinskii, Nikolai. 'Raboty, dostupnye dlia vsekh arestantov'. *Tiuremnyi vestnik*, no. 12 (1909): 1171–82.

Maksimov, S.V. *Sibir' i katorga*. 3 vols. Saint Petersburg: Tipografiia A. Transhelia, 1871.

Malsagoff, S.A. *An Island Hell: A Soviet Prison in the Far North*. London: A.M. Philpot, 1926.

Mandelstam, Nadezhda. *Hope against Hope: A Memoir*. Translated by Max Hayward. New York: Atheneum, 1983.

Markova, E.V. 'Doroga, kotoruiu ia ne vybirala'. *Radost'* 3 (1995): 126–33.

Markova, E.V. *Vorkutinskie zametki katorzhanki "E-105"*. Syktyvkar: Komi respublikanskii martirolog zhertv massovykh politicheskikh repressii "Pokaianie", 2005.

Materialy po voprosu o preobrazovanii tiuremnoi chasti v Rossii. Izdany Ministerstvom Vnutrennikh Del po svedeniiam, dostavlennym ot Nachalnikov Gubernii. Saint Petersburg: Tipografiia Ministerstva Vnutrennikh Del, 1865.

Mel'gunov, Sergei Petrovich. *The Red Terror in Russia*. London: J.M. Dent, 1925.

'O primenenii v 1914–1915 gg. truda katorzhnykh k dorozhnomu stroitel'stvu v Sibiri'. *Tiuremnyi vestnik*, no. 6–7 (1915): 1347–57.

Obzor Amurskoi oblasti za 1914 god. Blagoveshchensk: Amur. obl. stat. kom., 1915.

Obzor desiatiletnei deiiatel'nosti Glavnogo Tiuremnago Upravleniia. 1879–1889. Saint Petersburg: Tipografiia Ministerstva Vnutrennikh Del, 1899.

'Obzor preobrazovanii po tiuremnoi chasti pri novykh zakonodatel'nykh ustanovleniiakh (1906–1912 g.g.)'. *Tiuremnyi vestnik*, no. 10 (1912): 1581–701.

Otchtet po Glavnomu tiuremnomu upravleniiu za 1895 god. Saint Petersburg: Tipografiia S.-Peterburgskoi tiur'my, 1897.

Otchtet po Glavnomu tiuremnomu upravleniiu za 1899 god. Saint Petersburg: Tipografiia S.-Peterburgskoi tiur'my, 1901.

Otchtet po Glavnomu tiuremnomu upravleniiu za 1905 god. Saint Petersburg: Tipo-Litografiia S.-Peterburgskoi tiur'my, 1906.

Parshenskii, L. 'Pis'mo v redaktsiiu'. *Tiuremnyi vestnik*, no. 4 (1913): 703–4.

Pasynkov, N.N. 'Doklad prichislennogo k Ministerstvu Iustitsii koll. sov. N.N. Pasynkova po voprosu 6-mu perechnia voprosov, postavlennykh na obsuzhdenie s'ezda'. *Tiuremnyi vestnik*, no. 4 (1914): 885–87.

Perel', Iakov, and Naum Lagovier. 'Pravyi uklon v karatel'noi politike'. *Sovetskaia iustitsiia*, no. 3 (1930): 14–17.

Perel', Iakov, and Naum Lagovier. 'Pravyi uklon v karatel'noi politike' (continuation). *Sovetskaia iustitsiia*, no. 4 (1930): 14–17.

'Po povodu predstoiashchego preobrazovaniia katorgi i ssylki'. *Tiuremnyi vestnik*, no. 6 (1899): 246–53.

Poznyshev, Sergei. *K voprosu o preobrazovanii nashei katorgi*. Moscow: Pechatnia A.I. Snegirevoi, 1914.

Poznyshev, Sergei. *Osnovy penitentsiarnoi nauki*. Moscow: Iuridicheskoe izdatel'stvo Narkomiusta, 1923.

Rabochee i Krest'ianskoe Pravitel'stvo. "Article 284." *Sobranie Uzakonenii i Raspori-azhenii Rabochego i Krestianskogo Pravitel'stva RSFSR*, no. 19 (January 30, 1918).

'Raboty arestantov na Amurskoi zheleznoi doroge v 1913 godu v predelakh Amurskoi oblasti'. *Tiuremnyi vestnik*, no. 4 (1915): 933–43.

'Rech Iansona na 3-em soveshchanii sudebno-prokurorskikh rabotnikov'. *Sovetskaia iustitsiia*, no. 24–25 (1930): 1–2.

Salomon, Aleksandr. 'O. Sakhalin (Iz otcheta byvshego nachal'nika glavnogo tiuremnogo upravleniia A.P. Salomona)'. *Tiuremnyi vestnik*, no. 1 (1901): 20–53.

Salomon, Aleksandr. 'Rech' Nachal'nika glavnogo tiuremnogo upravleniia ha o. Sakhalin'. *Tiuremnyi vestnik*, no. 1 (1899): 9–11.

Salomon, Aleksandr. *Ssylka v Sibir'. Ocherk eia istorii i sovremennago polozheniia*. Saint Petersburg: Tipografiia S.-Peterburgskoi Tiur'my, 1900.

Sbornik materialov Tsentral'nogo Karatel'nogo Otdela. Moscow, 1920.

Shirvindt, Evsei, ed. *Klassovaia bor'ba i prestupnost'*. Moscow: NKVD RSFSR, 1930.

Sobranie uzakonenii i rasporiazhenii pravitelstva za 1920 g. Moscow: Upravlenie delami Sovnarkoma SSSR, 1943.

Solzhenitsyn, Aleksandr. *The Gulag Archipelago, 1918–1956: An Experiment in Literary Investigation*. Vol. 3 (New York: Harper Perennial Modern Classics, 2007 [1974]).

Stalin, I.V. *Sochineniia. Tom 13*. Moscow: Gosudarstvennoe izdatel'stvo politicheskoi literatury, 1951.

Svatikov, S.G. *Rossiia i Sibir': (k istorii sibirskogo oblastnichestva v XIX v.)*. Prague: Izd. Obshchestva Sibiriakov, 1929.

Tagantsev, Nikolai. *Russkoe ugolovnoe pravo*. Vol. 2. Saint Petersburg: Gos. Tip., 1902.

Tal'berg, D.G. 'Ssylka na Sakhalin'. *Vestnik Evropy*, no. 5 (1879): 218–51.

Tikhomirov, M.N., and P.P. Epifanov, eds. *Sobornoe ulozhenie 1649 goda*. Moscow: Izadatel'stvo Moskovskogo gosudarstvennogo universiteta, 1961.

Tiuremnoe delo v 1921 godu. Otchet Narodnogo Komissariata Iustitsii, po Tsentral'nomu Ispravitel'no-Trudovomu Otdelu, IX-mu Vserossiiskomu S'ezdu Sovetov R., Kr., i K. D. Moscow, 1921.

Tiuremnoe delo v R.S.F.S.R. Otchet Tsentral'nogo Karatel'nogo Otdela N.K.Iu. VII-mu S'ezdu Sovetov. Moscow, 1919.

Tiuremnoe preobrazovanie. Tom I. Ispravitel'nyi dom, zakliuchenie v kreposti i tiur'ma. Saint Petersburg, 1905.

Tretii Vserossiiyskiy s'ezd Professional'nykh Soiuzov. Moscow, 1921.

Trotsky, Lev Davydovich. *K istorii russkoi revoliutsii*. Moscow: Politizdat, 1990 [1930].

Trotsky, Lev Davydovich. *Sochineniia. Tom 15. Na puti k sotsializmu, khoziaistvennoe stroitel'stvo Sovetskoi Respubliki*. Moscow, Leningrad: Gosizdat, 1927.

Trudy I Vserossiiskogo s'ezda Sovetov narodnogo khoziaistva, 25 maia–4 iunia 1918 g. Moscow, 1918.

Ve Congrès Pénitentiaire International (Paris – 1895). Vol. 3: Rapports de la Première Section. Melun: Imprimerie administrative, 1896.

Vikharev, P. 'Arestantskie raboty'. *Tiuremnyi vestnik*, no. 8 (1895): 430–32.

Vinogradov, V., A. Litvin, and V. Khristoforov, eds. 'Vystuplenie F.E. Dzerzhinskogo Na Plenarnom Zasedanii 4-i Konferentsii Gubernskikh Transportnykh i Osobykh Otdelov Cheka Posle Nagrazhdeniia Ordenom Krasnogo Znameni (6 Fevralia 1920)'. In *Arkhiv VChK. Sbornik Dokumentov*, 141–48. Moscow: Kuchkovo pole, 2007.

'Vserossiskiii s'ezd rabotnikov penitentsiarnogo dela'. *Ezhenedel'nik sovetskoi iustitsii*, no. 41 (1923): 949–53.

Zhurnaly vysochaishe uchrezhdennoi Komissii o meropriiatiakh po otmene ssylki. Zasedaniia 3 iunia, 9 i 16 dekabria 1899 g., 10 ianvaria i 7 fevralia 1900 g. Saint Petersburg, 1900.

Secondary literature

Adak, Ufuk. 'Central Prisons (Hapishane-i Umumi) in Istanbul and Izmir in the Late Ottoman Empire: In-Between Ideal and Reality'. *Journal of the Ottoman and Turkish Studies Association* 4, no. 1 (2017): 73–94.

Adams, Bruce Friend. *The Politics of Punishment: Prison Reform in Russia, 1863–1917*. DeKalb: Northern Illinois University Press, 1996.

Alexopoulos, Golfo. 'Amnesty 1945: The Revolving Door of Stalin's Gulag'. *Slavic Review* 64, no. 2 (2005): 274–306.

Alexopoulos, Golfo. 'Destructive-Labor Camps: Rethinking Solzhenitsyn's Play on Words'. *Kritika: Explorations in Russian and Eurasian History* 16, no. 3 (2015): 499–526.

Alexopoulos, Golfo. *Illness and Inhumanity in Stalin's Gulag*. New Haven, CT: Yale University Press, 2017.

Alexopoulos, Golfo. *Stalin's Outcasts: Aliens, Citizens, and the Soviet State, 1926–1936*. Ithaca, NY: Cornell University Press, 2003.

Alexopoulos, Golfo. 'A Torture Memo: Reading Violence in the Gulag'. In *Writing the Stalin Era: Sheila Fitzpatrick and Soviet Historiography*, edited by Golfo Alexopoulos, Julie Hessler, Kiril Tomoff, and Joshua A. Sanborn, 157–76. New York: Palgrave Macmillan, 2011.

Anan'ich, B.V., R.Sh. Ganelin, B.B. Dubentsov, V.S. Diakin, and S.I. Potolov. *Krizis samoderzhaviia v Rossii, 1895–1917*. Leningrad: Nauka, 1984.

Anderson, Clare, ed. *A Global History of Convicts and Penal Colonies*. London: Bloomsbury Academic, 2018.

Anderson, Clare, and Hamish Maxwell-Stewart. 'Convict Labour and the Western Empires, 1415–1954'. In *The Routledge History of Western Empires*, edited by Robert Aldrich and Kirsten McKenzie, 102–18. London, New York: Routledge, 2014.

Andrew, Christopher M., and Oleg Gordievsky. *KGB: The Inside Story of Its Foreign Operations from Lenin to Gorbachev*. New York: HarperCollins, 1990.

Arkhimandritova, M.A., V.N. Borisov, and M.A. Bocharnikova. *Institut zakonodatel'stva i sravnitel'nogo pravovedeniia pri pravitel'stve Rossiiskoi Federatsii: Nezabyvaemye imena*. Moscow: Eksmo, 2010.

Arnold, David. 'The Colonial Prison: Power, Knowledge and Penology in Nineteenth-Century India'. In *Subaltern Studies VIII: Essays in Honour of Ranajit Guha*, edited by David Arnold and David Hardiman, 148–87. Delhi, Oxford: Oxford University Press, 1994.

Badcock, Sarah. 'From Villains to Victims: Experiencing Illness in Siberian Exile'. *Europe-Asia Studies* 65, no. 9 (November 2013): 1716–36.

Badcock, Sarah. *A Prison without Walls? Eastern Siberian Exile in the Last Years of Tsarism*. Oxford: Oxford University Press, 2016.

Barenberg, Alan. *Gulag Town, Company Town: Forced Labor and Its Legacy in Vorkuta*. New Haven, CT: Yale University Press, 2014.

Barenberg, Alan. 'Prisoners without Borders: Zazonniki and the Transformation of Vorkuta after Stalin'. *Jahrbücher für Geschichte Osteuropas* 57, no. 4 (2009): 513–34.

Barnes, Steven A. 'All for the Front, All for Victory! The Mobilization of Forced Labor in the Soviet Union during World War Two'. *International Labor and Working-Class History* 58 (October 2000): 239–60.

Barnes, Steven A. *Death and Redemption: The Gulag and the Shaping of Soviet Society*. Princeton, NJ, Oxford: Princeton University Press, 2011.

Baron, Nick. *Soviet Karelia: Politics, Planning and Terror in Stalin's Russia, 1920–1939*. London: Routledge, 2007.

Bassin, Mark. 'Inventing Siberia: Visions of the Russian East in the Early Nineteenth Century'. *The American Historical Review* 96, no. 3 (1991): 763–94.

Beaumont, Joan. 'Rank, Privilege and Prisoners of War'. *War & Society* 1, no. 1 (1983): 67–94.

Beer, Daniel. 'Blueprints for Change: The Human Sciences and the Coercive Transformation of Deviants in Russia, 1890–1930'. *Osiris* 22, no. 1 (2007): 26–47.

Beer, Daniel. *The House of the Dead: Siberian Exile under the Tsars*. London: Penguin Books, 2017.

Beer, Daniel. 'Penal Deportation to Siberia and the Limits of State Power, 1801–81'. *Kritika: Explorations in Russian and Eurasian History* 16, no. 3 (2015): 621–50.

Beer, Daniel. *Renovating Russia: The Human Sciences and the Fate of Liberal Modernity, 1880–1930*. Ithaca, NY: Cornell University Press, 2008.

Bell, Wilson T. 'The Gulag and Soviet Society in Western Siberia, 1929–1953'. Ph.D. dissertation. University of Toronto, 2011.

Bell, Wilson T. 'Was the Gulag an Archipelago? De-convoyed Prisoners and Porous Borders in the Camps of Western Siberia'. *The Russian Review* 72, no. 1 (2013): 116–41.

Berdinskikh, Viktor. *Istoriia odnogo lageria (Viatlag)*. Moscow: Agraf, 2001.

Berdinskikh, Viktor. *Spetsposelentsy: Politicheskaia ssylka narodov Sovetskoi Rossii*. Moscow: Novoe literaturnoe obozrenie, 2005.

Blum, Alain, Marta Craveri, and Valérie Nivelon. *Déportés en URSS: Récits d'Européens au goulag*. Paris: Éditions Autrement, 2021.

Blum, Alain, and Emilia Koustova. 'Negotiating Lives, Redefining Repressive Policies: Managing the Legacies of Stalinist Deportations'. Translated by Madeleine Grieve and Catriona Duthreuil. *Kritika: Explorations in Russian and Eurasian History* 19, no. 3 (2018): 537–71.

Boeck, Brian J. 'When Peter I Was Forced to Settle for Less: Coerced Labor and Resistance in a Failed Russian Colony (1695–1711)'. *The Journal of Modern History* 80, no. 3 (September 2008): 485–514.

Bonnell, Victoria E. *Roots of Rebellion: Workers' Politics and Organizations in St. Petersburg and Moscow, 1900–1914*. Berkeley: University of California Press, 1983.

Borisova, Larisa. *Voennyi kommunizm: Nasilie kak element khoziaistvennogo mekhanizma*. Moscow: Moskovskii obshchestvennyi nauchnyi fond, 2001.

Borodkin, L.I. 'GULAG v gody voiny: Mobilizatsionnaia ekonomika v ekstremal'nom rezhime'. *Ural'skii istoricheskii vestnik* 61, no. 4 (2018): 46–54.

Borodkin, L.I., P. Gregori, and O.V. Khlevniuk, eds. *Gulag: Ekonomika prinuditel'nogo truda*. Moscow: ROSSPEN, 2005.

Borodkin, L.I., and E.I. Safonova. 'Gosudarstvennoe regulirovanie trudovykh otnoshenii v gody nepa: Formirovanie sistemy motivatsii truda v promyshlennosti'. *Ekonomicheskaia istoriia. Obozrenie* 5 (2000). http://www.hist.msu.ru/Labs/Ecohist/OB5/borsaf.htm, last accessed 16 November 2023.

Bouvard, Josette. 'La commune de Bolchevo (1924–1938) ou la fabrique de l'Homme nouveau?' *La Revue russe* 39, no. 1 (2012): 69–80.

Brodskii, Iurii. *Solovki. Dvadtsat' let osobogo naznacheniia*. Moscow: ROSSPEN, 2002.

Brower, Daniel. 'Kyrgyz Nomads and Russian Pioneers: Colonization and Ethnic Conflict in the Turkestan Revolt of 1916'. *Jahrbücher für Geschichte Osteuropas* 44, no. 1 (1996): 41–53.

Bruno, Andy. 'Industrial Life in a Limiting Landscape: An Environmental Interpretation of Stalinist Social Conditions in the Far North'. *International Review
of Social History* 55, no. S18 (2010): 153–74.

Bugai, N.F. *L. Beria – I. Stalinu: "Soglasno Vashemu ukazaniiu…".* Moscow: AIRO-XX, 1995.

Bukharin, Nikolai. *Ekonomika perekhodnogo perioda, Chast I: Obschaia teoriia transformatsionnogo protsessa.* Moscow: Gosudarstvennoe sotsial'no-ekonomicheskoe
izdatel'stvo, 1920.

Bukharin, Nikolai. *The Politics and Economics of the Transition Period.* London,
New York: Routledge, 2003 [1979].

Bunyan, James. *The Origin of Forced Labor in the Soviet State, 1917–1921: Documents
and Materials.* Baltimore: Johns Hopkins University Press, 2019 [1967].

Buriak, Elena. 'Prinuzhdenie v organizatsii trudovykh otnoshenii v ramkakh
mobilizatsionnoi ekonomiki v pervye gody sovetskoi vlasti'. In *Mobilizatsionnaia
model' ekonomiki: Istoricheskii opyt Rossii XX veka*, edited by G.A. Goncharov
and S.A. Bakanov, 317–32. Cheliabinsk: OOO 'Entsiklopediia', 2009.

Chamberlain, Lesley. *Lenin's Private War: The Voyage of the Philosophy Steamer and
the Exile of the Intelligentsia.* New York: St. Martin's Press, 2007.

Cohen, Stephen F. 'Bolshevism and Stalinism'. In *Stalinism: Essays in Historical
Interpretation*, edited by Robert C. Tucker, 3–29. New Brunswick, NJ: Transaction
Publishers, 1999.

Cohen, Stephen F. *Bukharin and the Bolshevik Revolution: A Political Biography,
1888–1938.* Oxford: Oxford University Press, 1980.

Conroy, Mary Schaeffer. 'Health Care in Prisons, Labour and Concentration Camps
in Early Soviet Russia, 1918–1921'. *Europe-Asia Studies* 52, no. 7 (2000): 1257–74.

Corrado, Sharyl M. 'The "End of the Earth": Sakhalin Island in the Russian Imperial
Imagination, 1849–1906'. Ph.D. dissertation. University of Illinois at Urbana-
Champaign, 2010.

Craveri, Marta. 'Krizis GULaga: Kengirskoe vosstanie 1954 goda v dokumentakh
MVD'. *Cahiers du monde russe* 36, no. 3 (1995): 319–43.

Crompton, Jonathan. 'Resistance and Authority in Siberia, 1920–21: The Bolsheviks
and the Siberian Peasantry with Reference to the Novosibirsk Region'. *Revolutionary Russia* 10, no. 2 (1997): 1–24.

Daly, Jonathan W. 'Criminal Punishment and Europeanization in Late Imperial
Russia'. *Jahrbücher für Geschichte Osteuropas* 48, no. 3 (2000): 341–62.

Daly, Jonathan W. 'On the Significance of Emergency Legislation in Late Imperial
Russia'. *Slavic Review* 54, no. 3 (1995): 602–29.

Dameshek, L.M., and A.V. Remnev, eds. *Sibir' v sostave Rossiiskoi imperii.* Moscow:
Novoe literaturnoe obozrenie, 2007.

Danilov, V.P., and S.A. Krasil'nikov, eds. *Spetspereselentsy v Zapadnoi Sibiri: 1930–
vesna 1931 g.* Vol. 1. Novosibirsk: EKOR, 1992.

Danilov, V.P., and S.A. Krasil'nikov, eds. *Spetspereselentsy v Zapadnoi Sibiri: Vesna 1931–nachalo 1933 g.* Vol. 2. Novosibirsk: EKOR, 1993.

Danilov, V.P., Roberta Manning, and Lynne Viola, eds. *Tragediia sovetskoi derevni: Kollektivizatsiia i raskulachivanie. Dokumenty i materialy, 1927–1939.* 5 vols. Moscow: ROSSPEN, 1990.

David-Fox, Michael. *Showcasing the Great Experiment: Cultural Diplomacy and Western Visitors to Soviet Union, 1921–1941.* Oxford, New York: Oxford University Press, 2012.

Davies, R.W., Mark Harrison, Oleg Khlevniuk, and Stephen G. Wheatcroft. *The Industrialisation of Soviet Russia.* Vol. 7. London: Palgrave Macmillan, 2018.

Davoliūtė, Violeta, and Tomas Balkelis, eds. *Narratives of Exile and Identity: Soviet Deportation Memoirs from the Baltic States.* Budapest, New York: Central European University Press, 2017.

Davydov, M.A. *Dvadtsat' let do Velikoi voiny: Rossiiskaya modernizatsiya Vitte–Stolypina.* Saint Petersburg: Aleteiia, 2016.

De Vito, Christian G., and Alex Lichtenstein, eds. *Global Convict Labour.* Studies in Global Social History 19. Leiden, Boston: Brill, 2015.

De Vito, Christian G., and Alex Lichtenstein. 'Writing a Global History of Convict Labour'. In *Global Convict Labour,* edited by Christian G. De Vito and Alex Lichtenstein, 1–45. Leiden, Boston: Brill, 2015.

Demoskoff, A. Joy. 'Penance and Punishment: Monastic Incarceration in Imperial Russia'. Ph.D. dissertation. University of Alberta, 2016.

Denis, Juliette. 'Identifier les "éléments ennemis" en Lettonie: Une priorité dans le processus de resoviétisation (1942–1945)'. *Cahiers du monde russe* 49, no. 2–3 (20 September 2008): 297–318.

Dikötter, Frank, and Ian Brown, eds. *Cultures of Confinement: A History of the Prison in Africa, Asia, and Latin America.* London: Hurst, 2007.

Dzhekobson, M. [Michael Jakobson], and M.B. Smirnov. 'Sistema mest zakliucheniia v RSFSR i SSSR. 1917–1930'. In *Sistema ispravitel'no-trudovykh lagerei v SSSR,* edited by M.B. Smirnov, 10–24. Moscow: Zven'ia, 1998. Electronic version available at: http://old.memo.ru/history/nkvd/gulag/, last accessed 15 April 2022.

Dziak, John J. *Chekisty: A History of the KGB.* Lexington, MA: Lexington Books, 1988.

Elie, Marc, and Jeffrey Hardy. '"Letting the Beasts Out of the Cage": Parole in the Post-Stalin Gulag, 1953–1973'. *Europe-Asia Studies* 67, no. 4 (2015): 579–605.

Engelstein, Laura. 'Combined Underdevelopment: Discipline and the Law in Imperial and Soviet Russia'. *The American Historical Review* 98, no. 2 (1993): 338–53.

Ertz, Simon. 'Trading Effort for Freedom: Workday Credits in the Stalinist Camp System'. *Comparative Economic Studies* 47, no. 2 (2005): 476–91.

Ertz, Simon. *Zwangsarbeit im stalinistischen Lagersystem: Eine Untersuchung der Methoden, Strategien und Ziele ihrer Ausnutzung am Beispiel Norilsk, 1935–1953.* Berlin: Duncker & Humboldt, 2006.

Evans, Robin. *The Fabrication of Virtue: English Prison Architecture, 1750–1840*. Cambridge: Cambridge University Press, 1982.

Fedor, Julie. *Russia and the Cult of State Security: The Chekist Tradition, from Lenin to Putin*. Abingdon, New York: Routledge, 2011.

Fitzpatrick, Sheila. *Stalin's Peasants: Resistance and Survival in the Russian Village after Collectivization*. New York: Oxford University Press, 1996.

Foucault, Michel. *Surveiller et punir*. Paris: Gallimard, 1975.

Foucault, Michel. *Discipline and Punish: The Birth of the Prison*. New York: Vintage Books, 1995 [1977].

Frank, Stephen P. *Crime, Cultural Conflict, and Justice in Rural Russia, 1856–1914*. Berkeley: University of California Press, 1999.

Frierson, Cathy. 'Crime and Punishment in the Russian Village: Rural Concepts of Criminality at the End of the Nineteenth Century'. *Slavic Review* 46, no. 1 (1987): 55–69.

Frierson, Cathy A. *All Russia Is Burning! A Cultural History of Fire and Arson in Late Imperial Russia*. Seattle: University of Washington Press, 2002.

Gatrell, Peter. *A Whole Empire Walking: Refugees in Russia during World War I*. Bloomington: Indiana University Press, 1999.

Geifman, Anna. *Death Orders: The Vanguard of Modern Terrorism in Revolutionary Russia*. Santa Barbara, CA: Praeger Security International, 2010.

Gentes, Andrew A. *Exile to Siberia, 1590–1822: Corporeal Commodification and Administrative Systematization in Russia*. Basingstoke, New York: Palgrave Macmillan, 2008.

Gentes, Andrew A. *The Mass Deportation of Poles to Siberia, 1863–1880*. Cham: Springer International, 2017.

Gentes, Andrew A. 'Roads to Oblivion: Siberian Exile and the Struggle between State and Society in Russia, 1593–1917'. Ph.D. dissertation. Brown University, 2002.

Gentes, Andrew A. 'Vagabondage and the Tsarist Siberian Exile System: Power and Resistance in the Penal Landscape'. *Central Asian Survey* 30, no. 3–4 (2011): 407–21.

Gerlach, Christian, and Nicolas Werth. 'State Violence – Violent Societies'. In *Beyond Totalitarianism: Stalinism and Nazism Compared*, edited by Michael Geyer and Sheila Fitzpatrick, 133–79. Cambridge: Cambridge University Press, 2008.

Getty, J. Arch, and Oleg V. Naumov. *The Road to Terror: Stalin and the Self-Destruction of the Bolsheviks, 1932–1939*. New Haven, CT: Yale University Press, 1999.

Getty, J. Arch, Gábor T. Rittersporn, and Viktor N. Zemskov. 'Victims of the Soviet Penal System in the Pre-War Years: A First Approach on the Basis of Archival Evidence'. *The American Historical Review* 98, no. 4 (1993): 1017–49.

Geyer, Michael. 'The Militarization of Europe, 1914–1945'. In *The Militarization of the Western World*, edited by John R. Gillis, 65–102. New Brunswick, NJ: Rutgers University Press, 1989.

Geyer, Michael, and Sheila Fitzpatrick, eds. *Beyond Totalitarianism: Stalinism and Nazism Compared*. Cambridge: Cambridge University Press, 2008.

Gheith, Jehanne M., and Katherine R. Jolluck. *Gulag Voices: Oral Histories of Soviet Incarceration and Exile*. Basingstoke: Palgrave Macmillan, 2011.

Gibson, Mary. 'Global Perspectives on the Birth of the Prison'. *The American Historical Review* 116, no. 4 (October 2011): 1040–63.

Graziosi, Andrea. *The Great Soviet Peasant War: Bolsheviks and Peasants, 1917–1933*. Cambridge, MA: Harvard University Press, 1996.

Gregory, Paul R. *Terror by Quota: State Security from Lenin to Stalin (an Archival Study)*. New Haven, CT: Yale University Press, 2009.

Gregory, Paul R., and Valery Lazarev, eds. *The Economics of Forced Labor: The Soviet Gulag*. Stanford, CA: Hoover Institution Press, 2003.

Grigorov, A.I., and A.A. Grigorov. *Zakliuchennye Riazanskogo gubernskogo kontslageria RSFSR 1919–1923 gg*. Moscow: Tipografiia OOO "MID", 2013.

Gullotta, Andrea. 'A New Perspective for Gulag Literature Studies: The Gulag Press'. *Studi Slavistici*, no. 8 (2011): 95–111.

Hagenloh, Paul. '"Socially Harmful Elements" and the Great Terror'. In *Stalinism: New Directions*, edited by Sheila Fitzpatrick, 286–308. London: Routledge, 2000.

Hagenloh, Paul. *Stalin's Police: Public Order and Mass Repression in the USSR, 1926–1941*. Washington, DC: Woodrow Wilson Center Press; Johns Hopkins University Press, 2009.

Harris, James R., ed. *The Anatomy of Terror: Political Violence under Stalin*. Oxford: Oxford University Press, 2013.

Harris, James R. 'The Growth of the Gulag: Forced Labor in the Urals Region, 1929–31'. *The Russian Review* 56, no. 2 (1997): 265–80.

Hartmann, Anne. 'Concepts of the Criminal in the Discourse of "Perekovka"'. In *Born to Be Criminal: The Discourse on Criminality and the Practice of Punishment in Late Imperial Russia and Early Soviet Union. Interdisciplinary Approaches*, edited by Riccardo Nicolosi and Anne Hartmann, 167–96. Bielefeld: transcript, 2017.

Hoffmann, David L. *Cultivating the Masses: Modern State Practices and Soviet Socialism, 1914–1939*. Ithaca, NY: Cornell University Press, 2011.

Hoffmann, David L., ed. *Stalinism: The Essential Readings*. Malden, MA: Blackwell, 2003.

Hofmeyr, Isabel. 'South Africa's Indian Ocean: Boer Prisoners of War in India'. *Social Dynamics* 38, no. 3 (1 September 2012): 363–80.

Holquist, Peter. '"Conduct Merciless Mass Terror": Decossackization on the Don, 1919'. *Cahiers du monde russe* 38, no. 1/2 (1997): 127–62.

Holquist, Peter. *Making War, Forging Revolution: Russia's Continuum of Crisis, 1914–1921*. Cambridge, MA: Harvard University Press, 2002.

Holquist, Peter. 'State Violence as Technique: The Logic of Violence in Soviet Totalitarianism'. In *Stalinism: The Essential Readings*, edited by David L. Hoffmann, 127–58. Malden, MA: Blackwell, 2003.

Holquist, Peter. 'To Count, to Extract, and to Exterminate: Population Statistics and Population Politics in Late Imperial and Soviet Russia'. In *A State of Nations: Empire and Nation-Making in the Age of Lenin and Stalin*, edited by Ronald Grigor Suny and Terry Martin, 111–44. Oxford, New York: Oxford University Press, 2001.

Holquist, Peter. 'Tools for Revolution: Wartime Mobilization in State-Building, 1914–1921'. *Ab Imperio* 4 (2001): 209–27.

Holquist, Peter. 'Violent Russia, Deadly Marxism? Russia in the Epoch of Violence, 1905–21'. *Kritika: Explorations in Russian and Eurasian History* 4, no. 3 (2003): 627–52.

Hull, Isabel V. *Absolute Destruction: Military Culture and the Practices of War in Imperial Germany*. Ithaca, NY: Cornell University Press, 2006.

Iliukhov, Aleksandr. 'Sovetskaia model' vseobschego truda v 1918–1922 gg.'. In *Rabochie v Rossii: Istoricheskii opyt i sovremennoe polozhenie*, edited by D.O. Churakov, 182–99. Moscow: Editorial URSS, 2004.

Iudina, Svetlana. 'Pamiati Bolshevtsev', 5 November 2013. https://urokiistorii.ru/articles/pamjati-bolshevcev, last accessed 14 March 2022.

Iunge, Mark, Gennadii Bordiugov, and Rolf Binner. *Vertikal' Bolshogo Terrora. Istoriia operatsii po prikazu NKVD no. 00447*. Moscow: Novyi Khronograf, 2008.

Ivanova, G.M. *Istoriia GULAGa, 1918–1958: Sotsial'no-ekonomicheskii i politiko-pravovoi aspekty*. Moscow: Nauka, 2006.

Jahr, Christoph, and Jens Thiel, eds. *Lager vor Auschwitz: Gewalt und Integration im 20. Jahrhundert*. Berlin: Metropol, 2013.

Jakobson, Michael. *Origins of the Gulag: The Soviet Prison Camp System, 1917–1934*. Lexington: University Press of Kentucky, 1993.

Jolluck, Katherine R. *Exile and Identity: Polish Women in the Soviet Union during World War II*. Pittsburgh, PA: University of Pittsburgh Press, 2002.

Jones, Heather. 'Discipline and Punish? Forms of Violent Punishment in Prisoner of War Camps in the First World War: A Comparative Analysis'. In *Lager vor Auschwitz: Gewalt und Integration im 20. Jahrhundert*, edited by Christoph Jahr and Jens Thiel, 99–116. Berlin: Metropol, 2013.

Junge, Marc. *Die Allunionsgesellschaft ehemaliger politischer Zwangsarbeiter und Verbannter (1921–1935)*. Habilitation, Ruhr Universit¨at Bochum, 2007.

Junge, Marc. *Die Gesellschaft ehemaliger politischer Zwangsarbeiter und Verbannter in der Sowjetunion: Gründung, Entwicklung und Liquidierung (1921–1935)*. Berlin: Akademie Verlag, 2009.

Kenney, Padraic. *Dance in Chains: Political Imprisonment in the Modern World*. New York: Oxford University Press, 2017.

Kenney, Padraic. "'I Felt a Kind of Pleasure in Seeing Them Treat Us Brutally'": The Emergence of the Political Prisoner, 1865–1910'. *Comparative Studies in Society and History* 54, no. 4 (2012): 863–89.

Khaziakhmetov, E.Sh. *Sibirskaia politicheskaia ssylka, 1905–1917 gg: Oblik, organizatsii, revoliutsionnye sviazi.* Tomsk: Tomskii Gosudarstvennyi universitet, 1978.

Khillig, Getts [Götz Hillig]. 'A.S. Makarenko and the Bolshevo Commune'. *Russian Education & Society* 44, no. 9 (1 September 2002): 75–92.

Khlevniuk, Oleg. 'The Gulag and the Non-Gulag as One Interrelated Whole'. *Kritika: Explorations in Russian and Eurasian History* 16, no. 3 (2015): 479–98.

Khlevniuk, Oleg. *The History of the Gulag: From Collectivization to the Great Terror.* New Haven, CT: Yale University Press, 2004.

Khlevniuk, Oleg. 'No Total Totality: Forced Labor, Stalinism, and De-Stalinization'. Translated by Rhiannon Dowling. *Kritika: Explorations in Russian and Eurasian History* 16, no. 4 (2015): 961–73.

Khlevniuk, Oleg. 'Party and NKVD: Power Relationships in the Years of the Great Terror'. In *Stalin's Terror: High Politics and Mass Repression in the Soviet Union,* edited by Barry McLoughlin and Kevin McDermott, 21–33. London: Palgrave Macmillan, 2003.

Khlevniuk, Oleg. 'Prinuditel'nyi trud v ekonomike SSSR. 1929–1941'. *Svobodnaia mysl'* 13 (1993): 73–84.

Khlevniuk, Oleg. 'Zony sovetskoi ekonomiki. Razdelenie i vzaimodeistvie'. In *Istoriia stalinizma: Prinuditel'nyi trud v SSSR. Ekonomika, politika, pamiat',* edited by L.I. Borodkin, S.A. Krasil'nikov, and O.V. Khlevniuk, 38–54. Moscow: ROSSPEN, 2013.

Kiselev, A.F. *Profsoiuzy i sovetskoe gosudarstvo: Diskussii 1917–1920 gg.* Moscow: Prometei, 1991.

Klimkova, Oxana. 'Special Settlements in Soviet Russia in the 1930s–50s'. *Kritika: Explorations in Russian and Eurasian History* 8, no. 1 (2007): 105–39.

Kokurin, A.I., and Iu.N. Morukov, eds. *Stalinskie stroiki Gulaga 1930–1953.* Moscow: MFD, 2005.

Kokurin, A.I., and N.V. Petrov, eds. *GULAG (Glavnoe upravlenie lagerei). 1917–1960.* Moscow: MFD, 2002.

Kokurin, A.I., and N.V. Petrov, eds. *Lubianka. VChK–OGPU–NKVD–NKGB–MGB–MVD–KGB. 1917–1960.* Moscow: MFD, 1997.

Kolesnikov, A.D. 'Ssylka i zaselenie Sibiri'. In *Ssylka i katorga v Sibiri (XVIII–nachalo XX v.),* edited by L.M. Goriushkin, 38–59. Novosibirsk: Izdatel'stvo 'Nauka', 1975.

Kollmann, Nancy Shields. *Crime and Punishment in Early Modern Russia.* Cambridge, New York: Cambridge University Press, 2012.

Kotiukova, T.V., ed. *Vosstanie 1916 goda v Turkestane: dokumental'nye svidetelstva obschei tragedii. Sbornik dokumentov i materialov.* Moscow: Mardzhani, 2016.

Kotkin, Stephen. *Magnetic Mountain: Stalinism as a Civilization*. Berkeley: University of California Press, 1995.

Koustova, Emilia. '(Un)Returned from the Gulag: Life Trajectories and Integration of Postwar Special Settlers'. *Kritika: Explorations in Russian and Eurasian History*, 16, no. 3 (2015): 589–620.

Kowner, Rotem, and Iris Rachamimov, eds. *Out of Line, Out of Place: A Global and Local History of World War I Internments*. Ithaca, NY: Cornell University Press, 2022.

Krasil'nikov, S.A., ed. *Iz istorii zemli Tomskoi. 1933 g. Nazinskaia tragediia*. Tomsk: Volodei, 2002.

Krasil'nikov, S.A. *Serp i molokh: Krestianskaia ssylka v Zapadnoi Sibiri v 1930-e gody*. Moscow: ROSSPEN, 2009.

Krasil'nikov, S.A., ed. *Spetspereselentsy v Zapadnoi Sibiri*. 4 vols. Novosibirsk: EKOR, 1992, 1993, 1994, 1996.

Kreienbaum, Jonas. 'Deadly Learning? Concentration Camps in Colonial Wars around 1900'. In *Imperial Co-operation and Transfer, 1870–1930: Empires and Encounters*, edited by Volker Barth and Roland Cvetkovski, 219–36. London: Bloomsbury Academic, 2015.

Kühne, Thomas. 'Colonialism and the Holocaust: Continuities, Causations, and Complexities'. *Journal of Genocide Research* 15, no. 3 (2013): 339–62.

Kukushkin, Iu., and O. Chistiakov. *Ocherk istorii Sovetskoi Konstitutsii*. Moscow: Politizdat, 1987.

Landau, Julia. 'Specialists, Spies, "Special Settlers", and Prisoners of War: Social Frictions in the Kuzbass (USSR), 1920–1950'. *International Review of Social History* 60, no. S1 (December 2015): 185–205.

Lauchlan, Iain. 'Chekist Mentalité and the Origins of the Great Terror'. In *The Anatomy of Terror: Political Violence under Stalin*, edited by James Harris, 13–29. Oxford: Oxford University Press, 2013.

Lebedev, V.B., and E.V. Stepanova. 'V.A. Sollogub i ego eksperimenty v oblasti organizatsii truda arestantov'. *Vestnik instituta: Prestuplenie, nakazanie, ispravlenie* 23, no. 3 (2013): 82–87.

Leggett, George. *The Cheka: Lenin's Political Police. The All-Russian Extraordinary Commission for Combating Counter-Revolution and Sabotage (December 1917 to February 1922)*. Oxford: Clarendon Press, 1981.

Leidinger, Hannes, and Verena Moritz. *Gefangenschaft, Revolution, Heimkehr: Die Bedeutung der Kriegsgefangenenproblematik für die Geschichte des Kommunismus in Mittel- und Osteuropa 1917–1920*. Vienna: Böhlau, 2003.

Lindenmeyr, Adele. *Poverty Is Not a Vice: Charity, Society, and the State in Imperial Russia*. Princeton, NJ: Princeton University Press, 1996.

Litvin, Aleksei. *Krasnyi i belyi terror v Rossii: 1918–1922 gg*. Moscow: Eksmo, 2004.

Lohr, Eric. *Nationalizing the Russian Empire: The Campaign against Enemy Aliens during World War I*. Cambridge, MA: Harvard University Press, 2003.

Lucassen, Leo. 'A Brave New World: The Left, Social Engineering, and Eugenics in Twentieth-Century Europe'. *International Review of Social History* 55, no. 2 (2010): 265–96.

Manz, Stefan, Panikos Panayi, and Matthew Stibbe, eds. *Internment during the First World War: A Mass Global Phenomenon*. Abingdon, New York: Routledge, 2019.

Margolis, A.D. *Tiur'ma i ssylka v imperatorskoi Rossii. Issledovaniia i arkhivnye nakhodki*. Moscow: Lanterna VITA, 1995.

Marks, Steven G. *Road to Power: The Trans-Siberian Railroad and the Colonization of Asian Russia, 1850–1917*. Ithaca, NY: Cornell University Press, 1991.

Martin, Terry. 'The Origins of Soviet Ethnic Cleansing'. *The Journal of Modern History* 70, no. 4 (1998): 813–61.

Mathiesen, Thomas. *Prison on Trial*. Winchester, Portland, OR: Waterside Press, 2006 [1990].

McLoughlin, Barry, and Kevin McDermott, eds. *Stalin's Terror: High Politics and Mass Repression in the Soviet Union*. London: Palgrave Macmillan, 2003.

Mironov, Aleksandr. 'Trudovoe ispolzovanie zakliuchennykh osobykh lagerei MVD SSSR'. In *Istoriia stalinizma: Prinuditel'nyi trud v SSSR. Ekonomika, politika, pamiat'*, edited by L.I. Borodkin, S.A. Krasil'nikov, and O.V. Khlevniuk, 200–210. Moscow: ROSSPEN, 2013.

Morrison, Alexander. 'Russian Settler Colonialism'. In *The Routledge Handbook of the History of Settler Colonialism*, edited by Edward Cavanagh and Lorenzo Veracini, 313–26. Abingdon: Routledge, 2016.

Mosse, George Lachmann. *Fallen Soldiers: Reshaping the Memory of the World Wars*. Oxford: Oxford University Press, 1991.

Mühlhahn, Klaus. 'The Concentration Camp in Global Historical Perspective'. *History Compass* 8, no. 6 (4 June 2010): 543–61.

Mühlhahn, Klaus. 'The Dark Side of Globalization: The Concentration Camps in Republican China in Global Perspective'. *World History Connected* 6, no. 1 (2009). https://worldhistoryconnected.press.uillinois.edu/6.1/muhlhahn.html, last accessed 4 April 2022.

Murav, Harriet. '"Vo Glubine Sibirskikh Rud": Siberia and the Myth of Exile'. In *Between Heaven and Hell: The Myth of Siberia in Russian Culture*, edited by Galya Diment and Yuri Slezkine, 95–112. New York: Palgrave Macmillan, 1993.

Nachtigal, Reinhard. *Die Murmanbahn: Die Verkehrsanbindung eines kriegswichtigen Hafens und das Arbeitspotiential der Kriegsgefangenen (1915 bis 1918)*. Grunbach: Bernhard Albert Greiner, 2001.

Nachtigal, Reinhard. *Russland und seine österreichisch-ungarischen Kriegsgefangenen (1914–1918)*. Remshalden: Bernhard Albert Greiner, 2003.

Nachtigal, Reinhard. 'Seuchen unter militärischer Aufsicht in Rußland: Das Lager Tockoe als Beispiel für die Behandlung der Kriegsgefangenen 1915/16?' *Jahrbücher für Geschichte Osteuropas* 48, no. 3 (2000): 363–87.

Nagornaia, Oksana. *Drugoi voennyi opyt: Rossiiskie voennoplennye Pervoi mirovoi voiny v Germanii (1914–1922)*. Moscow: Novyi Khronograf, 2010.

Nakhtigal', Rainkhard [Reinhard Nachtigal]. *Murmanskaia zheleznaia doroga, 1915–1919 gody: Voennaia neobkhodimost' i ekonomicheskie soobrazheniia*. Saint Petersburg: Nestor-Istoriia, 2011.

Nakonechnyi, Mikhail. '"Factory of Invalids": Mortality, Disability, and Early Release on Medical Grounds in GULAG, 1930–1955'. Ph.D. dissertation, University of Oxford, 2020.

Neilson, Briony. 'The Paradox of Penal Colonization: Debates of Convict Transportation at the International Prison Congresses 1872–1895'. *French History and Civilization* 6 (2015): 198–211.

Nordlander, David J. 'Capital of the Gulag: Magadan in the Early Stalin Era, 1929–1941'. Ph.D. dissertation, University of North Carolina at Chapel Hill, 1997.

Nordlander, David J. 'Magadan and the Evolution of the Dal'stroi Bosses in the 1930s'. *Cahiers du monde russe* 42, no. 2–4 (2001): 649–66.

Nordlander, David J. 'Origins of a Gulag Capital: Magadan and Stalinist Control in the Early 1930s'. *Slavic Review* 57, no. 4 (1998): 791–812.

Oushakine, Sergei. 'Pole boia na lone prirody: Ot kakogo nasledstva my otkazyvalis''. *Novoe literaturnoe obozrenie* 71 (2005): 263–98.

Pallot, Judith. 'Forced Labour for Forestry: The Twentieth Century History of Colonisation and Settlement in the North of Perm' Oblast''. *Europe-Asia Studies* 54, no. 7 (2002): 1055–83.

Pallot, Judith. 'The Topography of Incarceration: The Spatial Continuity of Penality and the Legacy of the Gulag in Twentieth- and Twenty-First-Century Russia'. *Laboratorium: Russian Review of Social Research* 7, no. 1 (2015): 26–50.

Papkov, S.A. *Obyknovennyi terror: Politika stalinizma v Sibiri*. Moscow: ROSSPEN, 2012.

Papkov, S.A. *Stalinskii terror v Sibiri: 1928–1941*. Novosibirsk: Sibirskoe otdelenie RAN, 1997.

Pastor, Peter. 'Introduction'. In *Essays on World War I: Origins and Prisoners of War*, edited by Samuel R. Williamson and Peter Pastor, 113–17. New York: Brooklyn College Press, 1983.

Petrov, Nikita, ed. *Istoriia stalinskogo gulaga. Konets 1920-kh – pervaia polovina 1950-kh godov. Tom 2. Karatelnaia sistema: Struktury i kadry*. Moscow: Karatelnaia sistema: struktury i kadry, 2004.

Petrov, N.V. 'Vvedenie'. In *Istoriia Stalinskogo Gulaga: Tom 2: Karatel'naia sistema: struktura i kadry*, edited by N.V. Petrov and N.I. Vladimirtsev, 21–56. Moscow: ROSSPEN, 2004.

Phillips, Ben. *Siberian Exile and the Invention of Revolutionary Russia, 1825–1917: Exiles, Émigrés and the International Reception of Russian Radicalism*. New York: Routledge, 2022.

Piacentini, Laura, and Judith Pallot. "'In Exile Imprisonment" in Russia'. *The British Journal of Criminology* 54, no. 1 (2014): 20–37.

Pokrovskii, N.N., V.P. Danilov, S.A. Krasil'nikov, and Lynne Viola, eds. *Politbiuro i krestianstvo: Vysylka, spetsposelenie. 1930–1940*. 2 vols. Moscow: ROSSPEN, 2005, 2006.

Polian, P.M. *Ne po svoei vole… Istoriia i geografiia prinuditel'nykh migratsii v SSSR*. Moscow: OGI-Memorial, 2001.

Popova, Zhanna. 'Exile as Imperial Practice: Western Siberia and the Russian Empire, 1879–1900'. *International Review of Social History* 63, no. S26 (August 2018): 131–50.

Popova, Zhanna. 'Exiles, Convicts, and Deportees as Migrants: Northern Eurasia, Nineteenth–Twentieth Centuries'. In *The Cambridge History of Global Migrations*, edited by Marcelo J. Borges and Madeline Y. Hsu, 240–58. Cambridge: Cambridge University Press, 2023.

Popova, Zhanna. 'A Threatening Geography: Forced Displacement and Convict Labour in Western Siberia, 1879–1953'. Ph.D. dissertation. University of Amsterdam, 2019.

Popova, Zhanna, and Francesca Di Pasquale. 'Dissecting Sites of Punishment: Penal Colonies and Their Borders'. *International Review of Social History* 64, no. 3 (December 2019): 415–25.

Pujals, Sandra. 'When Giants Walked the Earth: The Society of Former Political Prisoners and Exiles of the Soviet Union, 1921–1935'. Ph.D. dissertation. Georgetown University, 1999.

Rachamimov, Alon. *POWs and the Great War: Captivity on the Eastern Front*. The Legacy of the Great War. Oxford: Berg, 2010.

Raeff, Marc. *Michael Speransky: Statesman of Imperial Russia 1772–1839*. Dordrecht: Springer, 1957.

Rat'kovskii, Ilya S. *Krasnyi terror i deiatel'nost' VChK v 1918 godu*. Saint Petersburg: Izdatel'stvo Sankt-Peterburgskogo Universiteta, 2006.

Remnev, Anatolii. 'Vdvinut' Rossiiu v Sibir'. Imperiia i russkaia kolonizatsiia vtoroi poloviny XIX – nachala XX vv.'. *Ab Imperio*, no. 3 (2003): 135–58.

Rendle, Matthew. 'Mercy amid Terror? The Role of Amnesties during Russia's Civil War'. *The Slavonic and East European Review* 92, no. 3 (2014): 449–78.

Rendle, Matthew. 'Revolutionary Tribunals and the Origins of Terror in Early Soviet Russia'. *Historical Research* 84, no. 226 (2011): 693–721

Retish, Aaron B. 'Breaking Free from the Prison Walls: Penal Reforms and Prison Life in Revolutionary Russia'. *Historical Research* 90, no. 247 (2017): 134–50.

Retish, Aaron B. 'Controlling Revolution: Understandings of Violence through the Rural Soviet Courts, 1917–1923'. *Europe-Asia Studies* 65, no. 9 (2013): 1789–806.

Robson, Roy R. *Solovki: The Story of Russia Told through Its Most Remarkable Islands.* New Haven, CT: Yale University Press, 2004.

Ryan, James. *Lenin's Terror: The Ideological Origins of Early Soviet State Violence.* Routledge Contemporary Russia and Eastern Europe Series 36. London: Routledge, 2012.

Ryan, James. 'The Sacralization of Violence: Bolshevik Justifications for Violence and Terror during the Civil War'. *Slavic Review* 74, no. 4 (2015): 808–31.

Sanborn, Joshua A. *Imperial Apocalypse: The Great War and the Destruction of the Russian Empire.* Oxford, New York: Oxford University Press, 2014.

Scheipers, Sibylle. 'The Use of Camps in Colonial Warfare'. *The Journal of Imperial and Commonwealth History* 43, no. 4 (8 August 2015): 678–98.

Scherer, John L., and Michael Jakobson. 'The Collectivisation of Agriculture and the Soviet Prison Camp System'. *Europe-Asia Studies* 45, no. 3 (1 January 1993): 533–46.

Schlögel, Karl. *Terror und Traum: Moskau 1937.* Munich: Hanser Verlag, 2008.

Schrader, Abby M. 'Branding the Exile as "Other": Corporal Punishment and the Construction of Boundaries in Mid-Nineteenth-Century Russia'. In *Russian Modernity: Politics, Knowledge, Practices,* edited by David L. Hoffmann and Yanni Kotsonis, 19–40. Houndmills, New York: Macmillan, 2000.

Schrader, Abby M. *Languages of the Lash: Corporal Punishment and Identity in Imperial Russia.* DeKalb: Northern Illinois University Press, 2002.

Schrader, Abby M. 'The Languages of the Lash: The Russian Autocracy and the Reform of Corporal Punishment, 1817–1893'. Ph.D. dissertation. University of Pennsylvania, 1996.

Schrader, Abby M. 'Unruly Felons and Civilizing Wives: Cultivating Marriage in the Siberian Exile System, 1822–1860'. *Slavic Review* 66, no. 2 (2007): 230–56.

Scott, James C. *Seeing Like a State: How Certain Schemes to Improve the Human Condition Have Failed.* New Haven, CT, London: Yale University Press, 1998.

Shafir, Nir. 'The International Congress as Scientific and Diplomatic Technology: Global Intellectual Exchange in the International Prison Congress, 1860–90'. *Journal of Global History* 9, no. 1 (March 2014): 72–93.

Shcherbakov, N.N. 'Chislennost' i sostav politicheskikh ssyl'nykh Sibiri (1907–1917 gg.)'. In *Ssyl'nye revoliutsionery v Sibiri (XIX v. – fevral' 1917 g.).* Vol. 1. Irkutsk: Irkustkii Gosudarstvennyi universitet, 1973.

Shcherov, Ivan. *Tsentroplenbezh v Rossii: Istoriia sozdaniia i deiatel'nost' v 1918–1922 gg.* Smolensk: Smolenskii gosudarstvennyi pedagogicheskii universitet, 2000.

Shearer, David. 'Elements Near and Alien: Passportization, Policing, and Identity in the Stalinist State, 1932–1952'. *The Journal of Modern History* 76, no. 4 (2004): 835–81.

Shearer, David. 'Modernity and Backwardness on the Soviet Frontier: Western Siberia in the 1930s'. In *Provincial Landscapes: Local Dimensions of Soviet Power, 1917–1953*, edited by Donald Raleigh, 194–216. Pittsburgh, PA: University of Pittsburgh Press, 2001.

Shearer, David. *Policing Stalin's Socialism: Repression and Social Order in the Soviet Union, 1924–1953*. New Haven, CT, Stanford, CA: Yale University Press, Hoover Institution Press, 2009.

Shearer, David R., and Vladimir Khaustov. *Stalin and the Lubianka: A Documentary History of the Political Police and Security Organs in the Soviet Union, 1922–1953*. New Haven, CT: Yale University Press, 2015.

Shelley, Louise. 'Soviet Criminology: Its Birth and Demise, 1917–1936'. *Slavic Review* 38, no. 4 (1979): 614–28.

Shirokov, A.I. *Dal'stroi v Sotsial'no-Ekonomicheskom Razvitii Severo-Vostoka SSSR (1930–1950-e gg.)*. Moscow: ROSSPEN, 2014.

Shteinman, Roza. 'Sibirskii revoliutsionnyi komitet'. Kandidat dissertation. University of Sverdlovsk, 1975.

Smele, Jonathan. *The 'Russian' Civil Wars, 1916–1926: Ten Years That Shook the World*. London: Hurst, 2016.

Smele, Jonathan D. *The Russian Revolution and Civil War, 1917–1921: An Annotated Bibliography*. London, New York: Continuum, 2003.

Smith, Iain R., and Andreas Stucki. 'The Colonial Development of Concentration Camps (1868–1902)'. *The Journal of Imperial and Commonwealth History* 39, no. 3 (September 2011): 417–37.

Sokolov, Andrei. 'Prinuzhdenie k trudu v sovetskoi ekonomike, 1930-e – seredina 1950-kh'. In *Gulag: Ekonomika prinuditel'nogo truda*, edited by Leonid Borodkin, Pol Gregori [Paul R. Gregory], and Oleg Khlevniuk, 17–66. Moscow: ROSSPEN, 2005.

Solomon, Peter H. *Soviet Criminal Justice under Stalin*. Cambridge, New York: Cambridge University Press, 1996.

Solomon, Peter H. 'Soviet Penal Policy, 1917–1934: A Reinterpretation'. *Slavic Review* 39, no. 2 (1980): 195–217.

Spierenburg, Pieter. *The Prison Experience: Disciplinary Institutions and Their Inmates in Early Modern Europe*. Amsterdam Academic Archive. Amsterdam: Amsterdam University Press, 2007 [1991].

Stanziani, Alessandro. 'La gestion des approvisionnements et la restauration de la gosudarstvennost'. Le Narkomprod, l'armée et les paysans, 1918–1921'. *Cahiers du monde russe* 38, no. 1 (1997): 83–116.

Stoler, Ann Laura. 'Epilogue – In Carceral Motion: Disposals of Life and Labour'. In *A Global History of Convicts and Penal Colonies*, edited by Clare Anderson, 371–80. London: Bloomsbury Academic, 2018.

Stucki, Andreas. '"Frequent Deaths": The Colonial Development of Concentration Camps Reconsidered, 1868–1974'. *Journal of Genocide Research* 20, no. 3 (3 July 2018): 305–26.

Sykes, Gresham M. *The Society of Captives: A Study of a Maximum Security Prison.* Princeton, NJ: Princeton University Press, 1958.

Tepliakov, A.G. *Mashina terrora: OGPU-NKVD Sibiri v 1929–1941 gg.* Moscow: AIRO-XXI, 2008.

Ther, Philipp. *The Dark Side of Nation-States: Ethnic Cleansing in Modern Europe.* New York: Berghahn, 2016.

Tikhonov, Aleksei. 'The End of the Gulag'. In *The Economics of Forced Labor: The Soviet Gulag,* edited by Paul R. Gregory and Valery Lazarev, 67–73. Stanford, CA: Hoover Institution Press, 2003.

Titov, Iu.P. *Khrestomatiia po Istorii Gosudarstva i Prava Rossii.* Moscow: Velbi, 2002.

Toth, Stephen A. *Mettray: A History of France's Most Venerated Carceral Institution.* Ithaca, NY: Cornell University Press, 2019.

Tsarevskaia-Diakina, T.V, ed. *Istoriia stalinskogo Gulaga. Konets 1920-kh – pervaia polovina 1950-kh godov. Spetspereselentsy v SSSR.* Vol. 5. Moscow: ROSSPEN, 2004.

Valk, S.N., and G.D. Obichkin, eds. *Dekrety Sovetskoi vlasti.* Vol. 1: 25 October 1917– 16 March 1918. Moscow: Gosudarstvennoe izdatel'stvo politicheskoi literatury, 1957.

Varese, Federico. 'The Society of the Vory-v-zakone, 1930s–1950s'. *Cahiers du monde russe* 39, no. 4 (1998): 515–38.

Viola, Lynne. 'The Aesthetic of Stalinist Planning and the World of the Special Villages'. *Kritika: Explorations in Russian and Eurasian History* 4, no. 1 (2003): 101–28.

Viola, Lynne. *Peasant Rebels under Stalin: Collectivization and the Culture of Peasant Resistance.* New York: Oxford University Press, 1999.

Viola, Lynne. 'The Question of the Perpetrator in Soviet History'. *Slavic Review* 72, no. 1 (2013): 1–23.

Viola, Lynne. *Stalinist Perpetrators on Trial: Scenes from the Great Terror in Soviet Ukraine.* New York: Oxford University Press, 2017.

Viola, Lynne. *The Unknown Gulag: The Lost World of Stalin's Special Settlements.* Oxford, New York, NY: Oxford University Press, 2007.

Viola, Lynne, V.P. Danilov, N.A. Ivnitskii, and Denis Kozlov, eds. *The War against the Peasantry, 1927–1930: The Tragedy of the Soviet Countryside.* Annals of Communism. New Haven, CT: Yale University Press, 2005.

Volgyes, Ivan. 'Hungarian Prisoners of War in Russia, 1916–1919'. *Cahiers du monde russe et soviétique* 14, no. 1 (1973): 54–85.

Wachsmann, Nikolaus. '"Annihilation through Labor": The Killing of State Prisoners in the Third Reich'. *The Journal of Modern History* 71, no. 3 (1999): 624–59.

Weiner, Amir, ed. *Landscaping the Human Garden: Twentieth-Century Population Management in a Comparative Framework*. Stanford, CA: Stanford University Press, 2003.

Weissman, Neil. 'Regular Police in Tsarist Russia, 1900–1914'. *The Russian Review* 44, no. 1 (1985): 45–68.

Werth, Nicolas. *Cannibal Island: Death in a Siberian Gulag*. Princeton, NJ: Princeton University Press, 2007.

Wheatcroft, Stephen G. 'The Crisis of the Late Tsarist Penal System'. In *Challenging Traditional Views of Russian History*, edited by Stephen G. Wheatcroft, 27–54. London: Palgrave Macmillan, 2002.

Whitewood, Peter. 'Failing to Create Revolutionaries: Polish POWs in Soviet Captivity, 1920–21'. *Revolutionary Russia* 35, no. 2 (2022): 185–205.

Worobec, Christine D. 'Horse Thieves and Peasant Justice in Post-Emancipation Imperial Russia'. *Journal of Social History* 21, no. 2 (1987): 281–93.

Wurzer, Georg. 'Die Kriegsgefangenen der Mittelmächte in Rußland im Ersten Weltkrieg'. Ph.D. dissertation. Eberhard-Karls-Universität zu Tübingen, 2000.

Yaney, George L. *The Urge to Mobilize: Agrarian Reform in Russia, 1861–1930*. Urbana: University of Illinois Press, 1982.

Young, Sarah J. 'Knowing Russia's Convicts: The Other in Narratives of Imprisonment and Exile of the Late Imperial Era'. *Europe-Asia Studies* 65, no. 9 (2013): 1700–715.

Zaionchkovskii, P.A. *Krizis samoderzhaviia na rubezhe 1870–1880-kh godov*. Moscow: Izdatel'stvo Moskovskogo universiteta, 1964.

Zavadski, Andrei, and Vera Dubina. 'Eclipsing Stalin: The GULAG History Museum in Moscow as a Manifestation of Russia's Official Memory of Soviet Repression'. *Problems of Post-Communism* 70, no. 5 (2023): 531–543.

Zemskov, V.N. 'GULAG (Istoriko-sotsiologicheskii aspekt)'. *Sotsiologicheskie issledovaniia* 6 (1991): 10–27.

Zemskov, V.N. 'Spetsposelentsy (po dokumentatsii NKVD–MVD SSSR)'. *Sotsiologicheskie issledovaniia* 11 (1990): 3–17.

Zemskov, V.N. *Spetsposelentsy v SSSR, 1930–1960*. Moscow: Nauka, 2003.

Zubov, Sergei. *M.N. Galkin-Vraskoi – nachalnik Glavnogo Tiuremnogo upravleniia Rossiiskoi Imperii (1879–1896 gg.)*. Saratov: Izdatel'stvo Saratovskogo Gosudarstvennogo Universiteta, 2007.

Index